GLAMORGAN HISTORIAN

STEWART WILLIAMS'

Glamorgan Historian

VOLUME ONE

•

COWBRIDGE · GLAMORGAN

D. BROWN AND SONS LIMITED

FIRST PUBLISHED, 1963
SECOND EDITION PRINTED IN
SWITZERLAND AND WALES, 1969

EMERITUS PROFESSOR WILLIAM REES

Regarded by scholars throughout the Principality as the doyen of Welsh historians, Professor Rees has published a number of valuable works including *South Wales and the March: A Social and Agrarian Study* (Oxford University Press, 1924); *The Union of England and Wales* (University of Wales Press, 1938); *Caerphilly Castle: A History and Description* (Cardiff, 1937); *An Historical Map of South Wales and the Border in the 14th Century* (Ordnance Survey, 1933); *An Historical Atlas of Wales from Early to Modern Times* (Faber and Faber, 1959); *Surveys of the Duchy of Lancaster in Wales* (University of Wales Press, 1953); *Cardiff: A History of the City* (Cardiff Corporation, 1962).

Foreword

by

EMERITUS PROFESSOR WILLIAM REES, M.A., D.SC.,
F.S.A., F.R.HIST.S.

THE present volume, the first of a new series of studies on the history of Glamorgan, projected by Mr. Stewart Williams and edited by him, will be warmly welcomed. Especially will the venture appeal to those who are already familiar with the Editor's previous four volumes on the Vale of Glamorgan, a series which met with a most favourable reception. It is now proposed to extend the scope of the studies into the wider context of the *shire* of Glamorgan with the object of presenting a more comprehensive picture of the region as a whole.

Throughout the course of the history of Wales the Land of Morgan has played a conspicuous part, participating to the full in the struggles and the aspirations of the Welsh people. Nevertheless, within the wider entity, it has ever retained an individuality of its own. For long it was an independent kingdom, having its own line of kings, its own social and literary traditions, its own folk life and customs. To our forefathers, the Vale of Glamorgan was looked upon as the Garden of Wales, its wealth enshrined in the favoured soil of the Vale, but, in the later age of coal and steel, men turned to the rich storehouse of mineral wealth hidden deep in its barren uplands. Broadly the history of the County is the story of this great transition from the peaceful pursuits of husbandry to the revolutionary development of modern industry with the accompanying transformation in men and manners.

The subject, indeed, offers a fruitful field of investigation, covering, as it does, the entire range of man's endeavour. It is a story rich in retrospect both in its human and its material qualities, a story which will be unfolded in its many parts. Here then is an opportunity to bring together the researches of many, thus to throw into clearer perspective the history of the County and help to create a lively interest in its past as the basis for the understanding of the present. With this end in view the Editor has sought the collaboration of writers versed in the various aspects of the subject. The variety of the material incorporated in the first volume, with the reproduction of many rare prints, maps and illustrations, is but a foretaste of what we may expect in subsequent volumes in the series. It is an enterprise, generous in its conception, which should command the support of all who have the cultural interests of the County at heart.

William Rees

INTRODUCTION

GLAMORGAN offers the student of local history an abundance of material and although much has been recorded it is equally true to say that there is a considerable quantity waiting to see the light of day, while fresh evidence is continually making necessary a revised approach to many beliefs which were once generally accepted.

In many ways this is an ideal time to launch a series of books devoted to the history of Glamorgan. Interest in the subject has never been greater and there is a paucity of literary media acceptable both to scholar and interested layman. As will be evident from their titles, the chapters dealing with Medical Men and Communications are part of a series which will be continued in future volumes. It is also my intention to publish more full size maps and other hitherto unpublished accounts of tours through Glamorgan.

Some of the contributors are very well known and all can be described as authoritative writers on their various subjects. For those who wish to know something more about them our "Notes on Contributors" provide some biographical details. I am personally indebted to all fifteen writers for generously collaborating in the preparation of this volume.

It is also most appropriate that I should mention here the debt of gratitude I owe to my friend Mr. T. J. Hopkins, the Archivist at Cardiff Central Library, for his untiring efforts towards the success of this project. Mr Roy Denning, too, has been extremely helpful at all times and is responsible for the index.

It will be obvious that illustrations play an important part in this volume and for their kindness in permitting me to use various old prints, maps, engravings, sketches and photographs, I am indebted to the British Museum, National Museum of Wales,

National Library of Wales, University of Wales Press Board, Cardiff Public Libraries, Pontypridd Public Libraries, Neath Antiquarian Society, Mr. Robin Herbert, Mr. V. C. Hardacre and the Western Welsh Omnibus Co. Ltd.

Finally, a special word of thanks to that distinguished historian, Emeritus Professor William Rees, who has kindly written a foreword to this series. I could wish for no better endorsement of my hopes and ambitions.

1, Crossfield Road,   STEWART WILLIAMS.
Barry.

CONTENTS

ILLUSTRATIONS

NOTES ON CONTRIBUTORS

THOMAS BEVAN, a native of Pontypridd, was educated at Howard Gardens High School and University College, Cardiff. He obtained his M.A. Degree in 1928 with a thesis on "The Industrial Development of the Llynfi, Ogmore and Garw Valleys with special reference to transport facilities in the area." For thirty-six years, until his retirement, he was Economics and Social History Master at Bridgend Grammar School. First Chairman, now Vice-President, of the Bridgend and District Local History Society.

GEORGE C. BOON took an Honours Degree in Latin at Bristol University, and from 1950-1956 was Archaeological Assistant at Reading Museum, where he concerned himself with the Silchester Collection. Since his appointment as Assistant Keeper of Archaeology at the National Museum of Wales in 1957 he has excavated widely on Roman sites in the Principality. His interest in the Roman period goes back to his schooldays, and he is the author of *Roman Silchester* (1957) and many papers on coins and Roman antiquities. He has been elected Fellow of the Society of Antiquaries and of the Royal Numismatic Society.

J. BARRY DAVIES was born thirty-four years ago in the parish of Pentyrch where his family have lived for 170 years. Although, regrettably he admits, he is of the first non-Welsh speaking generation, the musical farm names of the district influenced his youthful imagination, leading him gradually to a deep and abiding interest in the locality where he grew up. He is at present a Civil Servant living and working in Cardiff.

ROY DENNING, a Cardiffian, was educated at Cathays High School. He joined the staff of Cardiff Public Libraries in 1942 and has held posts in various types of libraries, scientific and public, since that date. Is at present Librarian of the Glamorgan College of Technology, Treforest. Fellow of the Library Association, with Honours in Historical Bibliography. Official observer for the National Museum of Wales for the Pontypridd-Miskin area. He has done research on William Thomas the diarist, and David Jones of Wallington, local historian.

R. W. D. FENN, a native of Surrey, was educated at Jesus College, Oxford, where he read Theology. He began to specialise in Welsh Church History in 1954 when he entered St. Michael's College, Llandaff. Ordained in 1956 he has served curacies at the Parish Churches of Swansea and Cardiff and is now Assistant Curate of Coity with Nolton, Bridgend. Besides Extra-Mural Lecturing in Welsh Church History for University College, Cardiff, he is at present engaged on a study of Episcopacy in the Celtic Churches and on an account of the impact of Methodism on an eighteenth century parish in the Vale of Glamorgan.

T. J. HOPKINS was born and bred in the Border Vale parish of Pendoylan. Educated at Cowbridge Grammar School, University College of Wales, Aberystwyth (First Class Honours B.A. Degree) and University College, London (Diploma in Archive Administration). He has been Archivist at the Central Library, Cardiff, since 1948. Exploring the Vale of Glamorgan has long been one of his main interests, and he also has an active connection with the Calvinistic Methodist (or Presbyterian) Church of Wales.

13

ELIS JENKINS is senior English Master at Neath Grammar School, Honorary Curator of Art at the Royal Institution of South Wales, Swansea, and a founder member of the Gower Society. In recent years he has become "more and more involved" with the Vale of Neath, a district for which he has written the official guide. His interest in the still unspoilt beauty of this historic valley, with its concentration of waterfalls, has taken him to private and public collections all over Britain in quest of the work of the English topographical artists who recorded these scenes from the mid-eighteenth century onwards.

A. G. PRYS-JONES, a native of Denbigh, was educated at Pontypridd Intermediate School, Llandovery College, and Jesus College, Oxford. After a brief period in business he took up teaching. Before World War I he taught in several English schools, and from 1919-1949 served on the Inspectorate of the Welsh Department of the Ministry of Education. A man of many talents—poet, historian, literary critic, broadcaster—he has published numerous books on a variety of subjects.

D. MORGAN REES is Keeper of the Department of Industry at the National Museum of Wales. A native of Aberaeron, Cardiganshire, he was educated at Rhondda County School, University College of Wales, Aberystwyth, and Gonville and Caius College, Cambridge, where he read Economics and History. H.M. Inspector of Factories in districts in Lancashire and the East Midlands and after the war in Cardiff and Newport. In 1949 he was appointed to the staff of the British Iron and Steel Federation as Area Training Officer, first in Lancashire and Cumberland, and then in South Wales and Monmouthshire. He joined the staff of the Museum in February 1959.

SIR FREDERICK REES was born at Milford Haven, Pembrokeshire, in 1883. In the course of his distinguished career he has had connections with five Universities, three of which—Wales, Edinburgh and Birmingham—have conferred upon him the Honorary Degree of Doctor of Laws. He is also a Honorary Fellow of Lincoln College, Oxford. He was Principal of University College, Cardiff, from 1929-1949, and has served on a number of Royal Commissions and Government Committees. He was knighted in 1945. Books he has written include *Studies in Welsh History* and *The Story of Milford Haven*.

ARTHUR J. RICHARD was educated at the University College of Wales, Aberystwyth. He is an M.A. (Wales) and a Fellow of the Society of Antiquaries. Ex-Headmaster of Whitchurch Grammar School and a Past President of the Cardiff Naturalists Society. He is a member of the Governing Body and Council of the National Museum of Wales. Was in charge of the excavations at Kenfig Castle and contributed a chapter on "Castles, Boroughs and Religious Houses" to the *History of Carmarthenshire*.

TOM RIDD is a History Graduate of the University College of Swansea. Upon completion of his period of professional training as a teacher, he returned to college as a full-time research student engaged upon a study of the municipal history of the borough of Swansea in the nineteenth century. His thesis was awarded the M.A. Degree of the University of Wales in 1955. For the next two years he served in the Royal Army Educational Corps and then, in 1957, he took up his present appointment as Assistant History Master at the Bishop Gore Grammar School, Swansea. He has written a number of articles for publication in *Gower* (the Journal of the Gower Society).

14

PETER H. THOMAS was born in Pontardawe. He received his education at Ystalyfera County Grammar School, University College, Cardiff, and the Welsh National School of Medicine. He now practises medicine as a General Practitioner in the Vale of Glamorgan and lives at Llantwit Major. His main interest outside his daily work lies in the field of medical history, an interest which has culminated in his appointment as honorary Curator of the Museum of the College of General Practitioners, London.

W. S. K. THOMAS was educated at Ystalyfera Grammar School and University College, Swansea, where he obtained a Diploma in Education in 1952. He returned to Swansea in 1954 to undertake research into the history of the town in the sixteenth and seventeenth centuries under the supervision of Professor Glanmor Williams. Research Assistant at University College, Swansea, 1957-58, he was awarded the PH.D. Degree of the University of Wales in 1958. He was appointed Senior History Master at Brecon Boys' Grammar School in September 1958.

MOELWYN I. WILLIAMS is Assistant Keeper in the Department of Printed Books at the National Library of Wales. He is an Extra-Mural Lecturer and Chairman, Mid-Wales Executive Committee, Workers' Educational Association. Born in Gilfach Goch, he was educated at University College, Cardiff. He is the author of a M.A. thesis on a sociological study of the Vale of Glamorgan. During World War II he served in the Royal Air Force and was granted a commission from the ranks. His publications include articles on the commercial history of Glamorgan. He is at present engaged on writing an agrarian history of Glamorgan.

15

THE INDUSTRIALISATION OF GLAMORGAN:
AN INTRODUCTION

by

D. MORGAN REES, M.A.

INDUSTRY has been growing and developing in the county of Glamorgan for four centuries. The valleys and ridges of the uplands saw the first stirrings of industrialisation early in the second half of the sixteenth century when their outcrops of ironstone and plentiful supply of trees and water encouraged, yes enticed, English ironmasters. During the early years of the first Elizabeth's reign, too, copper ores were being exported from Cornwall for smelting at Neath.

For more than a hundred years thereafter the furnaces and forges of the iron industry were scattered throughout the northern half of the county, and then with something of a suddenness there was an upsurge of industrialisation with industrial areas appearing as if to a set pattern. The alliance between coal and iron resulted in the emergence, as the eighteenth century progressed, of a great chain of ironworks at the heads of the valleys on the northern edge of the South Wales coalfield, Glamorgan's share being those at Merthyr and Aberdare. Simultaneously in the lower Swansea Valley and in the Neath and Port Talbot districts copper smelting works increased in number and Swansea itself, also engaged in spelter, gold, silver and nickel plating, came to be regarded as the world centre for non-ferrous metallurgy.

As steel superseded iron and the use of foreign ores became more and more important the long haul to the inland locations became too great a financial burden. Many companies failed to carry on and those that did built new works on the Glamorgan sea-board. The Glamorgan tinplate industry, an industry within the steel industry, had first developed on the coastal belt west of Port Talbot and in the east, and by the end of the nineteenth century the county had many works, most of them being fed their "tin bars" from steelworks, some founded specially for the purpose, on the same coastal locations. As this century came to an end the Swansea copper trade was in decline : richer ores were discovered in remoter regions of the world and the practice of smelting the ores at the copper mines grew.

In the meantime, coal in addition to being an important fuel had become an industry in its own right ; its impact on the pace of industrialisation is mirrored in its own rapidly increasing production and, as the years moved into the twentieth century, in the great demands it was making on increased means of transport. The ironmasters of Merthyr called for roads and canals to transport their finished iron ; the ironmasters and the coal owners had demanded railways, so that they could transport in greater bulk and more quickly, and then the coal industry itself had needed special lines to the sea to meet the export demand for its product. Transport itself then became an industry in Glamorgan ; a peak had been reached and with it a great industrial impetus was spent. The second quarter of the twentieth century witnessed the growth of a new industrial pattern which followed some years of inertia. The iron and steel industry began to develop integrated units as a new technological age emerged, but the county also acquired a new industrial resilience from the introduction of new industries grouped in industrial estates and placed strategically to meet the needs of certain localities which had suffered as the old order had changed. Glamorgan was no longer dependent on its basic industries.

During the Tudor period the ironmasters of south-east England were suffering from the stringent restrictions imposed upon the use of wood as a fuel for their works. They were attracted to Glamorgan, which was plentifully wooded, had ironstone easy to come by in outcrops at the heads of the valleys, and many rivers and mountain streams where waterwheels for driving the blowing apparatus of a furnace could be erected. Their coming was resented by such as Rice Merrick who, in 1578, wrote of the forests and woods of Glamorgan as natural features of the past since many of them by "the Iron Milles were spoyled and consumed". Their need to consume the trees for conversion into charcoal fuel, and the difficulty of maintaining constant supplies of this fuel, made it necessary for the furnaces to be established at considerable distances apart. The forge was also some distance from the furnace, usually some way downstream, to ensure for each a separate water supply. The picture of Glamorgan's sixteenth century industrialisation was, therefore, one of furnaces and forges widely distributed, an iron industry, in the words of T. S. Ashton, governed by "the tyranny of wood and water".

Ironmaking in blast furnaces began in Glamorgan during the 1550's. The Sussex ironmasters established their furnaces and complementary forges during these years in the valleys of the Taff and the Cynon. Ironworks were founded at Pontyryn and Pont-y-gwaith on the banks of the upper Taff ; a blast furnace at Dyffryn in the Cynon Valley might have been linked with a forge at Llwydcoed in Aberdare at this time. There was, too, a furnace at Cwmaman and a forge at Mountain Ash. Llanwonno had a furnace and there was another on the Taff near Castell Coch which was served by a forge at Rhyd-y-gwern in the Glamorgan part of the parish of Machen. Other furnaces operating in the county during the second half of the sixteenth century were situated at Llantrisant, Pont-y-gwaith in the valley of the Rhondda Fach, and Coity Anglia, near Bridgend. The ironworks at Pentyrch, under the direction of Edmund Mathew, was producing ordnance pieces and during the reign of Elizabeth I earned official displeasure for violating the ban on the export of arms. In 1574 Mathew was forced to give bonds to refrain from foreign trade in armaments, but in May 1600 the Cardiff Port Book showed that he was sending to London "48 pieces of ordinances called sakers and mynions. 48 tons weight". He was then prohibited from casting ordnance altogether, but persisted in doing so until the Privy Council ordered the destruction of the Pentyrch furnace in 1616.

A flourishing iron trade had been built up since the arrival of the English ironmasters. Iron was shipped to Sussex, to Worcestershire and to Dublin before 1570 and thereafter at the turn of the century from Cardiff to Gloucester, Bridgwater, Bristol, London, Porlock and Flushing and, indeed, from Newton to Minehead and other Channel ports. This trade fell away after 1600, because production increased in districts outside the county, where ironmaking had hitherto been conducted on a small scale, and many of the ironworks did not survive into the seventeenth century.

During the next one hundred and fifty years there was no great industrial growth in Glamorgan, only a few furnaces and forges were at work. In 1680 the Taff furnace was replaced by one at Caerphilly which was worked until the end of the eighteenth century. A new ironworks at Pentyrch was founded soon after 1740, while in the Neath area during this century ironworks operated at Bryncoch, Melin-cwrt, Aberdulais, Penrhiwtyn and Neath Abbey. At Cefn Cribbwr from about 1760 John Bedford, a silver medallist of the Royal Society of Arts, worked a furnace and forge carrying out many experiments on the use of coal in the smelting of iron. Doubtless there were other furnaces and forges, but it was a quiet period in the iron trade.

The copper industry played an important part in the growth of Neath and Swansea. It came first of all to Neath where a smelting-house was built in 1584 so that the copper ore of Cornwall could take advantage of the abundance of "sea-cole" available there. This was an early example of taking ore to the fuel, and as the industry developed so did it increase its demand for coal and indirectly create an export market, for the ore-ships were laden with coal on their return to Cornwall. Copper smelting was followed by lead smelting and the extraction of silver—the ores coming by sea from Cardiganshire—and as the seventeenth century ended Neath was an important industrial centre using coal for refining or smelting non-ferrous ores. Swansea, at this time an important port, began to develop its copper smelting industry at the beginning of the eighteenth century, it being first located, perhaps, at the "Llangavelach works in 1717". There followed ultimately a line of works between Landore and the newly founded village of Morriston, on the lower reaches of the Tawe ; works were also founded at Taibach and Cwmavon. For the most part the industry used Cornish ores, augmented by supplies from North Wales and Ireland, until the beginning of the nineteenth century when foreign ore was first imported. The industry then continued to expand until it reached its peak in the 1860's. Not only in Swansea but much farther afield works such as the Hafod, the White Rock and the Forest became well known.

During almost the same period the ironworks of Dowlais, Plymouth, Penydarren, Cyfarthfa and Abernant had become great names. A quotation from a technical journal of 1868 runs, "Dowlais! The name of no other place in Britain so strongly and fully expresses the tremendous power of iron and coal . . ." A new speed of industrialisation came to Merthyr and Aberdare with the alliance of coal and iron born of the use of coke in the smelting of iron and afterwards with the introduction of the steam engine. There developed a compulsive concentration of industry in these localities resulting from the easy availability of good coking coal and of ironstone which could be worked, as John Lloyd put it, "at slight expense in patches, by turning over, like a garden, the open mountain slopes". Limestone and stone for the furnaces were also available. As the eighteenth century was ending the ironworks were entering into a rapid development soon to take them to a great height of prosperity.

The great growth of the iron industry during the first half of the nineteenth century, and of the coal industry subsequently, is reflected in the development of transport in Glamorgan. The ironmasters of the sixteenth century had a transport problem. They exported pig iron and bar iron, the ultimate markets for their products being very far away because of the initial remoteness of their works from the home ports which shipped the iron to merchants in Bristol, Bridgwater, Gloucester, Dublin and London. It was a long and tedious business to convey the iron in trains of pack-horses or mules along the roughest of tracks to Cardiff and Newton (Porthcawl). This means of transport remained the same for two hundred years. There was no urgent need to improve it because the iron industry as it was then located fell away. Towards the end of the eighteenth century the position changed with almost an alarming swiftness and one of the great problems confronting the ironmasters was transport; whether they were producing cannon for the Navy, or bar iron for foreign markets, their first hurdle was from the works to the ports.

The first attempt at surmounting this came in the building of rough roads. It was said that Anthony Bacon, who used mule trains to Cardiff and Swansea from his Cyfarthfa works, was the leader in improving about 1767 a poor road from Merthyr Tydfil through Gelligaer and Caerphilly to Cardiff, although there is some doubt about the existence of this road. Be that as it may, a number of the Merthyr ironmasters were authorised to make a turnpike road down the Taff Valley from Merthyr to Tongwynlais where it joined the Cardiff turnpike road. Even on the improved roads a waggon drawn by horses could only haul two tons of iron and this form of land carriage was costing the ironmasters far too much as their production tonnages began to soar. The next step was the development of the Glamorganshire canal and after many altercations between the various parties concerned—Crawshay of the Cyfarthfa Works and Taitt of Dowlais Works quarrelled, as did Homfray of Penydarren Works and Crawshay, and Homfray and Taitt failed to agree—the Canal was eventually opened in 1794. Some of the Merthyr ironmasters were soon dissatisfied because they were still unable to transport their finished iron quickly enough due to the constant congestion of barges on the Canal between Merthyr and Abercynon, where there were as many as sixteen locks in a one mile stretch of the waterway. In 1799 the partners of the Dowlais, Penydarren and Plymouth ironworks agreed to build a tramroad from Merthyr to Abercynon so that this frustrating stretch could be by-passed ; this was opened in 1802 and became known as the Penydarren Tramroad.

The Aberdare Canal, built to serve the Hirwaun, Abernant and Aberdare ironworks, was opened in 1812 to join the Glamorganshire Canal at Abercynon, but for some years it carried only a little iron. The tonnages sent down the Glamorganshire Canal, however, illustrate how great was the development of the works in Merthyr. Malkin in his *Antiquities of South Wales*, published in 1803, said that "more than 200 tons of finished iron are sent down weekly to the port of Cardiff". This was at the rate of over 10,000 tons a year. In 1817 it was 39,000, in 1820 49,000, in 1823 50,000, and it reached a total of 132,000 tons in 1840 and just on 160,000 tons in 1848. During the first half of the nineteenth century the growth of the iron trade had been rapid ; by 1855 the Cyfarthfa Works had eleven blast furnaces, the Dowlais eighteen, Penydarren seven, the Plymouth five—and the population of Merthyr was 70,000.

Comparable transport developments became necessary with the industrialisation of the Neath and Swansea areas. Mackworth's canal was built between 1695 and 1700 to serve the Melyn lead and copper works about a mile below Neath ; a canal was built at the end of the eighteenth century to connect the Penrhiwtyn furnaces with the River Neath and 1799 saw the completion of the Neath canal, developed to carry coal for the export trade and to bring iron ore down to the Neath Abbey ironworks. In the Swansea area the first canal was the Llansamlet, which carried for a number of collieries, copper and spelter works to a wharf in the town, but eventually the greatest was the Swansea Canal which was opened in 1798 and served the growing coal industry and ironworks of the Tawe Valley. In 1810-11 this canal carried 140,000 tons of coal and, it has been estimated, about 390,000 tons of coal and culm in 1837-39, half or more being anthracite. The canal played its part in the development of Swansea as a port ; the population of Swansea increased from just below 7,000 in 1801 to just over 19,000 in 1841.

In an aside, yet as an introduction to the more intense industrialisation which followed the coming of the railways, the Penydarren Tramroad must be mentioned once again. It was on this tramroad, for a distance of 9½ miles, from the Penydarren Ironworks to the Glamorganshire Canal's landing stage at Abercynon, that a locomotive drew a load on rails for the first time in history. The date was the 21 February 1804. The locomotive was built by Richard Trevithick, a Cornish engineer working for Samuel Homfray at Penydarren, and its load, carried in five waggons, consisted of ten tons of iron and seventy men. The journey took four hours and five minutes.

In 1830 coal abandoned its subsidiary role. Hitherto the land-sale and export trade of coal depended upon amounts surplus to the requirements of the ironmasters, but in 1830 114,000 tons of coal was shipped on the Glamorganshire Canal. The basis of Glamorgan's economy was soon to move from iron to coal ; the county was to see the development of an enormous steam coal trade. Even in 1835 the pits of Dinas, in the Rhondda Fawr, were sending over 50,000 tons of coal by tramroad and canal to Cardiff. The carrying capacity of the canal was now far too low because in addition to the growth of coal tonnages the imports of iron ore were steadily increasing and the two-way traffic caused a congestion which became intolerable as more finished iron and coal sought transport on the canal to Cardiff. The agitation of the ironmasters and coal owners finally resulted in the passing of the Taff Vale Railway Company's Act in 1836, and the main line, Merthyr to Cardiff, was opened in 1841, followed by a branch line from Pontypridd to Dinas, Rhondda. In the meantime the West Bute Dock had been opened at Cardiff in October 1839 and the way was now open for the greater development of the coal trade in Glamorgan. Pits were sunk in the Rhondda Valleys, in the Aberdare and Taff Valleys, and there were developments in the Vale of Neath, in the Swansea

Valley and in other coal-laden locations in the county. By the mid-century coast-wise shipments of coal and exports from Cardiff and Swansea totalled just over a million tons and the consumption of coal by the iron industry and copper smelting industry was enormous. There had also been successful experiments in the Swansea Valley in the use of anthracite coal in the smelting of iron. During the next thirty years the foreign demand for Welsh coal became so great that the congestion at Cardiff became acute. A train of coal travelling from Pontypridd to Cardiff, a distance of about twelve miles, would take about eight or nine hours, so great was the pressure of traffic. The frustration which the ironmasters had known was now being experienced by the coal owners and it was not relieved until a new outlet for the coal of the Rhondda was provided by the Barry Railway and the opening of Barry Docks in 1889. By 1890 there was an outlet to Swansea with the completion of the Rhondda and Swansea Bay Railway and a further outlet had been provided by the Pontypridd, Caerphilly and Newport Railway. The Vale of Neath Railway had been opened in 1851 and ten years later provided with a dock at Briton Ferry, and the Swansea Valley industries were assisted by a railway which opened in 1860.

As the nineteenth century waned, the ironmasters and copper smelters were being superseded by the coal owners who were building up an industry to the exclusion of all others, so it appeared. Iron was giving way to steel following the discoveries of Henry Bessemer and the successful work of C. W. Siemens on steelmaking in open hearth furnaces at Landore. The works at Dowlais and Cyfarthfa turned to steelmaking, but most of the non-phosphoric ores required for the new processes had to be imported—haematite ores were being mined near Pontyclun and Taff's Well—and the transport costs of raw materials became almost prohibitive. Dowlais persisted into the twentieth century but the new pattern had been set by the opening of a new Dowlais works at Cardiff in 1891. Already, too, steel works which provided the tinplate trade with its steel were in production within easy reach of Swansea and other west Glamorgan ports, to be followed by others after the turn of the century. Some fifty years later one of Europe's greatest integrated iron and steel works was located on the coast of Glamorgan at Port Talbot ; a works planned to meet new needs and to employ new technologies.

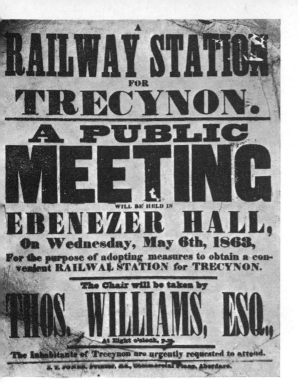

This 1863 poster illustrates the public desire for railway stations

Conjectural working model of Trevithick's Penydarren Tramroad locomotive

Blast Furnaces in course of contruction—Dowlais Works, Cardiff, 1889-91

Glamorganshire Canal Sea-Lock, Cardiff, 1891

Lewis Merthyr Colliery, Porth

Behinder receiving a pair of singles at Clayton Tinplate Works, Pontarddulais

General view of Aberthaw Cement Works

Aerial view of the Abbey Works of The Steel Company of Wales Ltd., Port Talbot

The development of the iron industry in Merthyr and Aberdare was closely followed by the emergence of a quarrying industry. Limestone was quarried to provide fluxing stone for the smelting process ; the continued expansion of the iron industry and afterwards the integration of ironmaking and steelmaking maintained for it a fairly constant demand. In recent times limestone quarrying has expanded greatly—at the end of the 1950's there were more than thirty quarries in Glamorgan—to meet the needs of the modern steel industry, the cement industry and the demand for road metal. The needs of building, as houses and industrial buildings were wanted in Merthyr and Aberdare in the days of the ironmasters, were satisfied by quarrying the coal measure sandstones. Certain of the quarries, which then produced the sandstone, are still being worked for building stone and road metal. Dolomite quarrying for the steel industry has been carried on for many years at Taff's Well and the industry's demand for silica bricks, for use as furnace and coke-oven linings, has been met over a protracted period by brick works at Morriston and Landore.

By the end of the nineteenth century the tinplate trade was safely located on the sea-board, primarily in western Glamorgan, near the ports. The hand mills were producing in and around the Neath and Port Talbot areas, in Swansea's hinterland at such towns as Morriston, Gowerton, Gorseinon, Pontardawe and Pontarddulais and continued to do so until their technological peace was disturbed by the coming of the strip mill. After World War II the steel strip mill put down at Port Talbot needed to be followed by a tinplating process which followed the same principle, and Glamorgan's first electrolytic tinning line came to be founded at Llangyfelach. In one sense this development in the tinplate industry brought an unwanted element into the continuing industrialisation of the county because it shattered a way of working familiar to many people and communities for more than fifty years.

Fortunately, Glamorgan had already been given an industrial cushioning to withstand such shocks. The decline of the coal industry, with the falling off of its export trade after World War I and an iron and steel industry merely marking time in the early thirties, had brought industrial depression and social distress. The successful cement industry already established at Aberthaw, Rhoose and Penarth had provided some compensation, but the crisis was acute and the formation of industrial estates—first known as trading estates—became a matter of official policy. The first factories of the new light industries were built at the Treforest Estate. In time they became established at Bridgend, Hirwaun and Fforestfach. Some of these factories and others founded separately on valley sites were able to provide alternative employment for displaced, disabled and redundant workers. The traditional skills of the workers of the county accepted successfully the challenge of the new industrialisation.

The years following the Second World War saw great technological developments in the original basic industries of Glamorgan. They saw, too, the introduction of brand new industries, industries which typified a new technological age—plastics, chemicals, nylon and terylene yarn, petroleum products, and machine tools—and the many other different industries which complete the complex industrial pattern which Glamorgan has achieved since the first days of ironmaking and copper smelting.

MUNICIPAL GOVERNMENT IN SWANSEA, 1485-1640

by

W. S. K. THOMAS, B.A., PH.D.

IN 1485, a date which conventionally we regard as the opening of the modern period, the borough of Swansea was already old, its corporation possessing valuable property rights and certain exclusive privileges. That the town was not to fade into impotence and decay like many another Welsh borough was due to its favourable topographical position, the nature of the charters which its lords had granted it at various times in the past, and to the character of its inhabitants—their pride in its existence, and their determination to preserve the corporate franchises. The next hundred and sixty years were to see great developments in the nature of its government, some of these being determined by national legislation, but all representing a direct response to the rapid economic advance of the town and its hinterland. It is with these developments of a constitutional kind that we shall be concerned in this chapter.

In the late fifteenth century the Somerset family through the marriage of Charles Somerset to Elizabeth, the daughter and heiress of William Herbert, the second Earl of Pembroke, acquired possession of the lordship of Gower. In 1532 Charles's eldest son, Henry Somerset, Earl of Worcester, for the sum of three hundred marks, granted a charter to Swansea which was practically a confirmation of an earlier charter granted by William de Breos in 1306. In seeking this charter the town was, in effect, seeking once again legal incorporation. But this charter is a most significant document in another way. It clearly demonstrates the hold of the lord on the town. Many towns, as a result of the decay of feudalism and the disappearance of the class of feudal barons, emerged from the Middle Ages freed from the control and exactions of their overlords. This was not so with Swansea. The town was the centre of the lordship and the overlord could hardly be expected to surrender all his rights in his own "capital".

27

Within a few years of the charter came the Act of Union which markedly affected the municipal development of Swansea. Its effects on the town can be discerned in four directions. Firstly, it made the existence of Swansea as a garrison town unnecessary ; secondly, the doors were thrown wide open to the admission of the Welsh into the town; thirdly, the Burgesses of the town were granted the right to participate in the election of Members to Parliament; and finally, a new significance was given to the influence of the lord within the borough.

The Act of Union made the existence of Swansea as a garrison town unnecessary because it abolished the Marcher-Lordships. These quasi-kingdoms were now turned into shires. As a result of this legislation, those boroughs like Llandovery or Kidwelly which had been founded as mere appendages to castles, decayed as corporate towns. Swansea, however, was well situated from the standpoint of trade and commerce. Even in the Middle Ages the town had developed as an important commercial and trading centre, and as the hub of the economic life of the seignory of Gower. Thus, although as a result of the Act of Union Swansea lost what importance it had possessed as a garrison town, the fact that it had developed a commercial life of its own was a positive guarantee against any likelihood of decay.

Another effect of the Act of Union was that since Welshmen now attained full equality with Englishmen they could enter fully into the life of the town. Henceforth they could participate in the economic life of the towns both of Wales and England, and these towns acted like a magnet on all classes. At Swansea, the Welsh had begun to enter the town in the late Middle Ages. They had helped to fill the vacuum caused by the sharp decline in its original population brought about by the Black Death, and a contracting economy in the later Middle Ages. Before 1536, however, their intrusion can be likened to a trickle. After 1536 this trickle became a stream.

The Act of Union also enabled Swansea to participate in the elections of Burgesses to Parliament conditionally upon the town contributing towards the payment of members' wages, even though this was ceasing as a general practice in England at this time, and almost certainly in the county of Glamorgan as well. At Swansea, as was the case generally in the Welsh boroughs, the right of election was vested in the duly admitted Burgesses. A study of the borough records throws some light on the question of Swansea's contribution towards the payment of members. From a receipt dated 27 August 1587 it appears that Swansea contributed £3 towards the expenses of George Lewis, its Member of Parliament, for two sessions.   The total sum due from the eight Glamorgan boroughs was £17 12s. 0d.

Finally, the Act of Union gave a new significance to the influence of the lord within the borough.   The class which desired membership of Parliament—the gentry—came to regard the manipulation of the parliamentary boroughs as their chosen field of activity. At Swansea there were three ways in which the electorate could be controlled : by controlling borough appointments, by limiting the number of Burgesses, and by the mass creation of non-resident Burgesses.   In the town, during this period, the operation of the first two methods can be discerned.

Corporate appointments at Swansea were made in the manorial Court Leet presided over by the Steward and Portreeve. The fact that the Steward was the lord's nominee enabled the lord to exercise considerable influence in that court since the Steward was not only responsible for swearing in the new officers and duly admitted Burgesses, but was responsible for the final selection of the Portreeve and, in all probability, of the other borough officers as well.

Another way in which the electorate was controlled at Swansea was by limiting the number of Burgesses. The fact that Swansea was already under the control of a manorial lord, who had a constitutional right of interference in its affairs, must have greatly facilitated the task of controlling the electorate which was generally quite willing to accept the guidance of the lord or his agent in political matters. The interests of the lord and the Burgesses seem to have coincided to a remarkable degree ; the lord wished to limit the electorate, for the smaller the body of Burgesses the easier it was to control ; the Burgesses could agree with this policy for the material benefits which went with burgess-ship were correspondingly increased.

The enjoyment of privileges was, indeed, an essential feature of corporate life and, since this was so, it may be as well at this point to indicate their general character.   Perhaps the most important of the privileges enjoyed by the Burgesses was the freedom from payment of tolls. There were "quayage", "wharfage" and "market dues"—tolls on merchandise brought into the town by land or sea by non-burgesses and levied upon all manner of commodities.There were also "keelage" dues on all vessels entering or leaving the port, and the "assize of ale", a tax on all public houses within the borough.

To this category of privileges also belonged the careful insistence on the right of exclusive trading within the borough. A bye-law introduced in 1569 stipulated that non-burgesses were not to follow any craft, or open any shop, in the town unless they had been licensed to do so by the Portreeve, Aldermen and Common Attorneys.

Equally important, at least until the close of the sixteenth century, was the insistence on communal trading. By an ordinance of November 1553 Burgesses were not allowed to board a vessel until the Portreeve had ascertained what merchandise she carried, and until he had entered the custom. The merchant, furthermore, was not to sell his goods to any "foreign" persons but only to Burgesses for the space of fifteen days. After the expiration of the fifteen days the merchant could "Carie away his ware att his pleasure".

An ordinance of 7 August 1555 enjoined that all goods entering the port, except those of a perishable nature, were to be taken to the town hall where the process of bargaining proceeded only among the Burgesses, and not until the Burgesses had made their choice were the goods to be released for the "foreigners" or "sensers".

Regulations affecting the sale of merchandise brought into the harbour continued to be made at intervals by the Corporation. On 15 October 1560 a regulation was made by which no Burgess was allowed to purchase a whole cargo. The visiting merchant was himself to retail his wares, though subject to the former regulation that they should first be offered, under the supervision of the Corporation officials, to the Burgesses of the town.

The enjoyment of borough property, again, was strictly confined to the Burgesses who alone could obtain leases of it, usually at low rentals. Thus on 24 January 1547 a Burgess by the name of Richard Yoroth leased six acres of land near St. Helen's for 99 years at a yearly rent of 3s. 4d. But the Burgesses also possessed valuable common and pasture rights. One such common was Cefn Coed which contained altogether about 200 acres and extended "in lengthe One Myll And in Bredthe half a Mill".

Such then were the privileges and rights of the burgess body, and it is now appropriate that attention should be devoted to the machinery by which they were administered. The essential features of this machinery were the Lord, Steward, Court Leet, Portreeve, a small executive Council, the Common Hall and finally the Vestry.

During the Middle Ages the lord had jealously maintained control over the town, and this for several reasons. In the first place, the town formed the "capital" of his seignory of Gower. Secondly, it was a source of influence for electoral purposes. And thirdly, and perhaps most important of all, it represented a valuable source of income derived from various sources including rents, fines and heriots, tolls on markets and fairs, assize of ale, mises and aids, and finally wrecks of sea and felons' goods.

The lords of Swansea throughout the whole period from 1492-1640 were the successive members of the Somerset family : Charles Somerset (1460?-1526), first Earl of Worcester; Henry Somerset (d. 1549), second Earl; William Somerset (1526-1589), third Earl; Edward Somerset (1553-1628), fourth Earl; and Henry Somerset (c. 1577-1646), fifth Earl and first Marquis of Worcester. The history of the Somersets, however, lies outside the purview of this chapter. Men of considerable influence in national politics, they never themselves resided in Swansea, and delegated their authority to Stewards. Nevertheless, they realized the importance of choosing as Stewards men of strong character and local influence. Three of these Stewards, Sir Matthew Cradock, Sir George Herbert and Sir Thomas Mansel, were men of especial eminence, and deserve to be briefly noticed.

Sir Matthew Cradock was the son of Richard ap Gwilym ap Evan ap Cradock Vreichvras and Jennett Horton of Candleston Castle, near Newton, in Glamorgan. A daring opportunist, he was a man of considerable business acumen as well as of military and naval skill. He was also a very ambitious man, and possessed acquisitive gifts of no mean order and from 1486 onwards office after office fell into his hands. Deputy Steward of Gower under Jasper, Duke of Bedford, he had in 1506, to all intents and purposes, become Steward under Charles Somerset, the first Earl of Worcester. He died in 1531 and was buried in St. Mary's Church, Swansea.

A kinsman of Charles Somerset, Sir George Herbert was the second son of Sir Richard Herbert of Ewias. Descended as he was from the great Herbert clan, he was full of their pride and courage. He could also be cruel and unscrupulous, and these traits of his character were strikingly demonstrated when he hanged a sixteen-year old boy for sheep stealing despite a strong denial of the felony by the boy's father from whom, apparently, the sheep were taken. However, against these more undesirable aspects of his character must be placed his patronage of the bards, for he had entertained in his household some of the leading poets of Glamorgan. On the dissolution of the religious houses he had purchased the landed possessions of the Hospital of St. David at Swansea. Typical of many of the gentry of the time he speculated in business ventures, and developed the coal mines around Neath. His home, the Place House, Swansea, was a considerable edifice in its day.

Sir Thomas Mansel was the eldest son of Sir Edward Mansel and Jane Somerset the daughter of Henry, second Earl of Worcester. Thrice sheriff of Glamorganshire between 1593 and 1623, he was also for many years a Justice of the Peace. It would appear that he was not always too assiduous in the performance of his duties, for in 1626 he had been denounced by the Council in the Marches of Wales for failing to observe the wishes of that jealous and autocratic body, apparently with regard to the licensing of ale-houses in Swansea. He died on 20 December 1631 and was buried at Margam.

A very important function of the Steward was to preside, with the Portreeve, over the Court Leet. There were two Courts Leet or Tourn Courts held annually in the town, one in the Spring (1 May) and the other in the Autumn (29 September). It was in these Courts Leet that the borough officers were elected and Burgesses admitted to the freedom. At the October Leet were chosen the Portreeve, Common Attorneys, Sergeants-at-Mace and subsidiary officials such as the Constables and the Layer-Keepers. At the Easter Leet the Stewards of the Burrows and the Stewards for the Mountain were elected, whose duty it was to supervise the common lands.

The Burgesses were admitted through the four channels of birth, marriage, apprenticeship and gift, and on admission had to pay a composition fee which in 1613 was fixed at 20s.— a regulation, however, that was not strictly adhered to for more than a few years.

The chief corporate officer for whose final selection the Steward

Swansea Castle (centre) from the river

Samuel and Nathaniel Buck, 1748

Windows of the Hospital of the Blessed David, Swansea

A sketch from a photograph of 1865 of the windows of the fourteenth century Hospital

The Place House, Swansea

From an engraving of about 1830 representing the Goat Street side of the House

was responsible, the Portreeve, exercised during his year of office functions of a most important nature. He was the Coroner of the Liberty; he was responsible for the distribution of bequests among the poor, his accounts being carefully audited ; he was responsible for collecting the rents and other dues payable to the lord ; he presided over the Court Leet, over meetings of the aldermanic body, and over the Vestry. A study of the names of those that occupied the office between 1485-1640 reveals, significantly enough, that the office was, to a very large extent, concentrated in the hands of a few of the foremost families of the town, particularly the Flemyngs, Francklens and the Sadlers.

A small executive council of twelve Aldermen, over which the Portreeve presided, had apparently emerged at Swansea during the later Middle Ages, though it is not until the sixteenth century that we first discern it in action. It is obviously impossible to date exactly the emergence of this council, for it probably evolved slowly for the purposes of town government. The burgess body must have been found rather unwieldly because of its size, and the advantages of a smaller body, composed probably of the ablest and most influential and opulent from among the Burgesses, must have become apparent at an early date. The twelve Aldermen did not co-opt themselves but were chosen from the ranks of the Burgesses by what was, ostensibly, popular election. Unfortunately, it seems impossible to determine how free these elections really were, but the fact that Aldermen held office for life probably led to a good deal of pressure for their own election from the wealthier and most prominent Burgesses.

Since the function of this council was to act as an executive, it was obviously desirable to maintain the full complement of twelve Aldermen, otherwise the pressure of business on those that remained would have become too great. Thus it was that during the sixteenth century attendance became compulsory, and an Alderman absent from town for a year and a day was dismissed from his aldermanship. A person could also lose his aldermanship for behaviour inimical to the best interests of the Corporation.

It would appear that the executive council was, in theory at least, subject to the general burgess body which evidently was responsible for general policy, because the actions of the council seem to have required the confirmation of the Burgesses. The general burgess body to which the aldermanic council was responsible met in Common Hall. Since at Swansea there were four avenues to the freedom, the number of Burgesses sitting in Common Hall would naturally, as a result, have varied from time to time. The Burgesses could not be identified with the entire town population but constituted a small proportion of the whole. Thus it would appear that in 1583 the number of Burgesses could hardly have exceeded 79. Since the population of the town at this time was about 1,000, the Burgesses would have formed 8 *per cent* of the total population. In 1634 they comprised 7 *per cent* of the population. This provides an entirely different picture from that presented by the town in the nineteenth century, because in 1833 the Burgesses formed 0.7 *per cent* of a total population of 15,621. Judged by this standard the town in the sixteenth and seventeenth centuries would appear to have had a far higher proportion of Burgesses among its citizens.

The Burgesses were not confined solely to any one class in the town, but were drawn from the ranks of craftsmen and shopkeepers, as well as from merchants. Furthermore, since the Corporation had the right to admit Burgesses by gift, strangers were occasionally admitted to the freedom though their rights were usually restricted.

A Burgess absent from the town for a year and a day was disfranchised unless he continued to pay his share of any tallages or taxes levied upon the town. The Corporation pursued this policy because it held that Burgesses continually absent from town were in no position to fulfil their obligations as burgesses, obligations enshrined in the oath they took when first admitted to the freedom. By this oath the Burgesses promised to be true, to be obedient to the Portreeve, to pay any tallages or taxes levied upon them, to maintain the privileges and liberties of the town, to acquaint the Portreeve and Aldermen of any developments that might endanger these liberties and finally to "Doe all other thinges y^t becometh a true Burges for to doe". Under this last obligation were included the duties of serving in any office, and of keeping watch and ward.

An essential qualification for burgess-ship was marriage, for in 1563 it was expressly stipulated in "an order for freemen" that "no man to be made burges exsepet he or they be fyrst maryde in matreymony". Furthermore, any person entering the town had to reside there for a year and a day before he could qualify for the freedom unless he was the son of an apprentice or a freeman.

But the Portreeve presided not only over the Court Leet and the Aldermanic Council. He presided also over the Vestry, the nerve centre of the parish, which had been selected by the Tudor sovereigns as the unit of local civil administration. Moreover, the Portreeve appointed and swore in the Church-wardens, so that in the government of the parish the Vicar seems to have been a mere cipher, and his name is never more than casually mentioned in either the Parish or Corporation Books. It has been possible to trace the functions of the Vestry at Swansea in several directions : in the maintenance of highways, in the relief of maimed soldiers and the prisoners in the county gaol at Cardiff, in payments to the Muster Master and the House of Correction, and finally in the destruction of vermin like rooks, crows, starlings, choughs, etc.

In the later sixteenth and early seventeenth centuries the borough had become increasingly exclusive. The government of the town was in the hands of a comparatively few, presumably wealthy, families who adopted a proprietorial attitude towards the rest of the inhabitants. This growing exclusiveness of the Corporation found expression, in the main, in the pre-occupation of the Corporation with the more profitable aspects of town life—the port, market and Corporation estate—and there is little evidence in its operations of any sense of responsibility to the population of the town as a whole, membership of the Corporation being regarded more as a privilege to be enjoyed than as carrying duties to be performed. Thus, only the minimum provision was made for such essentials as public health and education. The adverse effect of this was emphasised by the fact that the Corporation wielded authority over a very wide area, for the boundaries of the borough included the district bounded by the Brynmill stream, the Burlais Brook and the river Tawe, although the town itself, until the nineteenth century, was confined to a cluster of houses at the mouth and along the bank of the river. Still, perhaps we should not be too severe in our condemnation of the Corporation for failing to some extent in its responsibilities towards the townspeople, because a study of the Corporation accounts reveals that it only had a limited amount of money at its disposal. The Corporation had four main sources of income. These were rents, payments on admission of

Burgesses, profits of the port and fines for breaches of municipal regulations. In a typical year like 1629/30 the income from all these sources amounted to only £18 8s. 1d. The disbursements in this year were for repairs or other necessaries, or for relief of the poor, and amounted in all to £14 11s. 0d. Other indications of this growing exclusiveness of the Corporation are to be found in the greater self-consciousness of the Corporation as revealed in the emphasis laid on the dignity and decorous behaviour of its members and the purchase of maces; in the class conflicts that arose between the narrow oligarchy of wealthy ruling families on the one hand and the general body of poor inhabitants on the other ; and finally, in the attitude of greater independence which the Corporation adopted towards the lord by the early decades of the seventeenth century.

From the foregoing it can be seen that in the period 1485-1640 the character of municipal government at Swansea had been moulded primarily by two sets of circumstances, one set essentially local, and the other extraneous. Not only had the government of the town reflected the rapid development and expansion of the town's economy, but it had also responded to the central legislation of the times. Furthermore, it is interesting and instructive to note that while the town displayed many features which were essentially individualistic, many traits were revealed by it which were characteristic of the development of towns in general in the sixteenth and early seventeenth centuries. By 1640, though the actual framework of civic administration at Swansea was probably not dissimilar from what it had been at the end of the Middle Ages, it would appear that subtle changes had taken place in the working of that administration. Supreme power and authority had become increasingly concentrated in the hands of a few of the wealthier and more prominent among the town families, while to the non-burgesses the Corporation had acquired the appearance of a closed shop. The exclusiveness of town government at Swansea was to remain one of its most characteristic features right down to the nineteenth century.

THE CASTLES OF GLAMORGAN :

AN INTRODUCTORY STUDY

by

ARTHUR J. RICHARD, M.A., F.S.A.

THE first castles in Glamorgan were erected by the Normans during the conquest of the south-east by Robert Fitzhamon *c.* 1090 and the establishment of the lordship of Gower under Henry de Newburgh, Earl of Warwick, less than twenty years later. They were earth and timber structures, normally divided into two categories—the familiar motte and bailey, and the ring-motte or work. The former, perhaps earlier than the latter, consisted of a conical mound (the motte) partly or wholly artificial and surrounded by a ditch. The summit was flattened to receive a timber tower. Round the rim ran a stockade and at its base usually lay an enclosure, D or shield shaped, protected by a palisaded rampart and ditch (the bailey). Such mottes as have survived are widely scattered throughout the county and, as might be expected, stand on the fertile Vale and in river valleys.

A few occupied important sites—Llandeilo Talybont and Loughor guarded the approaches from the west, and Morganstown the route through the Taff Gorge, north of Cardiff, until, we imagine, it was replaced by Castell Coch in the thirteenth century.

Ring-works are single-banked and ditched enclosures ; one may be seen near the church at Llanilid and others in Gower. Two of the latter have been excavated—Old Castle Camp, Bishopston, by the late Col. Morgan[1] and Castle Tower, Penmaen, by Mr. Leslie Alcock.[2] The rampart of the Old Castle was 6 ft. high and 5 ft. wide at the top, and had a diameter of 25 yds. The ditch measured 20 ft. across and was 7 ft. to 8 ft. deep. A section cut

1 *Archaeologia Cambrensis,* July 1899.
2 *Morgannwg,* vols. III-V.

through the bank exposed impressions of a double row of stakes which Mr. Alcock suggests formed part of staging borne by the rampart. Castle Tower stands on a promontory overlooking Three Cliffs Bay. Here were found traces of a burnt gatehouse and two halls of different dates, the earlier built of timber and the other of dry walling four or five courses high. In both cases the only datable material was some mediaeval pottery. We are warned that such castles may be adaptations of existing fortifications. Other earthworks which may belong to this class are the elliptical enclosure at the north-east angle of the Iron Age fort at Caerau-super-Ely and "Y Gaer" north of Trehill, St. Nicholas, not far from a conical motte.

That motte castles were capable of presenting a stout and, at times, successful resistance may be gleaned from the fact that in an attack on a castle belonging to Henry Beaumont near Swansea in 1116 Gruffydd ap Rhys managed to burn the outworks (*i.e.* the bailey) but failed to take the tower. He was more successful at Oystermouth, which he burned outright causing William de Londres to leave his castle, cattle and riches.[3] Fire was the greatest danger; in 1215 Rhys Ieuanc reduced the castle of Loughor and took that of Hugh de Villers at Llandeilo Talybont "passing the garrison and castle through fire and sword". He then proceeded to conquer all the other castles of Gower.[4]

It was, therefore, inevitable that the more important structures should be rebuilt in stone. At Cardiff, caput of the lordship of Glamorgan, the new castle was built on the existing mound and the result was a shell-keep. This was in the second half of the twelfth century. The Norman invaders had found the Roman fort in ruins and having thrown up the motte and wooden tower they built up the walls on Roman foundations on the western and south western fronts. The rest of the walls they covered with a great earthen bank. Now the stockade was replaced by a stone curtain forming a twelve-sided keep with walls 6 ft. thick, against the inside of which were built lean-to structures. In the thirteenth century a new entrance was added and the "Black Tower" and the parapetted wall that connected it with the keep were constructed. The great hall and octagonal tower, which form the oldest part of the

3 *Brut y Tywysogion.*
4 *ibid.*

residential block, date from the first half of the fifteenth century and in all probability stand on the site of the original hall.

To the twelfth century, too, belong the massive rectangular keeps so admirably exemplified at Goodrich in Herefordshire. Kenfig was such a castle. Its sides measured 46 ft. by 44 ft. and were 11 ft. thick. As was usual the entrance lay on the first floor. Other characteristics were the pilaster and clasping buttresses and wide-jointed masonry. One only of the original corners remains, the north-eastern, and this was buried to the level of the vault of the basement; the others were removed when extensive alterations were made in the late thirteenth century. Normally such heavy structures were built where no motte existed. It is possible, however, that here the keep stands on the site of the original motte,[5] part of which was removed to raise the level of the existing bailey to the top of the plinths, except on the north-east side where the summit is about 7 ft. higher. There was extensive reconstruction during the late thirteenth and early fourteenth centuries. An entry in the *Annales de Margan* recording an attack on Kenfig in 1232 states that the tower was still encircled by a ditch and palisade (sepe). At the end of the century the latter gave way to a plain wall which served as a revetment to the mound, and the south wall was rebuilt from the plinth upwards. At the same time the basement was vaulted and a new entrance made at ground level. In the first half of the fourteenth century a corridor was added projecting into the outer bailey and leading to a drawbridge. This outer enclosure was unusually large, about eight acres in extent. May it have contained the "town within the gates" mentioned in the same account?

At the beginning of the thirteenth century came the circular keeps built either on ground level as at Pembroke or on solid mounds as at Skenfrith. Such a tower existed at Treoda in Whitchurch, where the motte has been flattened to within 5 ft. of the ground; it was probably built early in the fourteenth century. According to G. T. Clark there was another at Llanquian (Lancovian) with a diameter of 64 ft. At the time of its demolition in 1895 the round motte at Afan carried about 40 ft. of walling which might easily have formed part of a round building.

The lay-out at Kenfig is definitely that of the motte and bailey;

5 I am indebted to Mr. C. N. Johns for valuable help in working out this hypothesis.

at Coity and Ogmore[6] we are reminded of the ring-work. The keep stands to one side of the entrance and the curtain follows the line of the rampart. Keep and bailey form one defensive structure. The earlier of the towers mentioned is that at Ogmore which dates from *c.* 1130; the foundations of the cellar belong to the same century but the rest of the masonry to that which followed. The outer ward, which carried no curtain, also dates from the thirteenth century.

One of the most prominent features of castles was the hall. The remains of such a building erected in the thirteenth century may be seen against the north curtain at Ogmore; that at Coity was constructed in the fourteenth century and was situated on the first floor. It was supported by pillars. At Penrice[7] in Gower the domestic buildings were ranged along the north-west side between the circular keep and the gatehouse. The last-named is most interesting; it consists of three towers, two of which project their length beyond the curtain to form and protect a passage leading to the third immediately to their rear and linking them together. They are rectangular in shape and have rounded corners; a similar structure may be seen attached to the keep on its western side and the ruins of yet another stand further to the north-east. The eastern side of the circular keep was protected by a "chemise"; it was roofed and battlemented and had but one floor. It has been suggested that its original purpose was to enfilade the front of the hall.

The strongest of all the castles was Caerphilly, begun in 1271.[8] Its main features are the artificial lakes, the concentric plan and the gatehouses. The first were created by damming the stream which flowed on the southern side and the waters of the marsh which lay to the north. This was achieved by the erection of a curtain wall 380 yards long and strengthened by buttresses and bastions. About half-way along its length stood a gatehouse protected by a hexagonal barbican, isolated by the moat that ran along the front of the barrage. Behind this long wall were two platforms, the southern much wider than the northern. The flanks rested on gravel banks; at the southern end was a gatehouse and at the northern a postern gate protected by portcullis and drawbridge. Beyond the curtain

6 Described by Sir Cyril Fox as "Ring Castles". *South Wales and Monmouthshire regional guides to ancient monuments, vol. IV (H.M.S.O.).*
7 D.J.C. King and J.C. Perks : *Arch. Camb.*, 1961.
8 For a description of this castle see Dr. W. Rees' *Caerphilly Castle.*

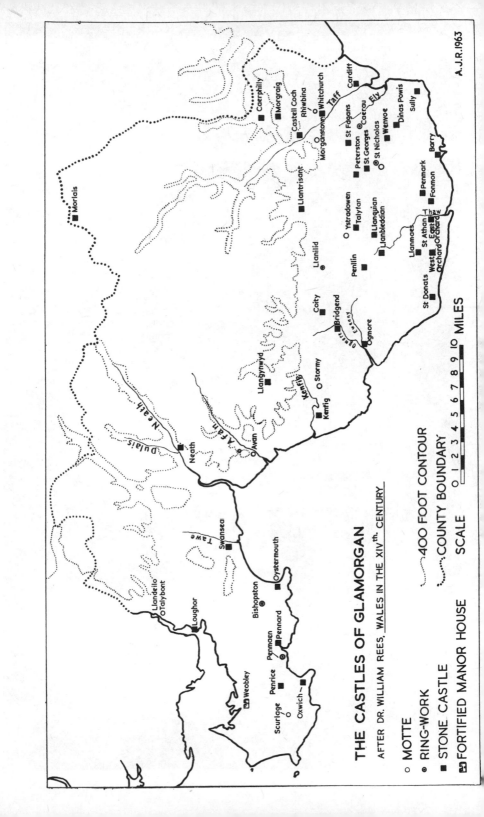

THE CASTLES OF GLAMORGAN

AFTER DR. WILLIAM REES, WALES IN THE XIVth CENTURY

- ○ MOTTE
- ⊙ RING-WORK
- ■ STONE CASTLE
- ▣ FORTIFIED MANOR HOUSE

.... 400 FOOT CONTOUR

∙∙∙∙∙∙ COUNTY BOUNDARY

SCALE 0 1 2 3 4 5 6 7 8 9 10 MILES

A.J.R. 1963

Morlais
Caerphilly
Morgraig
Castell Coch
Rhiwbina
Whitchurch
Morganstown
Cardiff
Llantrisant
St Fagans
Caerau
St Georges
St Nicholas
Wenvoe
Dinas Powis
Sully
Peterston
Penmark
Barry
Ystradowen
Talyfan
Llanquian
Llanbleddian
Fonmon
Thaw
St Athan
Llanmaes
Egst
West
Orchard
Orchard
Penllin
Llanilid
St Donats
Coity
Bridgend
Ewenny
Ogmore
Llangynwyd
Kenfig
Stormy
Kenfig
Neath
Avan
Neath
Nedd
Pwlais
Tawe
Swansea
Oystermouth
Bishopston
Pennard
Penmaen
Weobley
Penrice
Oxwich
Scurlage
Loughor
Llandeilo
Talybont

Caerphilly Castle

Photograph by H. Tempest (Cardiff) Ltd.

Cardiff Castle

**Plan of
Moated Mound**

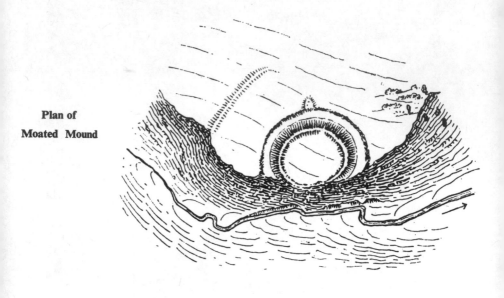

—— BISHOPSTON, GOWER ——

Section of Moated Mound

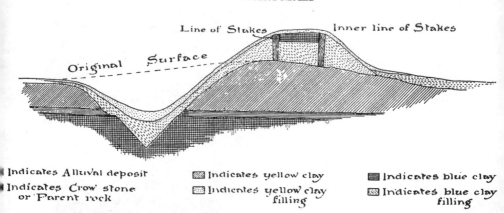

Line of Stakes   Inner line of Stakes

Original   Surface

Indicates Alluvial deposit   Indicates yellow clay   Indicates blue clay
Indicates Crow stone   Indicates yellow clay   Indicates blue clay
or Parent rock   filling   filling

Scale of Feet

10   5   0   10   20   30   40

Terrill
del

and separated from it by the inner moat was the main structure, concentric in plan and consisting of two wards, both entered through gatehouses at eastern and western ends.   At the angles of the outer ward are bastions rather than cylindrical towers which was the case in the inner ward, and it should be noted that its walls are low and that it is narrower than the inner—all of which was part of the general scheme of defence.   The inner ward was the principal stronghold; the east gatehouse was more elaborate and formidable than any other and was both fortress and residence.   It had three floors. On ground level were guardrooms flanking the entrance passage and above these stood the chamber from which the portcullises were raised and lowered.   On the second floor was the main chamber measuring 55 ft. long by 21 ft. wide; it had a great fireplace and was lighted by two long windows.   A small chapel with ribbed vault adjoined it at the southern end.   Communication with other parts of the castle was afforded by the rampart walk which was vaulted on its southern side.   The great hall lay to the south and had solars to the west and buttery and chapel to the east; the kitchen and servant quarters were contained in a semi-circular tower which jutted out into the outer ward.   On this side, too, was a covered passage leading from the hall to a water gate.   The architectural details of this range belong to the fourteenth century, as witness the ball-flower ornament on the jambs of the hall windows and door frame.   The western approach to the castle was guarded by the hornwork, three acres in extent and surrounded by the waters of the lakes.   Access from the west lay over a drawbridge leading to a gateway situated between two half-round bastions while communication with the outer ward was provided by another bridge worked from the western gate of the ward itself.

On the ridge which separated the commote of Cibwr from the rest of Senghenydd and not far east of the road that runs from Cardiff to Caerphilly past Thornhill lie the ruins of Castell Morgraig.[9]   The plan is hexagonal with a rectangular keep projecting from the east angle and D shaped towers from the others. It has been suggested that the castle was never completed; if this be so it does not stand alone, for the same is probably true of Llanblethian, where practically all that remains above ground is an early fourteenth century gateway.

9   *Cardiff Naturalists' Society Transactions*, vol. XXXVIII.

The castles at Caerphilly, Cardiff and Castell Coch were restored by the Marquesses of Bute. Among the residences that have been inhabited for a very lengthy period are Fonmon and St. Donat's. The nucleus of the former was a rectangular "keep" or hall of late twelfth or early thirteenth century date. Lateral extensions were made from the thirteenth century onwards to Jacobean times. St. Donat's was built by the Stradlings in the late thirteenth or early fourteenth century on the concentric plan, but much of the castle was modernised during the first half of this century.

A glance at the distribution map will show that the castles resolve themselves into two major groups, one extending westward from Cardiff as far as Kenfig and another in Gower with Swansea as base. Between them lay the lands of the Cistercian monasteries at Margam and Neath and the Welsh lordship of Afan. There are no traces of the original stronghold at Swansea; it stood immediately north of the existing building, no part of which is earlier than the thirteenth century. There have been extensive alterations to the site, but the mediaeval portion of the south block is a domestic structure especially associated with Henry Gower, Bishop of St. David's during the years 1328-47. Arcaded parapets similar to that at Swansea may be seen at the episcopal palaces at St. David's and Lamphey.[10]

There are but two castles in the upland region—those at Llangynwyd, near Maesteg, and Morlais, two miles north of Merthyr. The latter, generally believed to have been the cause of the trouble between the lords of Glamorgan and Brecon in the reign of Edward I, stood at the northern tip of the Uwch Caiach commote of Senghenydd near the disputed boundary between the two lordships.[11]

The exact nature of some of the castles has yet to be determined. Weobley was a fortified manor house and is so described in a document dated 1409. The emphasis is on the domestic side and the main rooms disposed around the comparatively small courtyard are the hall, kitchen, bakehouse and chapel. The windows of the solar and hall are large and one of them is an exact counterpart of the long windows in the hall at Stokesay Castle, Shropshire.

It has been repeatedly emphasised that castles were more than

---

10. W. Ll. Morgan. *Castle of Swansea.* D. B. Hague. *Gower*, vol. IX, 1957.
11. G. T. Clark. *Mediaeval Military Architecture*, vol. II, pp. 312 *et seq.*

military strongholds : they were centres of administration and economic development. They wrought great political and social changes; the lordship replaced the commote[12] and the towns and religious houses that followed must have helped to consolidate the hold already secured.

12 Dr.William Rees. "The Lordship of Cardiff". (*Cardiff Naturalists' Society Transactions*, vol. LXIII.), and Presidential Address, *Arch. Camb.*, 1961.

For plans see Ministry of Works Guides and G. T. Clark. *Med. Milit. Arch.*

I am indebted to Mr. G. Howard Davies for drawing the distribution map which accompanies this chapter.

ARTISTS IN THE VALE OF NEATH

by

ELIS JENKINS, B.A.

TO its inhabitants, the Vale of Neath is a broad gentle valley extending north-eastwards from the estuary at Briton Ferry to Pont Nedd Fechan, about fourteen miles upstream; to the specialist exploring the region for its geology, its caves, forests, archaeology or trout, this area is usually extended to embrace about thirty square miles of upland across which half-a-dozen tributary streams course like veins till they converge near Pont Nedd Fechan to form the River Neath. The wide valley with its quiet pastures and water meadows flanked by steep hills, and the upper region with its many ravines, water-falls and fissured limestone beds, combine to offer another specialist, the pictorial artist, an incomparable subject for his pencil and brush.

Although the beauties of this district had been observed since about 1600 by occasional visitors who had come from England or North Wales as botanists or antiquaries, the mass invasion did not begin till the second half of the eighteenth century, when the Vale, in common with many other remote parts of Britain, was discovered by a new kind of traveller, the topographical artist. Until this time, travelling in this country had been undertaken only for such exigencies as war, commerce or sheer subsistence, for the physical conditions were such that movement from place to place for pleasure was not only unthinkable, but sometimes even impossible. Roads were only a little better than they had been in Chaucer's day; inns were unreliable and, not infrequently, dangerous places for strangers, their landlords or landladies unhelpful, and the means of transport uncomfortable.

By contrast, the seat of a centralised government in London had found its focal point not only in parliament but in an urbane life which reached its highest expression in the clubs and coffee-houses whose sophisticated conversation ranged from the epigram

44

to what Lamb called "the diffuser graces of rhetoric". To the Augustans, wit found its consummation in the heroic couplet, the portrait in oils, and the formal classical landscape.

Then came breaking into the life of these two Englands the industrial, social and cultural upheavals which by comparison with the slower tempo of earlier changes might well be called revolutions. At this remove of time it is interesting to observe that soon after 1750 the people of England were going around in greater numbers than ever before in time of peace, the countrymen to the town in search of sheer subsistence, the townsmen to the country in quest of the picturesque.

The poets and the artists also were early on the move. While Gray, Thompson, Collins, Cowper and Dyer were finding inspiration in country scenes, and at the same time replacing the couplet with new and more flexible forms of expression, the artists were leaving London and the large cities on foot or horseback in such numbers as to suggest an exodus of biblical dimensions. Almost in procession they made for the furthermost parts of Britain, seeking picturesque scenes, and particularly that admixture of the old, the wild and the remote which made such an appeal to the town-bred artist as representing what came to be known as the Gothic.

Many reasons have been put forward to explain the upsurge of romantic feeling that sent the eighteenth century artists of western Europe to look for inspiration far from the towns. It has been usual to say that since well-to-do young men were prevented by war and revolution from completing their education with the Grand Tour of the Continent, they accepted as a substitute the discovery of remoter Britain. But as England was not involved in war with any European country for the twenty-five years preceding the last decade of the century, and there seems during that time to have been no political hindrance to the conventional Tour, one must look for other causes for the interest in landscape, ruins and rustics that had been evident fifty years earlier not only in England but in France and Germany as well. Among these may have been the mass imitation we call fashion, an infection by new ideas which we call "something in the air", or some manifestation of the swing between extremes which Carlyle describes as "action breeding reaction, reaction expending itself", the extremes in this case being the two ways of life represented by town and country.

In a short account of the topographical painters in Wales in the eighteenth century, reasons for their sudden activity are perhaps less positive than the fact that they found their material at its most congenial in Scotland, the Lakes, Yorkshire and Wales. The invasion of Wales was a pincer-movement, with the northern prong reaching out from Chester to the coastal castles and Snowdonia, and the southern alternating between an entry by way of Abergavenny or Newport. In the south, either way led to Neath : the north-of-the-valleys route to Merthyr and the Vale of Neath, the Newport route along the "Via Julia Maritima" via Cardiff, Cowbridge and Margam. As the end was a string of castles that included Swansea, Loughor, Kidwelly, Laugharne and a dozen others down to Pembroke, there was always a convergence at Neath, which had the advantage too of fifteen waterfalls around Ystradfellte, and a few more, together with water-mills and old bridges, in the main valley. Indeed, Ystradfellte provided the greatest concentration of fast-moving water and deep ravines in Britain, and by 1820 Aberdulais Mill and Baglan Bay had been depicted more often than any other provincial subject except perhaps Windsor Castle.

An examination of the collections of watercolour drawings in the National Library at Aberystwyth, the National Museum at Cardiff and the British Museum, and of the municipal galleries at Newport and Swansea, reveals a wealth of material that is quite astonishing. Nearly all the established artists from the mid-eighteenth century onwards came to the Neath district to record the rich variety of scene from fishermen's huts on the coast at Briton Ferry to the waterfalls above Ystradfellte, from the ruins of Neath Abbey and Castle to the Mill at Aberdulais. Anthony Devis, J. M. W. Turner, H. Walmesley, Paul Sandby, Thomas Rowlandson, Nicholas Pocock, J. "Warwick" Smith, Thomas Barker, H. Grimm, J. Laporte, H. Gastineau, Joshua Chrystall, W. de la Motte, Tom Girtin and John Varley are only a few of the many established topographers whose Neath drawings are preserved; and with these must be placed a smaller group of artists whose work is more strongly localised, men like Thomas Baxter, William Weston Young, Thomas Rothwell and Thomas Hornor, who did little work in other regions and whose stay in the district was extended.

The drawings of some of these artists, such as those of Payne,

Turner and James Bourne, were largely in small sketch-books, which were intended as visual reminders when some subjects were to be worked up into finished watercolours or paintings after the return to London or some other town in the south. Many of these sketches would be translated into engravings, the demand for which in the London print-shops during this period provided a steady income which was later to make a patron a little less indispensable. The work of other artists like Devis and Varley is represented by larger and less perfunctory drawings, perhaps only because their South Wales sketch-books have not survived, and we see only the London end of their work. Lastly were the isolated oil-paintings by Richard Wilson, Charles Deane and John Baker Pyne, who, if we may make the distinction, had more artist than topographer in their make-up; and there are also the well-known engravings by Paul Sandby and Walmesley, most of the preliminary sketches for which do not appear to have survived.

Nearly all these artists were Englishmen painting their way through the Principality under patronage (like Sandby) or for remunerative end-products such as book-illustration—it was the great age of travel-books—or engravings for sale in the print-shops that abounded in the city, especially around St. Paul's. At this time there were not many Welsh artists working in Wales, which lacked a tradition in painting and had few well-to-do patrons; indeed, in the period under consideration, only the Wynns of Wynnstay and Thomas Johnes of Hafod gave any considerable encouragement to the arts. The Welsh genius may have expressed itself more agreeably in that by-way of dramatic art, the sermon, for the puritan and the artist have either been uncomfortable bedfellows or have led a Cox-and-Box existence : when one is in, the other is out; which may explain the fine flowering of the arts in Wales with the decline in nonconformity around the turn of this century.

The first delineation of any Neath subject was a rough pen-and-ink sketch of St. Thomas's Church by Thomas Dinely, one of the two gentlemen-at-arms who in 1684 attended the first Duke of Beaufort on his triumphal Progress through Wales on his appointment as Lord President of the Council of Wales and the Marches. The next was in 1741, when the brothers Samuel and Nathaniel Buck recorded the Abbey and the Castle in their series of engravings—the well-known long horizontal panels with a printed title along the upper edge and several lines of cursive description below. The original sketch for the engraving of the Abbey is in the custody of the Neath Antiquarian Society, and, like its engraving, bears little resemblance to the external reality. It has sometimes been maintained that the topograhical artist did little more than record the outward face of a scene much as the camera did a hundred years later. This is manifest nonsense, as anyone can see by looking at a dozen representations of Neath Abbey or Aberdulais Mill; for although the work of the less talented lacks imagination, that of the more competent is highly individual in its treatment, while the very best, such as Turner's "Ewenny Priory" in the National Museum, has something of the consummation of the poet's dream, the light that never was on sea or land. Clearly, then, there is much variety in both the approach and the achievement of these artists, and if at one end we find the draughtsman content to record the scene without imposing much of his own personality on it, at the other there is not only Turner but J. C. Ibbetson, who, though always lumped with the topographical artists, was really more interested in people than in places.

In this profusion of artists who came to Neath, Turner stands head and shoulders above the others much as Shakespeare does over the other Elizabethan dramatists. In 1795, at the age of twenty, he made his second visit to Wales, following the coast road from Newport to Pembrokeshire and adhering closely to the itinerary and the recommended subjects and even inns which some friend or mentor had written inside the cover and on the flyleaf of his handsomely bound South Wales Sketchbook, now in the British Museum. Although some of the pages seem to have been torn out (either by Ruskin or his students, some think), at least one page must surely have been of Neath Abbey, for there is no sketch of any scene between Neath town and Kidwelly, and Neath Abbey was one of the London guide's recommendations. There are ten pages depicting scenes in or near Neath, which is exactly half the twenty South Wales drawings that have survived. Of these, four are of waterfalls, including those of Melincourt and Aberdulais, three are of watermills, including the pencil-sketch of Aberdulais Mill, and the remaining three are of coastal scenes at the Baglan Bay end of Briton Ferry. It is curious that although Turner must have passed through Briton Ferry on his way to Neath, the drawings of

eath Castle, 1807

By permission of Robin Herbert, Esq.

by George Bradshaw

eath Abbey, Town of Neath and Gnoll House, *c.* **1770**

18th century Artist

Gateway of Neath Castle, *c. 1790*

by J. "Warwick" Smith

By permission of the National Library of Wales

By permission of Neath Antiquarian Society

Neath Castle, *c. 1765*

by or after Richard Wilson

(*Right*) Aberdulais Falls

by William Weston Young

By permission of the National Museum of Wales

Left) **Aberdulais Falls, 1795**

by J. M. W. Turner

By permission of the British Museum. Turner's "South Wales Sketch Book", Ref. XXVI.9.

Porth-yr-Ogof, looking out towards Ystradfellte, 1819

by Thomas Hornor

Briton Ferry from Lord Jersey's home, 1818

by Thomas Bax

Lime Kiln near the mouth of River Neath, 1806

by William Pay

scenes in the Vale precede those of Baglan Bay, which may mean that the valley excursion was made on the day of his arrival at Neath, after which he spent the night at the Castle Hotel, and the next day crossed the Ferry to Jersey Marine, thereby missing Neath Abbey, but taking in Briton Ferry on his way to Swansea and the west.

There is some evidence that Turner later used some of these sketches for finished watercolours, but even in the sketch-book, especially where some colour-wash has been applied as in the coastal scenes and two of the waterfalls, the result is unforgettable. Particularly striking in the Melincourt drawing is the concentration on essentials by a young man confident in his reserve of a powerful visual memory, with the pencil work vignetting away, and a colour-wash of blue "dragged" on the cascade in the centre.

In this short survey it may appear that Turner has been given a disproportionate amount of attention, but, with such a long queue of visiting artists waiting their turn, it seemed necessary to begin with a general account of the incursion, extending to Turner the special mention appropriate to a giant, and close by singling out two or three men whose names will always be associated with the delineation of the district.

Thomas Hornor was a landscape gardener in London in the early years of the eighteenth century; he claimed to have discovered a new way of transposing to a plane surface an accurate representation of large estates. The publication of an account of his system and an advertisement in a South Wales newspaper appear to have brought him several commissions from the Neath district, so that between 1816 and 1820 he compiled a number of huge brass-bound albums of watercolours with interleaved descriptive matter in a beautiful copperplate hand. A typical album contains about two dozen watercolour drawings of scenes on the river Neath from the estuary at Briton Ferry to the waterfall region above Pont Nedd Fechan (corrupted by these very English travellers to "Pontneathvaughan" and since accepted by the class-conscious Welsh); but some albums include a supplementary illustrated tour, described in word and picture, down the Taff Valley from Merthyr to Cardiff, and along the coast to Briton Ferry to complete the round journey.

In 1925, Rhys Phillips in his *History of the Vale of Neath* used two pages to describe one of these "sumptuous albums", but, as was his way, did not reveal where it was to be found. In 1957, one of the albums, once the property of the Duke of Sutherland, was broken up for sale in Newport, and its forty drawings dispersed among two or three dozen new owners. Since then, continued search has brought to light the existence of seven more Hornor albums, all complete, and the remains of an eighth, making at least nine in all. Four of them are in Welsh national or municipal collections, one in the British Museum, and two in private ownership. No other region in Britain has been more assiduously recorded, nor more beautifully presented, for the alternation of attractive watercolours and meticulously penned descriptive matter is achieved with skill and even humour. Some of the albums have the drawings in the two tones of sepia and blue; others use the full range of available, or at least necessary, colours; and all have some of the illustrations, such as the inset cartouche of the river estuary, in monochrome. The most extraordinary feature is the resemblance between the contents of the albums, for not only is the manuscript account of the journey to the Vale reproduced verbatim at least eight times, but the drawings are almost identical from album to album, except for small variations such as the number and grouping of figures, or the detail of cloud formations and light conditions. That is to say that the viewpoint and layout for each picture are the same, the former being often marked on a special frontispiece map of the tour. If some of the drawings seem perfunctory and lacking in vitality, we must remember that for some five years he turned out at least nine or ten versions of each scene, for in addition to the Albums there are a number of watercolours given to the Neath Antiquarian Society in 1921 by Lady Stanley, a Neath woman and widow of the explorer of Africa. They include not only some very attractive panoramas of Briton Ferry and the estuary, but one faded version of an Album regular—Briton Ferry church.

Hornor worked during the heyday of the cult of panoramas, and eight of his albums include as a special endpiece a folded panorama of the Vale of Neath, which when extended shows a most imposing scene running from Cadoxton to Ystradfellte. Neath town itself is not visible, being concealed by an abutment of rock below Melincourt, but the Mumbles Head is discernible in the gap on the left, and the Carmarthen Van near the rock framing on the right. The panorama from the largest album is over nine feet long, and represents in every respect an imposing performance; and certainly impressive evidence of the successful application, in the hands of an artist as well as an inventor, of his much-advertised apparatus for "delineating the countryside". The smaller panoramas of the Briton Ferry district displayed in the Neath Public Library are also very attractive, and one of them shows an idiosyncrasy of Hornor's—a partiality for depicting a scene by moonlight.

At his best, Hornor is as good as any of his contemporaries except Turner, Girtin and the few who could soar; even at his poorest he is never banal, always competent and interesting, and as Neath's very special delineator, well deserving the space we have given him.

William Weston Young is another of Neath's "particulars". He came from Bristol in 1797 as a newly-wed in his twenty-first year to lease Aberdulais Mill. In six years he was bankrupt through speculating in East Anglian corn just prior to one of the Vale of Neath's good harvests. After that we hear more of him in connexion with Swansea earthenware and Nantgarw china, some of which he decorated without distinction, but also without the incompetence of the "Laddres Fall" on the National Museum plate attributed to him. After a life of varied activity and fortune in Newton, Worcestershire and elsewhere, he came to Neath again, to publish in 1835 the little *Guide to the Scenery and Beauties of Glyn Neath* (by which he meant the Vale of Neath, not Glyn-neath town), a rare and much-coveted book, whose fifteen small hand-coloured etchings testify to his dedication to a beautiful valley, if not to his genius. But Young was certainly talented, and his versatility in work and play, as well as his strength in adversity, made him much loved both during his life-time and posthumously. As he seldom signed his drawings, much of his work must be lost in anonymity, but there are some two dozen authenticated topographical watercolours depicting scenes in Swansea, Neath and the Neath Valley, and also parts of the Glamorgan coast near Porthcawl; a collection of sepia drawings, with long manuscript captions, in the National Museum of Wales; a refreshing album of fourteen scenes from the Vale, mostly rivers and waterfalls, in the National Library at Aberystwyth; and (in private ownership) some meticulously executed bird drawings, including a white owl, an eagle and a jay, which may have been copied from a late eighteenth century book. There is in Worcestershire a group of more fluent drawings of the Vale which the writer has seen in monochrome reproduction, but which suggest that, though Young sometimes could produce rather earthbound work, his best shows both skill and great charm.

In contrast to Young, whose output was considerable, two other artists employed at the Cambrian Pottery in Swansea made only brief excursions to Neath. In 1791 Thomas Rothwell, who was employed as engraver at the works, produced a number of engravings of local scenes which includes one of Vernon House, Briton Ferry. These prints, published by Coles and Haynes, are both scarce and mysterious, for they do not appear to have been used as designs on any of the pottery of the period, though some of them were transferred to some kind of plaster-of-paris base so fragile that fewer than half a dozen examples are known to have survived, among which are the one of Vernon House, the view of the Pottery itself, and a most interesting one of Aberdulais Mill, which, as the only version on paper informs us, was based on an early eighteenth century painting now lost.

Thomas Baxter, who came to Swansea from Worcester as a china decorator during the short-lived porcelain period, and whose work is now as much prized as it is scarce, published in 1818 in a brown paper cover a set of six engravings of local scenes. All but one are of Swansea, the exception being a view of Briton Ferry church. At about the same time, Baxter made many pencil-and-wash drawings of places in Swansea, the Mumbles and Briton Ferry. With two exceptions, those that have survived are shared between the Royal Institution of South Wales in Swansea and Mr. Kildare Meager, and their number, even when added to the total of the engravings, is probably less than that of the pieces of china supposed to have been decorated by this gentle and discriminating artist.

Baxter's watercolour of the garden of Vernon House, of which there are two copies, and which may have been commissioned by the owner, is more finished than the pencil-and-wash drawings of Swansea, and is also closer to the manner of his decoration on china. But in a sense drawings are more fragile than porcelain, for while the pieces of Swansea porcelain painted by Baxter probably look exactly as they did when they left the factory around 1818, the drawings (save for the one that has remained in the obscurity of an album) have faded so badly that they are now almost pencil sketches only. Even in our galleries, too many watercolours that should dwell in darkness have seen such a great deal of light that the freshness and colour of the artist's vision is now subdued to his draughtsmanship. So it may be a blessing that the limited wall-space of so many of our public and private galleries is being taken over for the display of phrenetic wallpaper patterns, and so driving the lowly topographers into the reserve collections in the basements. But they are there for the discriminating lover, with a curator or keeper or private trustee who seems ever willing to share his pleasure. As was said at the beginning, England (without Wales in this context) has really got something here.

POLITICS AND RELIGION IN THE VALE OF GLAMORGAN DURING THE CIVIL WAR

by

J. F. REES, M.A.(OXON).

" ALL Wales is the nursery of the King's infantry". So wrote a contemporary. This provides the key to the course of events in Glamorgan during the Civil War. When Charles I raised his standard at Nottingham on 22 August 1642, and thus declared open war on Parliament, he found that, while horsemen rallied to him in good numbers, he was lacking in foot. It was therefore decided to march towards the borders of Wales where active recruiting was already in progress. Commissions of Array had been issued to the leading gentry, who were for the most part firm Royalists, authorising them to raise forces. In the Vale of Glamorgan, then the most populous part of South Wales, there was a closely related group of families—Stradlings of St. Donat's, Bassetts of Beaupré, Aubreys of Llantrithyd, Carnes of Ewenny and Mansels of Margam. They readily responded to the King's summons.[1]

The plan of campaign was to make a direct attack on London, the chief source of Parliament's strength, and so endeavour to bring the struggle to a speedy conclusion. The King left his headquarters at Shrewsbury on 12 October with this end in view ; but his army was intercepted by the Parliamentary forces under the command of the Earl of Essex in Warwickshire. There the battle of Edgehill was fought on the 23 October. The first levies from Glamorgan were engaged. They had been hurriedly recruited and were untrained and ill-equipped. They suffered heavy casualties ; of their officers William Herbert of Cogan Pill, the Member of Parliament for Cardiff, was killed and Sir Edward Stradling of St. Donat's was taken prisoner. The battle checked the impetus of the

---

1 The influence of these families may be judged from the fact that they supplied some twenty of the High Sheriffs of the County in the first half of the seventeenth century.

advance on London. The Royalists did not reach its outskirts until 12 November when they were faced with such formidable opposition they had perforce to withdraw to winter quarters at Oxford.

Meanwhile, William Seymour, Marquis of Hertford, who had been appointed Lieutenant-General of the western counties, including South Wales, had landed at Cardiff from Minehead with a small company on 3 October. He was welcomed by William Herbert of Grey Friars and with his help took possession of the Castle. Steps were then taken to raise recruits throughout South Wales. Parliament was quite unable to counter Hertford's efforts for it had no supporters who could help to enforce the Militia Ordinance, its reply to the King's Commissions of Array. Hertford, however, did suffer one rebuff. A group of South Pembrokeshire gentry, when summoned to meet at Carmarthen, refused to do so ; an indication that the Parliament had some support there. The Royalists are said to have raised seven thousand men. They were assembled at Cardiff on 4 November and "with colours flying and drums beating" they set out to join the King at Oxford. They had if possible to avoid detection by the Parliamentary garrisons at Gloucester and Hereford and had reached as far as Tewkesbury when they were overtaken by forces from Hereford on the 16 November. Hertford's horsemen are said to have offered a strong resistance ; but the Welsh foot, who are described as "ragged and inexperienced", were thrown into confusion. Some twelve hundred surrendered and after admonition were sent home, their officers being retained.[2] Hertford was forced to retreat. But he made a second attempt to reach Oxford and did so with some two thousand men just before Christmas. He did not return.

The King's strongest supporter in South Wales—in fact, one of the wealthiest men in the country—was Henry Somerset, Marquis of Worcester, who lived in semi-feudal state at Raglan Castle. He had given Charles considerable financial backing. His eldest son, Lord Herbert of Raglan, was anxious to play an active part in the war, but the family was Catholic, and the King, in deference to the strong opinion among his supporters, had issued a proclamation

2 Prisoners were an embarrassment during the war. It was impossible to provide camps for them on a large scale. Men were offered service in Ireland or were even trans-shipped to the West Indies ; officers were largely exchanged, except in extreme cases.

which debarred Catholics from bearing arms. After the withdrawal of Hertford, however, he decided to recognise the services of the Somerset family by giving Lord Herbert a commission as Lieutenant-General in South Wales. This seemed the only way of retaining it as a recruiting ground. Lord Herbert, whose enthusiasm always outran his discretion, declared that he would at his own expense raise a sufficient force to take Gloucester, the Parliamentary occupation of which was a serious hindrance to the movement of troops from South Wales to England. With fifteen hundred foot and five hundred horse, probably mainly from Monmouthshire, an approach was made as far as Highnam in the middle of February. While they encamped there they were surprised by the Parliamentary General, Sir William Waller, who had crossed the Severn without being noticed, and were forced to surrender on 24 March. Nothing daunted, Lord Herbert made a second attempt to raise forces against Gloucester when the King decided in August personally to lay siege to it. He claims to have supplied four thousand foot and eight hundred horse, again at his own expense. But Gloucester held out until Essex by forced marches from London was able to relieve it. The failure to reduce Gloucester had serious consequences. It meant the relative isolation of South Wales.

After all these depressing experiences it is not surprising that recruiting in South Wales was becoming difficult. The Welsh levies, badly equipped and largely untrained, had been as one contemporary says "a continual sacrifice to the sword!" The King's need, on the other hand, was getting more urgent. When Parliament concluded an alliance with the Scots the Royalist position in the North of England was seriously threatened. To raise an army to meet this emergency Prince Rupert was given special powers in Wales. It was no longer a matter of depending on the personal influence of the gentry. Resort had to be made to impressment. For this purpose English officers were appointed. Sir Charles Gerard, who had seen service on the Continent, became commander in South Wales. Sir Timothy Tyrrell with an English garrison was placed in Cardiff Castle. The Glamorgan gentry were to resent these appointments and they soon found the financial exactions imposed a heavy burden. But they had to acquiesce. When Rupert was defeated at Marston Moor in July 1644 it was obvious that the Royalist cause had suffered a serious set-back. This was accentuated by the defeat at Naseby in the following summer. There the Welsh levies had fought until it was obvious that the position was hopeless and they then surrendered in whole companies. To show the extent of the victory the prisoners were marched through the streets of London. In Tothill Fields, Westminster, they were preached to in Welsh by the Puritan, Walter Cradock. About seven hundred were induced to join for service in Ireland ; others agreed not to fight again and were sent home.

The King was still buoyed up by news of the series of brilliant victories won by Montrose in Scotland and by persistent hope of ultimate help from Ireland. But for the moment he turned to South Wales to repair his losses at Naseby. Five days after the battle he was at Hereford. A conference of the Commissioners of Array from the South Wales counties was called at Abergavenny. They assured him that they could supply him with infantry. He retired to Raglan and waited for them to fulfil their promises. The Commissioners found that they were unable to do so. The conduct of Sir Charles Gerard and his officers had aroused general discontent. The King went to Cardiff on 16 July to exert his personal influence; but he was so disheartened by his reception that he contemplated leaving South Wales and joining Rupert at Bristol. This plan was discussed between the King and his advisers at Crick where Rupert joined them. It would have been adopted had not the Welsh gentry pleaded with Charles to remain in South Wales. A new danger had arisen. The Scots army had reached Hereford and laid siege to it. A rumour was put about that Parliament intended to reward the Scots for their services by grants of land in Wales. This was obviously intended to stimulate recruiting. The King went so far as to assert that it had. In a letter to the Sheriffs of the North Wales counties he told them that the South Wales counties had unanimously entered into an association to resist and repel the Scots. This was a complete misrepresentation of the position. As the Commissioners were making such little headway it was decided to instruct the Sheriffs to call out the *posse comitatus*—all the able-bodied men—from the ranks of these a force might be more speedily formed. The levies of Glamorgan, some four thousand strong, were representative of public opinion. It provided an opportunity to air grievances. On 29 July the King met them at St. Fagan's. They presented their demands—among them that Cardiff Castle should be entrusted to a Glamorgan gentleman and the present Governor, Sir Timothy Tyrrell, and the English garrison should be removed, and that the arrears of the charges imposed by Gerard should be remitted. The nature of these demands is sufficient proof that they were formulated by the gentry. The meeting was adjourned to the following day when they reassembled on Cefn Onn. The King capitulated ; Timothy Tyrrell was removed and Sir Richard Bassett of Beaupré was appointed as his successor. Emboldened by this success they demanded that Gerard should be deprived of his command in South Wales. Again the King had to comply. He now realised that the position in Glamorgan was hopeless. On 5 August he crossed the hills to Brecon, taking his mid-day meal at Llancaiach, the home of Edward Pritchard.

The command in South Wales was entrusted to Sir Jacob Astley. He could make no headway. Glamorgan, he reported, was in such a disturbed condition that no help could be expected from it. "It must be power", he declared, "to rule this people and not entreaties with cap in hand to such as deserve the halter". The confusion in the Autumn of 1645 is understandable. The King's cause was obviously in eclipse. Bristol was surrendered by Rupert. Montrose was decisively defeated in Scotland. The King's attempt to strengthen Chester had ended in disaster. Royalists everywhere had to face the painful problem of adjusting themselves to the changed situation. The Glamorgan gentry had been united in the demand for the removal of Sir Charles Gerard. But their loyalty was unshaken. They now found, however, that new leaders had arisen who were prepared to join the winning side. Bussy Mansel of Briton Ferry, a grandson of Sir Thomas Mansel of Margam, a youth of twenty-two, was given command of the Parliamentary forces in the County. Edward Pritchard of Llancaiach, who had strong Puritan leanings, replaced Sir Richard Bassett as Governor of Cardiff Castle. More important with regard to the future was Philip Jones, the captain of the Swansea garrison. He was to become the virtual dictator of Glamorgan. The opposition to this new alignment was in a weak position. The new leaders could call upon the Parliamentary forces in South Pembrokeshire for support, for they had, under the leadership of Rowland Laugharne, succeeded in resisting all attempts to reduce them. Taking advantage of the decline of the Royalist power Laugharne invaded Carmarthenshire which yielded on 12 October. In the next month he received the complete surrender of Breconshire.

The gentry of the Vale objected strongly to the religious policy pursued by the victorious party. Under the command of the Sheriff, Edward Carne of Ewenny, they made an armed protest in February 1646. They alleged that there had been a general agreement in the previous year to keep all parties out of Glamorgan and that this understanding had been broken. Then the purpose was to remove "insupportable grievances" which had been due to the conduct of Sir Charles Gerard and his soldiers. This had been achieved. But the movement, they alleged, had since been diverted to other ends by the action of a few. Men of no social standing had been placed on the County Committee, while baronets, knights and other gentlemen had been passed over. The County's monthly contribution had been raised from £67 to £162. These points might not arouse general indignation. A wider issue was raised on a manifesto which the clergy in each parish were asked to read to their people and where necessary to explain in Welsh. It included two passages of special significance. "The Common Prayer Book", it was asserted, "had been commonly traduced and on several Sundays its use had been altogether omitted at Cardiff, surely a forecast of its final rejection if some had their desires". This was amplified by the statement that "schismatics of several kinds are of greatest trust with some in chiefest places of the government in this County, whereby our souls and lives our liberties and estates must be at their desire". Carne marched towards Cardiff and demanded that Pritchard should surrender the Castle. Pritchard reported the situation to Laugharne and prepared to hold out until relief came. On the 16 February a ship arrived in the river Taff and fired six shots to indicate that relief was on the way. Carne realised that he could not proceed with the siege. The parties entered into negotiation. It was agreed that the countrymen should return to their homes, promising not to take up arms again unless summoned to do so under warrant of Bussy Mansel, the Parliamentary commander. No objection was to be made to the use of the Prayer Book. Although Carne had accused Pritchard of calling Laugharne into the County, he had himself sought help from Monmouthshire. According to one account the rival forces came into conflict ; but the details are vague. Carne himself was sent as a prisoner to Bristol. He made full submission later in the year and a heavy composition was imposed on him for his delinquency.

Many other gentry felt that the position in 1646 was so hopeless that it would be discreet to acknowledge their past conduct and petition to compound for their delinquency. Naturally they tried to minimise the part they had played. Some said that they had been nominated as Commissioners of Array without being asked ; which was probably true. The question was whether they had acted in that capacity. Sir Richard Bassett stated that when he was made Governor of Cardiff Castle he dared not refuse because the King was present with a force. But six weeks later, when summoned by some of the gentry and freeholders, he had yielded it up without any resistance on condition that he should go where he pleased. Sir John Aubrey of Llantrithyd had only done what others had done and could not help being made a Commissioner of Array. Sir Edward Thomas of Bettws (near Bridgend) excused himself as he was old and lame and unable to travel. Walter Thomas, former Portreeve of Swansea, admitted that he had armed the inhabitants ; but he also was old and confined to his bed. His son, William Thomas of Danygraig, represented himself as the victim of circumstances ; he was made Sheriff when Gerard was in power but he subsequently surrendered to Laugharne. Whatever their pleas in extenuation they were all fined a sum based on the estimated value of their estates. It is understandable that they would follow the course of events in the hope that they would not have to pay. The War was over but it was not at all clear what the terms of the settlement would be. The King had been a prisoner of the Scots since May 1646 and had been negotiating with them about the future form of Church government without any prospect of agreement. Recognising at last the futility of the proceedings the Scots handed Charles over to Parliament in January 1647. The Presbyterian members there were anxious to disband the Army and were ready to treat with the King. Division between Parliament and Army played into his hands. In June the Army took the bold step of seizing his person. The news of this coup reached Glamorgan. It seemed to some of the gentry of the Vale an opportune moment to stage a demonstration against the County Committee. They met at Cowbridge on 13 June and issued warrants to the High Constables of the Hundred of Miskin to summon all able-bodied men to assemble there with their arms. This they claimed they did in the names of the King and Sir Thomas Fairfax, the Commander of the Army. They wrote to assure Laugharne, who was at Carmarthen, that their action was not intended to be any disrespect to him. Information had reached them that the County Committee intended to seize some of them and they had to act for their own security. It is clear that the old quarrels about sequestrations and religion were at the back of the movement. Laugharne described the leaders as "ancient malignants of a deep stain" who had no grievances. The County Committee, he declared, had justly administered the Ordinances of Parliament. But that was the rub. Between one and two thousand appear to have joined in a march towards Cardiff. Edward Pritchard in answer to a letter sent to him, signed by the chief leaders, naturally asked them by what authority they had disturbed the peace of the County. Their demands in the letter were that they should enjoy their liberties and estates as fully as they had before the setting up of the Committee and that taxation should be suspended until the outcome of the present discussions between King, Parliament and Army was ascertained. Laugharne acted promptly to suppress the rising. This was not difficult because some of the gentry did not approve of it and the common people were averse to a renewal of the fighting. On the approach of Laugharne's men the leaders took to flight. Prominent among the names appended to their manifestoes were those of Sir Richard Bassett and Sir Edward Thomas, both of whom had petitioned for permission to compound in the previous year. The brothers John and Thomas Stradling were also involved. It is curious to find the name of Sir Thomas Nott sometimes leading all the rest. He does not appear to have had any connection with Glamorgan. He was from Worcestershire and was known as an eminent Royalist. Probably he had come to South Wales to report the state of affairs in England and help to instigate a rising. There was also a suspicion that Judge Jenkins of Hensol (then a prisoner in the Tower) had done something to inspire it. But it did not need much encouragement to give vent to the smouldering discontent among the gentry of the Vale.

The next year seemed to offer them a golden opportunity. Parliament issued an order for the disbanding of supernumeraries, a heading under which Laugharne's troops came. John Poyer, the governor of Pembroke Castle, refused to surrender that stronghold. His defiance was supported by part of the forces of Colonel Rice Powell who had been Laugharne's right-hand man throughout the War. The Royalists were quick to take advantage of this mutiny of their erstwhile opponents. As the former Parliamentarians advanced from West Wales and entered Glamorgan they gathered an increasing number of supporters. Now there seemed a chance of taking Cardiff Castle which the risings in the past two years had failed to do. Fairfax had sent Colonel Thomas Horton to deal with the trouble in Pembroke. He was in Brecon when he was alarmed to learn of the threat to Cardiff. By forced marches through difficult country he managed to reach Llandaff and thus throw himself between Powell's forces and Cardiff. Laugharne, who had been absent in London, now hastened to the scene. He was in a difficult position. On two previous occasions he had suppressed Royalist disturbances in the Vale. Now he affected to believe that Horton was to blame for what had happened. He demanded to know by what authority he had entered into a district which had been ascribed to him by Parliament. Horton could only reply that he was acting under the command of Fairfax against Poyer and Powell who had defied the order to disband. He expressed his surprise that Laugharne had not chosen to assist him in crushing a movement that challenged the authority of Parliament. These exchanges were of no avail. For whatever reason Laugharne had decided on his course of action. He had a week-end to organise the composite force of which he now assumed the command ; for it was known that Cromwell was on his way with reinforcements. The advantage of numbers was on his side. These included his own men—the supernumeraries—who had had much experience of fighting and a large body of countrymen who had been collected by Powell in his advance through the Vale. The total number probably amounted to eight thousand. Horton appears to have had not more than three thousand, but they were disciplined troops. Laugharne prepared for battle early in the morning of Monday, 8 May, marching from St. Nicholas in the direction of St. Fagan's. Horton's account of the engagement gives a clear picture of how he ordered his forces. Unfortunately there is no corresponding account of Laugharne's tactics. Horton admits that the issue was fiercely contended for two hours before his men gained the advantage.   Then resistance ceased.   Over a hundred officers were taken prisoner and about three thousand men.   Four thousand clubmen (countrymen) are said to have been dispersed.   Tradition has greatly exaggerated the number killed in the action.   Laugharne and Powell escaped to Pembroke and Tenby respectively and prepared to be besieged.   Pembroke held out against Cromwell himself until 11 July.

After this defeat the Vale had to submit to the policy of the Puritan party.   The Army was in control and it was dominated by the sects—Baptists and Independents—and the Church was in a very drastic sense disestablished.   It is significant that Horton acknowledged the debt he owed to Philip Jones for all his help. He also commends the "constant-minded" Edward Pritchard and Bussy Mansel.   New men were now definitely in control.   The County Committee had the power to sequester the livings of "scandalous" clergy and put others in their place. The exercise of this power had been one of the causes of the risings in the previous two years.   "Scandal" as interpreted by the Puritans was a wide term.   It covered delinquency, *i.e.* open support of the Royalists, insufficiency, especially in regard to preaching, plurality and moral defects of character.   There was ample room for the application of these principles in the Vale for Puritanism had made little or no progress there.   Before the war it had made some impression in Cardiff where William Erbury, Vicar of St. Mary's, had been accused before the Court of High Commission of irregular practices and forced to resign, while his curate, Walter Cradock, had been deprived of his licence by the Bishop of Llandaff, but the only "gathered church" at this time was that at Llanvaches, near Chepstow, which was the first Independent cause in Wales.   Walter Cradock had ministered there.   When war broke out the members fled to Bristol, and later to London.   In 1641 Cradock supported a petition to Parliament for more preachers for Wales and he continued to press this need.   This was ultimately met by the appointment of three itinerant ministers to preach in Welsh in South Wales—Henry Walter, Richard Symonds and Walter Cradock himself.   It is worthy of note that Henry Walter, like Cradock, was closely associated with Llanvaches.   The fortune of war had opened a way for the Puritans to preach "the Word" in South Wales.   The three itinerants were voted maintenance of £100 a year out of the revenues of the Deans and Chapters of Llandaff and St. David's. The parochial clergy on the other hand were subject to enquiry as to their "sufficiency" and thirty-five were ejected from their livings in Glamorgan before the more stringent examination which followed the passing of the Act of 1650. Puritan nominees were usually selected to fill the vacancies. But the majority of episcopal clergy were not removed. What was happening, however, must have caused general alarm among them. The Church had been disestablished and partially disendowed. What would be the next step? The answer came when the "Rump" Parliament passed the *Act for the better Propagation and Preaching of the Gospel in Wales*. This superseded all previous enactments. It provided for the appointment of seventy-one Commissioners, any five or more of whom were authorised to summon before them any clergyman who had been charged with "Delinquency, Scandal, Malignancy or Non-residency". If found guilty they were to be ejected from their benefices. Their places were to be filled by men recommended by a body of Approvers. Prominent among the Commissioners were Philip Jones, Edward Pritchard and Bussy Mansel. At the head of the list of Approvers were Henry Walter, Walter Cradock and Richard Symonds. The operation of the Act was limited to three years. During that period twenty incumbents were ejected in Glamorgan. The charges against them were mostly Delinquency or Insufficiency This is in marked contrast with what happened in Monmouthshire where forty-five were ejected. In ten cases the charge was Drunkenness. Perhaps the Commissioners were more lenient in Glamorgan.

The period from the outbreak of the Civil War to the lapsing of the *Propagation Act* (1642-1653) were years of strain and stress in the Vale of Glamorgan. It is difficult, however, to assess the effect of the War and its sequel. There were repeated recruiting drives which must have been a drain on the man-power ; but round figures have to be regarded with caution. Since prisoners were not generally retained it is probable that there was a good deal of double reckoning. Then heavy fines were imposed on the gentry as composition for their delinquency. If paid, they must have had a crippling effect on their estates ; but to what extent cannot be ascertained. All the evidence goes to show that the gentry, despite their difficulties, remained Royalist at heart. They did not change sides, though many at times may have wished that it were possible

Herbert House as it was in 1805. Part of this ruin still stands in Grey Friars, Cardiff. It was an Elizabethan residence, a plan of which is shown on Speed's Map of Cardiff, 1610

Llancaiach, the home of Edward Pritchard, as it was in 1889

Drawing by David Jones of Wallington

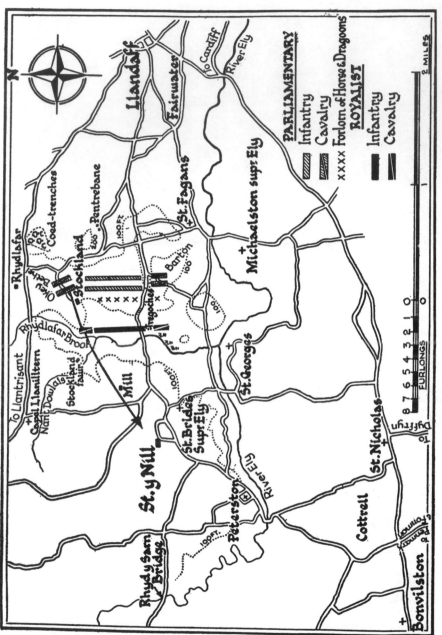

The Battle of St. Fagan's, 8th May, 1648

Reproduced, by permission, from Sir Frederick Rees's *Studies in Welsh History* (University of Wales Press, Cardiff).

to maintain neutrality.   The crisis of 1645, when they resisted the
King to his face and compelled him to dismiss Sir Charles Gerard,
was a protest against the excesses of the English officers who had
been nominated by Rupert in his anxiety to impress and equip men
without delay.   It is a most interesting incident.   One of the King's
supporters shrewdly remarked at the time that to negotiate with the
King before obeying his commands was a dangerous innovation.
But the gentry were not concerned with general principles.   They
wanted particular grievances redressed.   That their loyalty was
unshaken is proved in the following years, when although the
position was well-nigh hopeless, they were prepared to snatch at
any chance to embarrass the Parliamentary party.   As to religion
they were staunch upholders of the Church and strongly resented
the attack which the Puritans directed against it.   Their partiality
for bishops aroused the suspicion of Captain Robert Moulton,
who with the Parliamentary ships was keeping a close watch on
Glamorgan.   He reported to the Speaker of the House of Commons
that there was a group at St. Donat's which included Archbishop
James Ussher of Armagh,[3] Bishop Pearce of Londonderry and
possibly Bishop Mainwaring of St. David's.   The Commons thought
this concentration of bishops sufficiently suspicious to order their
arrest and that of their host Major-General Stradling.   They might
have noticed also that Francis Mansel, ejected principal of Jesus
College, Oxford, had sought refuge in the Vale and was at one time
the guest of the Aubreys of Llantrithyd.[4]

In the years following the battle of St. Fagan's until the restoration of the Monarchy in 1660 the civil government was largely in
the hands of Philip Jones, while Bussy Mansel held a succession of
military commands.   Philip Jones enjoyed the special confidence of
Cromwell to whom his extensive knowledge of Welsh affairs was
invaluable.   Many charges were brought against him, particularly
with regard to the administration of the *Propagation Act*.   His

---

3   James Ussher was the father-in-law of Sir Timothy Tyrrell and was at Cardiff
Castle when it was handed over to Sir Richard Bassett in 1645.   He was
obliged to move and had spent his time in the harmless occupation of
examining the books in the extensive library at St. Donat's.

4   It is worthy of note that there are few references to Catholics in the Vale.
The only Catholic family among the gentry was that of the Turbervilles of
Penllin and their various branches.   In the list of those killed at the battle
of St. Fagan's the name of Captain Turberville occurs with the addition
"a Papist".

purchases of property were criticised. He no doubt had opportunities for acquiring land in the unsettled condition of the times. Fonmon, of which his family is still in possession, was the bankrupt estate of a Parliamentarian when he bought it. Neither Philip Jones nor Bussy Mansel had strong religious convictions. They were politicians of the school which was characterised in the next generation as "trimmers". Of this their subsequent careers are sufficient proof. Philip Jones was Sheriff of Glamorgan in 1671 and Bussy Mansel was returned as Member of Parliament for the County in 1679. Whether Edward Pritchard displayed comparable flexibility—or whether he survived to the Restoration—is not known. He was older than the other two, for he was Sheriff in 1637 when they were not out of their 'teens. As a Puritan—and a Baptist—he may have had inconvenient convictions in the changed circumstances.

AUTUMN STORM : GLAMORGAN COAST

The wild sea hurls its ancient anger
Against the stubborn ramparts of the shore,
Like some vain Emperor whose monstrous pride
Demands new conquests, launching host on host
In thunder at the long beleaguered land.

There is no plunder here : the harassed trees
Have signalled their surrender to the winds,
Those loud marauders galloping through groves
With gusty sabres, seeking crinkled gold :
And whirling high the tributes of defeat
From ransacked treasuries, they toss and fling
The coloured coinage madcap to the world,
Like roaring, lusty, reckless prodigals,
Not caring where their lavish largesse falls.

And I, secure within my neutral cloak,
Anonymous amid anarchic elements,
Await and watch, enthralled by awe and wonder,
The fury of the white embattled waves,
And hear above the tumult of their onset
The high, victorious voices of the winds
Shrilling their challenge to the heedless stars.

A. G. PRYS-JONES.

THE ROMAN ARMY IN GLAMORGAN

by

GEORGE C. BOON, B.A., F.S.A., F.R.N.S.

IN Roman times, Glamorgan was part of the territory of the Silures, whose eastern boundary probably lay on the Wye, not far from which their little walled capital of *Venta*, Caerwent, was to rise. Tacitus describes the Silures as powerful, warlike, and in personal appearance swarthy and curly-haired. For nearly thirty years they remained, by force of arms and circumstance, outside the first, Severn-Trent frontier of the new province of Britain ; and, under the leadership of Caratacus—the Belgic chieftain who had fled westward after an initial defeat in Kent in A.D. 43—they harried Roman positions in the border so that legions were urgently sent in 49 to keep them at bay. Even after the subsequent defeat of Caratacus, resistance continued, and was favoured by the increasing difficulties of the Roman high command in Britain and then by civil war abroad. In 71, however, the Romans were able to begin a series of forward movements which culminated in the conquest of Highland Britain, as far as the Moray Firth, by 84. The conquest of the Silures was effected by the governor Julius Frontinus in 74-8 ; our only historical record of a brilliant campaign is one sentence of Tacitus, who makes especial mention of the difficulties of the terrain, but—as we shall see—the basic strategy of the conquest can be glimpsed archaeologically, in our own Glamorgan estuaries and uplands.

Two of the four legions involved in the invasion of Britain in 43, the Second Augustan and the Twentieth, were allotted to the permanent garrison of Wales—each with a base at the roots of the Welsh peninsula, the Second at Caerleon-on-Usk, *Isca*, and the Twentieth at Chester, *Deva*. Dependent on each legion were a dozen or more auxiliary regiments, scattered in forts strategically sited throughout Wales to maintain a military stranglehold on the natural routes of communication within the mountainous hinterland (fig. 1). Seven of these forts, held by regiments nominally 500 or

68

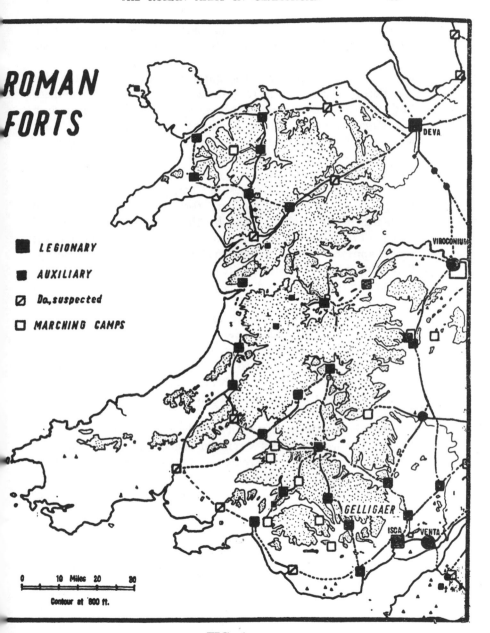

ROMAN FORTS

■ LEGIONARY

■ AUXILIARY

▧ Do., suspected

☐ MARCHING CAMPS

DEVA

VIROCONIUM

GELLIGAER

ISCA

VENTA

0   10   Miles   20   30

Contour at 600 ft.

FIG. 1.

1,000 strong—infantry, cavalry or part-mounted—are known in Glamorgan. One, at Gelligaer above Ystrad Mynach, has been extensively excavated. The sites of two are uncertain, and the rest have been partly explored. The purpose of the forts of the west and north of Britain was to protect the rich lands of southern England from the marauding tribesmen of the hills—and those in Glamorgan also sheltered the urban and romanised rural life which grew up along the southern seaboard, matching developments across the Channel in Gloucestershire and Somerset.

The map suggests the strategy of conquest. Firstly, we notice the estuarine siting of the fortress at Caerleon, closely paralleled by the positions chosen for auxiliary forts at Cardiff, Neath and Carmarthen and probably also by the two unlocalised sites of *Bomium* (? Ogwr estuary) and *Leucarum* (? Pontarddulais) whose names appear in a third-century road-book, the *Antonine Itinerary*. Secondly, since each excavated site has produced evidence of occupation in the conquest period, it is pretty clear that the invasion of 74-5 was seaborne, and possibly in several divisions designed, by a series of pincer-movements, to link up inland.

Today, our main routes inland from, say, Cardiff or Neath, lie along the valleys. Then, however, aboriginal forest encumbered the valley-bottoms, thinning out to scrbu or open moor mainly on the uplands. It is on the uplands, therefore, that we should expect to find the earliest traces of imperial Rome ; and aerial survey and fieldwork enable us to do so.

Sarn Helen, the Roman road from Neath fort (*Nidum*; the fort lies partly beneath the Boys' Grammar School and partly beneath an adjacent housing-estate, where two of its stone gateways are still to be seen) across the Fforest Fawr and down to the fort at Aberyscir ("Brecon Gaer"—*Cicutio*, partly excavated in 1924-5) climbs the west side of the Vale of Neath and, after passing the auxiliary fort at Coelbren (partly excavated in 1904) traverses the faint remains of a rectangular enclosure near Ystradfellte. This is a Roman marching-camp, and at 21 acres was large enough to house a sizeable force under the cramped conditions of active service. On the east side of the Vale of Neath, three others have recently come to light, linked by an ancient ridgeway (Cefn-y-ffordd). The first is near Tonna, opposite and above Neath fort, and already 800 ft. above sea-level : it occupies 61 acres, and was obviously the base-camp for an army

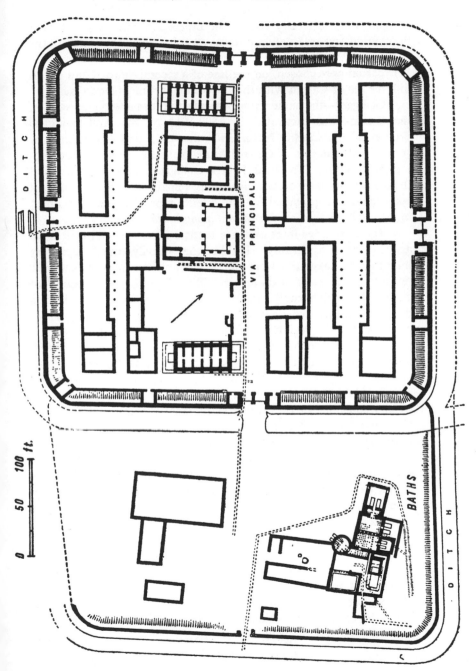

FIG. 2.

of more than legionary size. The others are near Aberdare and Pontypridd and are smaller. It was on some such penetration of the *Blaenau* that sites for permanent auxiliary forts at Gelligaer and Penydarren were chosen, on the line of a secondary road laid out to link the sea at Cardiff with the important fort at Brecon Gaer.

Gelligaer—the name itself bespeaks the former wooded state of the terrain—was excavated in 1899-1913 by the Archaeological Section of the Cardiff Naturalists' Society ; and the reports by John Ward, Curator of Cardiff Museum, are a classic of archaeological literature. To this day, little Gelligaer, its Roman name and the name of its garrison both lost to us, remains a perfect example of accommodation provided for the smaller type of infantry regiment in the auxiliary forces—the *cohors quingenaria*.

The auxiliaries increased the tactical efficiency of the Roman army very considerably. Unlike the heavily-armed legionary infantry, the auxiliaries were not Roman citizens and in fact their reward for 25 years' arduous and ill-paid service was a grant of citizenship, which each man received in the form of a bronze diploma—an attested copy of the original filed at Rome. These diplomas list the regiments having men due for the grant at any particular time, and as several of them have been found in Britain they throw considerable light on the army establishment of the province. One, of A.D. 103, was found at Malpas in Cheshire and lists four cavalry regiments and eleven cohorts of foot. One of the cavalry units, the *Ala* of Spanish Vettonians, was stationed at Brecon Gaer about 100, and this suggests that the other regiments too may have been in the Caerleon Command of the Second Augustan Legion, for Brecon has produced stamped tiles of the Second Legion and was therefore most probably under the Legion's control. The regiments are drawn mainly from the Balkans, Gaul, the Low Countries, and Spain, and were more lightly-armed than the legionaries (pl. IA), retaining, in many cases, the traditional arms of their homelands.

Gelligaer fort (fig. 2) is about 400 ft. square and nearly 3¾ acres in extent ; it lies (just behind St. Cattwg's church) at the tip of Cefn Gelligaer at about 770 ft. above sea-level, commanding a bleak and distant southerly prospect. The defences were massive : a V-cut ditch, the upcast from which formed the rampart, which was faced externally with a stout wall, and revetted by masonry along its inner

Plate I A. Battle scene on Trajan's Column. *Left :* legionaries, under their company standard-bearers, in reserve. *Middle :* auxiliary cavalry and, *Right :* auxiliary infantry attacking. Their raised hands held metal spears originally. About A.D. 107

By permission of the National Museum of Wales

Plate I B. North gateway of the late Roman fort at Cardiff (now restored) from within; note the projecting massive towers and the deeply recessed narrow gateway. Defensive fortification, to be contrasted with Gelligaer type of gateway (fig. 3) with its flush-fronted towers and wide (double) passageways designed for offensive movements

Fig. 3. Axonometric sketch for a reconstruction of the S.W. Gateway, Gelligaer

Fig. 4. Partial restoration of fragments of a dedicatory inscription from the S.E. Gateway, Gelligaer. Drawn by the author in consultation with R. P. Wright, Esq., F.S.A. The two final lines, which may have mentioned the regiment in garrison, are missing except for part of a numeral. Reads : *To the Emperor Caesar Nerva Trajan, son of the deified Nerva, Augustus, Conqueror of the Germans and the Dacians, High Priest Holder of Tribune's Power, Father of his Country, Consul for the fifth time* . . . (A.D. 103-111)

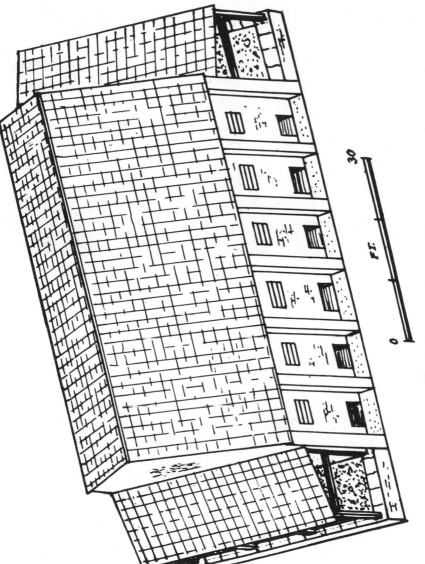

Fig. 5.   Axonometric sketch of a reconstruction of a granary, Gelligaer

Plate II A. Circular dry-heat room (*laconicum*) added to the regimental bath-house, Gellig
Foreground : cheeks of the furnace, with collapsed arch. *Within :* rubble of the colla
suspended floor and several collared box-tiles from the insulation of the vault

By permission of the National Museum of Wales

Plate II B. Granary near the N.W. Gate, Gelligaer. The figure stands on one of the cross-w
which supported the floor; behind him is the end wall of the building and beyond it a cov
loading bay and raised platform in front of the door

side. Calculation suggests that the wall was in the region of 13 ft. high, to which another 5 ft. for the battlements should be added. Each side was centrally pierced by a double gateway, with arches turned in calcareous tufa probably quarried at Pontsticill ; the passageways were deeply recessed, and flanked by guard-chambers carried up into towers connected by a gatehouse (fig. 3). There were also corner turrets, and one interval turret between each corner and gateway. Inscriptions from the north-west and south-east gates, although fragmentary, tell us that the defences were completed in the 5th consulship of the Emperor Trajan, A.D. 103-11 (fig. 4).

A wide roadway ran around the inside, delimiting the densely built-up area within, which was traversed by a main street (*via principalis*) running north-west to south-east. This street was flanked by the administrative block. Centrally, and facing another street (*via praetoria*) leading from the north-east gate, lay the headquarters-building (*principia*) with its enclosed courtyard containing a well for emergency use, its assembly-hall, and its suite of rooms to the rear—the middle room being the regimental shrine, where the standard would be laid up and the pay-chest kept. On the left of this was the residence of the commandant (*praetorium*), the prefect of the cohort ; beyond, one of the two stoutly-buttressed granaries (*horrea*) with ventilated floors. On the right of the headquarters we find the workshops and yard (*fabrica*) and the other granary. Here (pl. IIB and fig. 5) the grain would be stacked as it arrived in the form of tribute (*annona*) from the conquered tribes of lowland England : the two granaries are capable of holding, by calculation, a year's supply of the soldiers' staple foodstuff.

The front division of the fort (*praetentura*) contains four oblong barrack-blocks (*centuriae*), a pair on either side of the *via praetoria*. The other two, in the rear section of the fort (*retentura*) behind the headquarters, lie one on either side of the *via decumana* leading from the south-west gate, and complete the requirement for the housing of the six centuries of eighty men which probably formed the actual complement of the cohort. The broader, end sections of the *centuriae* mark the centurion's quarters ; the stud partitions which once divided the rest into narrow cubicles (*contubernia*—each perhaps for a section of eight men) have vanished. The stone partition within the broader end may mark off the quarters allotted to the three junior officers in the century, namely the *optio* (second in command), *signifer* (standard-bearer) and *tesserarius* (clerk).

Such an arrangement of buildings is within narrow limits standard and, with the differences imposed by the needs of the various kinds of regiments, can be found all over the Roman Empire —but nowhere, let it be added, more clearly than in Britain.

Outside the fort there was a two-acre annexe, fortified at some late period : the principal building within it was the regimental bath-house (*balneum*) over 90 ft. long, with a good-sized cold plunge, and rooms for moist (*calidarium*) and dry (*laconicum*) heat—this is the circular building (pl. IIA) added to the plan at some period. The heating-system was by hypocaust ("heat below"), where the heat produced by a furnace fired from outside circulated under, and warmed, the raised floor—sometimes, as we learn from ancient writers, to an uncomfortable pitch. In the walls there were narrow chimney-flues of tile to provide the necessary draught ; and (as experiment has shown) when once the immense thermal capacity of the structure had been overcome, this method of heating (used very often for houses) seems to have been reasonably efficient.

Much more must be said if the picture of Gelligaer is to be a complete one : but that space forbids. There was, for example, a well-built tile-kiln in the present churchyard, where most of the many thousands of tiles used in the fort and its environs were baked ; then, further away, we find the five-acre earthen enclosure which some regard as a labour-camp occupied during the construction of the fort, or its rebuilding in stone. Some practice-camps, where the troops were taught the art of entrenchment, have been noted a mile or so away at Heol-ddu-uchaf.

Of the other Glamorgan forts, I can pause only at Cardiff. Here, finds postulate the presence of an auxiliary fort, perhaps only of earthwork-and-timber construction, as was normal at the conquest-period and even later. The extant structure, however, belongs to a later fort, of a different type. The curtain-wall of the Castle is largely a reconstruction of the final phase of the defences of this fort, and was so built at the instance of the third Marquess of Bute. At the bottom of the walls, outlined in red stone, the courses of small Lias limestone masonry that are the Roman basis for the restoration can be seen to this day. The fort, girt with a wall 10 ft. thick with an earthen rampart behind, encloses 8¾ acres, and had only two gateways, north and south. As originally planned, however, its appearance was rather different. There were no bastions and projecting gate-towers, and the corners were rounded in the old Roman way exemplified at Gelligaer. In Wales there is at present no known parallel to this kind of fort ; but along the south-east coast of England, the "Saxon Shore", there is more than one such. At Reculver, a recently-found inscription suggests that the type was being built as early as the first part of the third century—a surprise for scholars. Then, at Cardiff, the wall was later rebuilt much as the Marquess thought, although his internal gallery is rather unlikely. The main features to note are the multangular bastions and gate-towers with their side-embrasures, placed for *ballista* (spring gun) crossfire ; the ditch beyond has gone. Similar defences can be seen at Caerwent to this day, and in that case were certainly built after 330. At Cardiff, as at the later Saxon Shore forts like Richborough, a late third or early fourth century date seems likely for this type of structure (pl. IB). Practically nothing is known of the interior of the fort, but occupation continued down to 383, as coins show, and during this time repairs were carried out.

The fort guarded the Channel seaboard—the English side no less than the Welsh, for it must in part have served as, or at least sheltered, a naval base—perhaps the same *reliquatio classis* whose commandant dedicated an inscribed mosaic at the late Roman temple of Nodens at Lydney. Beginning in the third century, and reaching a climax in the fourth, came the piratical raids from Ireland which brought about a development of the previously static and inward-looking system of Welsh defence. Both the Caerleon-Carmarthen coastal road and its inland links with Brecon Gaer were kept in good order from about 240 onwards, for there are milestones bearing the names of emperors from Gordian III (238-44) to Constantine II Caesar (317-37). This can only have been to expedite troop-movements to trouble-spots along the coast or, as ever, inland. Numerous late coin-hoards in Glamorgan and else-where attest the reality of the threat, and the coin-list from the Llantwit Major Roman villa suggests that economic farming became impossible some years before the withdrawal of troops by Magnus Maximus in 383 completed the story of the military occupation of South Wales. Only at *Venta*, behind the almost impregnable walls with their blocked gateways, did a Romanized pattern of life continue down to the end of the century and perhaps beyond.

POSTSCRIPT

As this article was in the press, Mr. J. M. Lewis of the Inspectorate of Ancient Monuments identified an eighth auxiliary fort north-west of Caerphilly Castle. In a classic section, elements of the defences and of an internal building have been revealed in the vicinity of a Civil War earthwork. The discovery, which will be published by Mr. Lewis in due course, shows that the Romans, like the Red Earl after them, did not fail to grasp the strategic importance of Caerphilly amid a hostile terrain, and also throws new light on the course of Roman roads in the Gelligaer-Caerleon and Gelligaer-Cardiff area.

THE PARISH OF PENTYRCH

by

J. B. DAVIES

PENTYRCH is a large rural parish of some 4,500 acres, lying about seven miles north-west of Cardiff towards Llantrisant. Physically dominated by the Garth mountain to the north, it extends from the river Taff in the east to Croesfaen in the west and lies astride a carboniferous limestone ridge, with the edge of the coalfield on one side and the farthest limits of the "Border Vale" on the other. Besides Pentyrch itself the parish includes the hamlets of Gwaelod-y-garth, Creigiau and part of Croesfaen.

The rocks and the soil of this district have from man's first appearance here been determining factors in the history of the parish. The carboniferous limestone, covered by a light, well-drained soil, supported in prehistoric times a moderate forest mainly of beech and oak, vestiges of which remain to this day. Light upland soils such as this were ideal for neolithic farmers whose ploughs could do no more than scratch the surface and were therefore unable to deal with heavy soils. A glance at the map today shows an area totally cleared of trees from the village up to the edge of the Garth Wood. Here, on Cefn Colstyn Farm, a flint axe head was found some years ago, and there can be little doubt that this was the earliest cultivation settlement in the parish. These neolithic farmers probably lived in caves on the Little Garth, one of which has from time to time yielded human and animal bones, worked flints, fragments of bronze and other articles. No doubt these caves have a long occupational history. The tumuli on the Garth hill, which are a land mark for miles around, afford further evidence of prehistoric man in Pentyrch, while a cromlech survives at Caeryrfa Farm in Creigiau. An ancient hilltop or "British" way traverses the parish from Radyr, linking an iron age homestead at Llwynda-ddu with the "Caerau" fort at Rhiwsaeson in Llantrisant and passing on its way the cromlech at Caeryrfa.

By Roman times it is more than likely that the cave dwellers had discovered and begun to work the ironstone in the Little Garth, the presence of which was a matter of cardinal importance, though not in the long run decisive, in the history of Pentyrch. It was probably not until much later that the significance of the coal abundantly occurring in the parish came to be realised, and it was not until the sixteenth century that the coal and iron combination began to challenge the agricultural and pastoral predominance of the economy.

When St. Cadoc came to this small secluded valley in the sixth century he may have found a bond village grouped around a "magic well". The inhabitants would have been farming the clearings on the Little Garth which perhaps belonged to the chieftain living at Llwynda-ddu. St. Cadoc may have made the sign of the cross over the well, which has ever since been known as Ffynnon Catwg, and founded the little church hard by, still dedicated to him. The stream which rises from the well is known as Nant Gwladus, perhaps after St. Gwladus the mother of St. Cadoc.

When the Normans came to Glamorgan, Pentyrch was part of the Welsh lordship of Miskin (Meisgyn) and the little bond village was probably part of the Welsh lord's demesne. By 1262 it had been granted to one Henry de Sully for one quarter of a knight's service. This appears to have been an encroachment, perhaps at Henry de Sully's initiative, on the Welsh lordship. The manor subsequently reverted to the chief lord and remained thereafter grouped with Clun as a member or submanor of Miskin.

The extant sixteenth and seventeenth century surveys give no mutual boundaries for Pentyrch, Clun and Miskin, and are inconsistent in putting tenements in Miskin one year and in Pentyrch another. The surveys do show, however, that the copyholds and demesne lands of Miskin were in three main groups, one in Pentyrch, the second in Llanilltern and the third in Llantwit Fardre and Llantrisant. The distribution of demesne and copyhold land in Pentyrch shows fairly clearly how the manor was originally organised. The village was centred on the church, as it is to-day, and probably de Sully built himself a timber hall on the rock overlooking the church beside the present vicarage. Surrounding the village were parcels of demesne land belonging to the lord, and copyhold lands, which were the holdings of former serfs whose services had long been commuted for money payments. The present day King's Arms (in the seventeenth century known as Cae Colman), Forlan and Cefn Colstyn, among other holdings, comprised an area of copyholds intermixed with demesne land bounded by the village on the west, the free lands of Pantycaerau, Llwynda-ddu and Graighir on the south, the Garth Wood on the east and the free lands of Ton Mawr and Cefn Bychan on the north. Some of these free lands, particularly the latter, may well have been encroachments, licensed or otherwise, on the lord's waste. To the north and west of the old village lay a second parcel of copyhold and demesne land comprising Pen-y-garn, Caerwal and Llwynyreos, while to the south of the village lay a third block, Gwaun Gwladus, Gwaun Trewern and "Gocket". The two former parcels represent the open arable fields and the latter is obviously the open meadow. To this limited extent, therefore, it is possible to outline the boundaries of Pentyrch manor. Some of the copyholds of Pentyrch remained until the early 1930's when they were converted into freeholds under the Enfranchisement Act of 1926.

The northern and western parts of the parish with their heavier, less permeable soils were, under the primitive conditions of agriculture then prevailing, more suitable for stock raising than for arable farming and here are found the freehold tenements held by the Welsh "aristocracy" of the lordship of Miskin.

One such tenement was settled in the twelfth century by Cynfyn ap Cynfyn, who was displaced by the Normans from the lordship of Ystrad Yw in Breconshire. This tenement of Penllwyn Cynfyn included the seventeenth century farms of Penllwyn, Creigiau and Caeryrfa. One of Cynfyn's descendants was Cadwgan Fawr, who, when Miskin was seized by the chief lord, stood out for and secured the rights and customs of the Welsh freeholders.

Another descendant of Cynfyn was Glamorgan's earliest historian, Rhys Meurug (Rice Merrick) of Cotrel, who in his *Booke of Glamorganshires Antiquities*, written in 1578, made the following statements :—

Madog, another of the Sonnes of Justyn, possessed the greater part of the Landes between Taff and Eley, being of the Lordship of Myskin, which, during the discord betweene the Glamorganians and the Conquerours lay wast, of which a great part discended to Kynwrig".

"Of Kynwrig discended Jevan vap David Llen Yghan vap Llen vap Kynwrig . . . whose inheritance was divided among his 4 Sonnes, viz . . . the house of Llanvayr . . . to Jankyn, his eldest Sonne. The house of Pencoyd and Pant y Corred . . . to Thomas his 2d Sonne. The House of Rydlavar . . . to Llen his 3d Sonne. The house of the higher Radyr . . . to Morgan his fourth and youngest Sonne".

These extracts throw light on the history of Pencoed, Pantygored and Castell y Mynach, the latter not mentioned by Rice Merrick, which are three stone houses, in close proximity, of early fifteenth century date. Pencoed is in Llanilltern, just outside Pentyrch parish.

According to Clark's *Limbus Patrum*, Robert Mathew, who was Coroner of Glamorgan in 1425-26, second son of Sir Mathew ap Evan of Llandaff, married Alice, daughter and co-heiress of Jenkin Thomas ap Evan David of Pantygored ap Llen Ychan ap Llen ap Cynfrig etc. "She was the heiress of Castell-y-Mynach". Later, we learn from the same source that Robert's grandson, Robert ap William Mathew of Castell y Mynach, married another heiress of the same family—"Alice d. and h. of John Thomas ap Thomas of Pant-y-corred (Miskin and Mounton) ap Evan ap David ap Ll. Ychan, from Madoc ap Jestyn. Alice had Pant-y-corred, Pant-Llech, Coed-Philip-Franc, Bryn-Rhydd and lands in Llantwit-Vardre", some of which is still owned by her descendant Mr. Wingfield. Much of this genealogical information is obviously corrupt, but since the importance of Welsh oral genealogies lay in their function of providing "title deeds" to land ownership it can be assumed that the basis of the truth, at least, is to be found in them.

Apart from the name, there is no evidence for the monastic origin of Castell y Mynach. The house, which is the most important in the parish, was from the fifteenth to the eighteenth century the home of eight generations of the Mathew family. Nothing in the building can with certainty be dated earlier than this period of domestic occupation. Robert was succeeded by William who was succeeded by another Robert, the latter still living apparently as late as 1540. His son was William Mathew who died in 1550. They were small gentlemen, owning at this date just Castell y Mynach, Pantygored and Maesmawr in Pentyrch, together with some land in Llantrisant and a moiety of the manor of Caerau, much of their land having

Castell y Mynach, *c.* **1940** *Photograph by V. C. Hardacre*

"Mathew Tew" bench, Castell y Mynach *Photograph by V. C. Hardacre*

Pentyrch in the thirteenth/fourteenth centuries

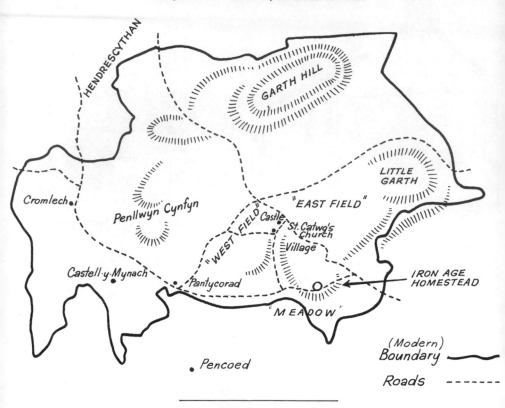

Pentyrch in the sixteenth/seventeenth centuries

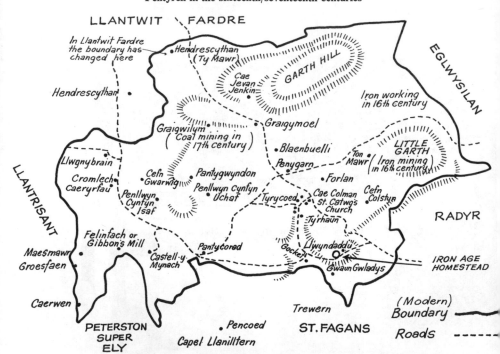

been divided during the fifteenth century by the practice of gavelkind. It was, however, a valuable holding, and yet during the sixteenth century the family were not in a dominant position in the parish. This was probably due to minority successions. Robert Mathew the younger must have enjoyed the estate for many years, but his son William died in 1550 only a few years after succeeding, while Miles, the next holder, left a posthumous son, Humphrey Mathew, which put the estate under trusteeship for twenty-one years. It was during the middle years of the sixteenth century that the more powerful Radyr branch established their influence in Pentyrch, buying up freehold lands and taking out leases of the demesne. In the Cwmllwydrew area, and towards the river Taff, they established their iron workings and we learn that in 1574 Edmond Mathew was in trouble with the Privy Council for exporting ordnance in violation of a monopoly held by one Ralph Hogge. Again in 1602, the Privy Council ordered "that especiall care be had to put downe Edmond Matthewes esquier for casting any Ordnaunce at his ffurnace neere Cardiff in Wales because from that place very easilie they may be carried into Spayne. And if a due accompte maie be taken for Ve or VI yeares last past, all or the most parte of Thordnaunce w'ch he hath made w'thin that tyme shall be fownde to have been stolne beyonde Seaes, and the officers of that Porte are very poore men, and such as dare not displease him.

Among Edmond Mathew's enterprises were "forges, ironworks and coal mines", and to evade the ban on his manufactures Mathew leased the works to a Cardiff merchant, Peter Samyne. By 1616 the Privy Council had caught up with Samyne's activities and found him guilty of illegally exporting ordnance. This time the ironworks were apparently put down in earnest, since we find in 1625 Bristol merchants unsuccessfully petitioning the King to appoint officers "to cast and make one hundred pieces of ordnance yearely at Cardiff where the best ordnance is reputed to be made, the same to be vended in the City of Bristol, Barnstaple and other places within the river of Severne".

It is unlikely that these early industrial activities had much effect on the local economy. The parish remained predominantly agricultural, but something of the future had been foreshadowed and the local abundance of coal, iron ore and timber had a potential which was unlikely to be forgotten.

Early in the seventeenth century the Mathews of Radyr sold their lands in the area, while the Castell y Mynach branch rose to the peak of their influence under Thomas Mathew, J.P., who was Sheriff of the County in 1613. Probably taking full advantage of his offices, Thomas progressively acquired much of the copyhold and freehold land in the parish in addition to renting all the demesne, much of which eventually seems to have become converted into his descendants' freehold possession. This Thomas Mathew is perhaps the "Mathew Tew" whose reputation as a bullying squire and a terror to all the farmers has been handed down in the locality. His boast was that his golden guineas, laid side by side, would stretch from Castell y Mynach to Pentyrch. He was, so the legend runs, done to death by a cottager in Efail y Castell, who, bearing some grudge, placed a shoemaker's awl under a cushion on a bench which Mathew usually sat upon. This bench has since been preserved in Castell y Mynach. It is perhaps not without significance that this Mathew appears in the Court of Star Chamber, accused, among other things, of "perjury in the Consistory Court of Llandaff use of false measures in buying barley; refusal to licence ale houses that did not sell his ale; other misconduct . . . in office".

From the existing house it would appear that it was Thomas Mathew who made the last significant aggrandisement of the family home. The house, as it survives, is L shaped, one wing being the original fifteenth century stone hall, probably built by Robert Mathew the Coroner, which was subsequently altered and enlarged by the insertion of a first, and at one time apparently a second storey, and the addition of a great chimney on the south gable. This alteration is probably of sixteenth century date. The second wing is of early seventeenth century style and was probably added by the above Thomas Mathew. A remarkable Renaissance mural in one of the upstairs rooms bears the date 1602, while over one of the barn doors is the date 1616, with the initials T.M., coupled with Kt. for Katherine his wife, the daughter of Sir Rowland Morgan of Bedwellty.

In the main hall of the house is a fine Royal Stuart coat of arms, which has not unnaturally fostered the legend in the district that the fugitive King Charles took refuge here. There is no record of a Royal visit to Castell y Mynach, but it is not improbable since Humphrey Mathew, Thomas's son, was, despite the Parliamentary sympathies of his overlord, the Earl of Pembroke, a staunch Royalist in common with most of his neighbours in the county.

Pentyrch men may have taken part in numerous engagements on behalf of the Royal Cause during the Civil Wars, including no doubt, the fight at St. Fagan's. Miles, a younger brother of Humphrey Mathew, may have had Pentyrch men with him at the Battle of Edgehill, where he commanded the Life Guard and ". . . with a reserve behind a haystack made opportunity for His Majesty and the Duke of York to escape". Miles, as appears from State papers of the Restoration period, had his horse shot under him and was robbed of all his goods, whereupon he retired into the mountains of Wales.

Meanwhile, Humphrey had been taken prisoner at Pembroke Castle, doubtless with some of his tenants' sons in service with him, and for his delinquency one third of his estate was sequestered. Humphrey compounded with a fine of £1,500.

The seventeenth century in Pentyrch was very much the century of the Castell y Mynach family. In the sixteenth century they had been freeholders among their peers, but during the years between 1595 and 1608 they reduced the number of freeholders in the parish by half and whittled those away during their ascendant years when they were Squires in residence. Their line ended with Cecil Mathew, who died in 1720 and was the last owner of the estate to live at Castell y Mynach. She married Charles Talbot, who became Lord Talbot of Hensol and from whom the estate descended to Lord Dynevor, who settled it on one of his daughters when she married Col. Wingfield, in whose family it remains. The nucleus of the estate has been handed down, if the early genealogies can be believed, through some 900 years to the present Mr. Wingfield.

One representative of a cadet branch of the Mathew family was resident in Pentyrch until his death in 1754. He was Thomas Mathew of Llwyn-y-brain Fawr, son of William Mathew of Meiros, Llanharan, who had inherited Llwyn-y-brain from his mother. He left it to his servant and reputed son, Thomas Joseph, who was thus, until about 1780, when he sold the property to the Rev. R. T. Rickards, Vicar of Llantrisant, the last resident freeholder in the parish. At the start of the eighteenth century most of the parish was owned by residents, but by the end of the century it was almost all in the possession of absentee landlords.

The great industrial development which led in the nineteenth century to an all out challenge to the agricultural nature of the parish, began in 1740 when Nicholas Price the elder, a tanner and publican, of the *Boar's Head*, Caerphilly, later of Pontypandy, his son Nicholas, and Thomas Lewis of Llanishen, leased land from the second Lord Talbot at £5 10s. 0d. a year for 99 years whereon to build a new forge and re-estabish the iron industry in Pentyrch. The late Mr. Edgar Chappell has an admirable account of this industry in his *Historic Melingriffith*, but he was rather hazy about its origin in 1740 and about Nicholas Price whom he assumed to have been but a manager. David Jones of Wallington, however, has among his notebooks a copy of the original lease cited above.

Mr. Chappell surmised that the family of Nicholas Price had some connection with the Prices of Tynton, but in fact they were related to the Prices of Watford. Nicholas Price was an ancestor of the well remembered eccentric, Dr. Price of Llantrisant.

Preserved in the County Record Office is a cash book kept by Thomas Vaughan, manager, during the years 1791-92, which shows the works under the direction of William Lewis, son of Thomas Lewis, while the buildings belonged to the executors of William Price, a younger son of Nicholas the elder.

This interesting document goes far towards bringing the industry to life for us. We have a picture of some half a dozen highly skilled men, finers and drawers, earning from £7-£11 a month and employing their own labour. We see farms, collieries and iron ore mines run in association with the works, and charcoal burners, or wood colliers, as they were called, cutting, cording and coking timber in many parts of the county. In Radyr, Cilynys, Rhydhelig, Cefn Colstyn, Creigiau, Tyla Morris and more distantly at Llanharan, Llantrisant, Garth Maelwg, Wenvoe, Machen etc., timber was being cut to feed this comparatively small ironworks.

By 1803 Benjamin Malkin could describe Pentyrch in the following terms :—

> ". . . about Pentyrch, are very extensive collieries among the hills, which likewise abound in iron ore, and are thought to be capable, by the application of industry and enterprize, of rivalling Merthyr Tydfil in quality and copiousness. The country, as in all such neighbourhoods, is wild and black ; and one of the largest mountains in Glamorganshire overhanging these

mines gives a magnificence to the sooty complexion of the scene . . ."

In 1805 the ironworks were transferred to R. G. Blakemore and Co., the owners of the Melingriffith Works, and the rate of development during the nineteenth century became even more rapid. One furnace was rebuilt in 1815 and the forge adapted for increased production, while in 1830 a second furnace was built. Output rose from 2,001 tons in 1829 to 3,904 tons in 1839, and 6,977 tons in 1846.

In 1837 the management passed to Blakemore's nephew, T. W. Booker, who died in 1855, leaving three sons, on one of whom, Thomas William Booker, fell the management of the works at the age of twenty-eight. He made a brave effort, but economic circumstances were against him, and despite the introduction of numerous improvements, things became worse, and a Limited Company was formed in 1872.

At this time the Pentyrch Section of the Company comprised, according to the prospectus :—

"Collieries, Limestone Quarries, Brickworks, Coke Ovens, Foundries and Forges for coke and charcoal bars, 3 melting furnaces, 9 fineries in the charcoal department and 4 melting furnaces. Puddling furnaces and 7 Balling furnaces in the Puddling department with full equipment. Also fitting, smith, millwright and pattern making Shops".

There were also (besides an almost new Brickworks with a capacity of 30,000 bricks per week), workable minerals exceeding 44 million tons of coal and 4½ million tons of argillaceous iron stone. The coal output was over 100,000 tons per annum and the iron stone over 15,000 tons, both capable of increase.

No doubt the prospectus was unduly optimistic, but, on the face of it, all seemed clear for the realisation of Malkin's prophecy of 1803 that Pentyrch stood fair to rival Merthyr in production. By this time, however, the works were facing the rivalry of steel and proposals for converting to the Bessemer Steel process came to nothing for lack of capital. Furthermore, it was found that imported Spanish ores were preferable to the native product for steel manufacture. In 1878 the West of England and District Bank, the majority shareholders, failed and the Company was liquidated. The Pentyrch manager, Henry Jeffreys, tried to get the workers to accept a ten per cent reduction in wages in order to keep the works going.

This they did after a bitter strike, the only one in the history of the works, but the low wages and short time led to widespread starvation and soup kitchens had to be opened and bread handed out to children in school. By 1888 the works were completely closed down. About 1890 they were leased for sheet iron manufacture and worked spasmodically until 1915, but Pentyrch's industrial career was halted, and today the only activity to rival agriculture is quarrying.

All this industrial growth was, of course, reflected in the population and was responsible for considerable changes in the face of Pentyrch. Population rose rapidly from 470 in 1801 to 2,182 in 1881. When the nineteenth century opened the parish was divided for administration into two hamlets, Garth and Castle. Garth Hamlet comprised mainly the old village centred on the church, scattered farm houses and a community of squatters' cottages on the Garth Hill occupied mainly by coal miners. The parish almshouses were also on the Garth, near Warren, and there was the growing community of iron workers' houses near the River Taff. Castle Hamlet had no nucleated settlement. The biggest farms of the parish were mainly here, Castell y Mynach, Pantygored, Maesmawr etc., all between 100 and 200 acres.

As the century advanced Gwaelod-y-garth developed into a living community of mine and iron workers, and survives as a thriving hamlet within the parish. Nearer the old village, in the area known as Twynyrodyn, Henry Lewis, Esq., of Greenmeadow started, about 1850, to grant leases of small building plots on Pen-y-garn Farm, where the hamlet of Pen-y-garn thus developed. This part is now being redeveloped by Cardiff Rural District Council.

Except at Tyn-y-coed where extensive coal mining was carried on continuously from the sixteenth century, Castle Hamlet was largely unaffected by the industrial growth, since the division between the hamlets roughly followed the boundary between the edge of the coalfield and the "Border Vale". In the 1880's, however, the Barry Railway was laid through this part of the parish and on Creigiau Farm was built a station around which grew the hamlet of Creigiau.

The scars of industry are very little apparent in Pentyrch. Coal mining was never intensive enough to have changed the skyline with abandoned tips, and that apart coal mining is an industry which leaves few marks behind it. The iron industry was concentrated near the river Taff, but now the ruins of the old works have been largely cleared away and modern council houses stand on part of the site.

The parish today is mainly agricultural and residential, the population is maintained at its present level largely by dormitory dwellers, and the pressure of such development is high. Indeed the County Council now proposes to establish in this beauty spot a dormitory town of some 20,000 inhabitants.

It seems that town planning, combined with the proximity of over-populated Cardiff, can succeed, where geology and geography failed, in destroying the age-old rural and agricultural nature of Pentyrch. We Pentyrch natives, who love every field and farm of our parish, cannot help being sad at the thought that the deadening hand of twentieth century planners can change those lovely fields into a featureless housing estate.

Visible monuments of history are not numerous in Pentyrch, but it is hoped that the foregoing outline, while inevitably omitting much of interest, does give some indication of the growth and development of the local community.

OCTOBER EVENING
(IN THE VALE OF GLAMORGAN)

The purple tapestries of dusk
Hung glittering and glowing in the high
Broad marches of the vivid evening sky :
And all the Vale like soft, blue velvet lay
In folded distances.   Deep inland from the sea
To the bare uplands where the brown hills ride
Above the mists of autumn like tall ships,
Each field, each hedge, each gracious tree
Stood etched, it seemed for ever, in that air
Of stilled, ecstatic eventide . . .
As if some wandering angel, unaware,
Had left a glimpse of the ultimate Kingdom there
In final, tranquil beauty, and set free
To pierce the dimness of our mortal sight,
A vision of our immortality :
A facet of infinity to light
The blest perfection which the mystics know,
Holy as silence of new-fallen snow,
Serene and flawless as a precious gem.

And through the glowing dusk, an early star
Gave token of that realm where all things move
In ageless wisdom and immortal love :
Where death and sorrow and the year's decay
Throw no chill shadows on eternal day,
Where men grown cold in wintry journeying
Walk in the warm, green solace of the Spring.

A. G. PRYS-JONES.

MEDICAL MEN OF GLAMORGAN :

(1) Dr. WILLIAM MORGAN (1750-1833)
by
PETER H. THOMAS, M.D.

"Physic of Metaphysic begs defence,
And Metaphysic calls for aid on Sense !
See Mystery to Mathematics fly ! "

ALEXANDER POPE

THIS article—the first of a series describing the activities of outstanding medical men having connections with Glamorgan— is penned in the hope that it will awaken and stimulate interest in a vigorous Welshman who must surely rank with the "greats" of the scientific world. We are fortunate in that Miss Caroline E. Williams, a grand-niece of our worthy, has left us a vivid account of his long life in a rare and fascinating book *A Welsh Family* (London, 1893), while more recently M. E. Ogborn, Joint Actuary of the Equitable Assurance Society, in his work *Equitable Assurances* (London, 1962) has given us another mine of information. These two books form the primary sources for any study of William Morgan's life and work. There are also a great number of secondary sources, some of which will be cited in the body of our article and others listed in the bibliographical note with which we shall conclude. Turning to local histories we find that H. J. Randall's *Bridgend* (Newport, 1955) gives William Morgan the prominence he so richly deserves. There were five William Morgans in five successive generations of the family, and in order to distinguish our worthy from his father, grandfather, son, and grandson, H. J. Randall refers to him in regal fashion as William Morgan the third. We ourselves shall adopt a slight variation of this method, using Roman cardinal numbers in place of the ordinals.

William Morgan I lived at Parc-gwyllt—now a hospital—in the parish of Coity. He had nine children by his wife Elizabeth John, one of whom was William Morgan II (1708-1772). This boy was given an education of a high order which included a good grounding in classics. Later, he succeeded Dr. David Richards of Oldcastle as a doctor in the town of Bridgend. There is no doubt that William Morgan II was an excellent family doctor who practised his healing art in the best of medical traditions. Not only was he the leading physician in the town, but his professional skill was also very much in demand throughout the surrounding parts of the county. He is pictured as "riding everywhere with his pharmacopoeia in his saddle-bags, and dispensing his medicines to gentle and simple from the still-room of his hosts". At the age of thirty-six he was a widower without offspring living in a lovely house at Newcastle in the higher part of Bridgend. It was at this stage of his career that he fell in love with and later married a patient by the name of Sarah or Sally Price. Her mother, Catherine, was the second wife of Rhys Price (1673-1739), a dissenting minister who lived at Tynton near Llangeinor in the Garw Valley, and has derived fame from the fact that he was an uncle and guardian of the "Maid of Cefn Ydfa". Catherine, in turn, was the daughter of the fore-mentioned Dr. David Richards. At the time of Sally's marriage in 1744, her brother, the Reverend Richard Price, had probably just embarked on his life's work as a dissenting minister at Stoke Newington. Later he was to become a great celebrity not only in the world of religion, politics, and philosophy, but also as a mathematician grappling in a brilliant way with the questions of probability as applied to life assurance and annuities. Price's mathematical brain was put to good use by the Equitable Life Assurance Society whose offices he visited almost daily for many years in the capacity of financial adviser. His work on this subject was really an extension of that of his predecessors John Graunt, Sir William Petty, Edmund Halley, and in particular James Dodson who described the working of an insurance society on principles which are as valid today as when he conceived them in 1756 (*British Medical Journal*, 1962, vol. II, p. 1109). Hence William Morgan's marriage to this young, clever, and attractive woman resulted in a life-long link of mutual help and friendship between the two families —a link which was to be of immense value for nearly half a century.

The matrimonial union of Sally and William was blessed with seven children, three sons and four daughters. Our main concern is with their third child and eldest son, William Morgan III, born on 26 May 1750. For many years the Morgans led a very busy and happy life at their home in Newcastle, but unfortunately Dr. Morgan's shrewdness and scholarship did not extend to money matters. To this important aspect of life he displayed an unaccountable and surprising sang-froid. He was not wealthy and hated mean people. Of his brother-in-law John Price he asserted firmly : "I am ashamed to reflect that brother John has long professed the Christian religion attended with so little Christian charity". Long afterwards his eldest son used to remark, "What a fortune my father would have made if he had charged for his physic what doctors do now". By 1769, Dr. Morgan's partner, Mr. Sidney, had retired, and so he became anxious, in view of his own advancing years and the consequent increasing burden of general practice, that his son should complete his training as a doctor and then join him as an assistant. William Morgan III was a pupil at Cowbridge Grammar School at the time of the death of the headmaster, Daniel Durel, in 1766, and must have continued for a short while under his successor, the Reverend Thomas Williams (L. J. Hopkin-James, *Old Cowbridge*, pp. 266-7). It seems that he left Cowbridge about 1767 and began to familiarise himself with the day-to-day routine of a practice under the aegis of his father. But in a letter to Richard Price, who had now become a Doctor of Divinity and a Fellow of the Royal Society, the father lamented the fact that William seemed to prefer academic learning to a science such as pharmacy. The two years training necessary to become a physician was beyond the limited means of the ageing doctor who at last was becoming very concerned about the future of his wife and family.

At this juncture we find William Morgan III, a young man of nineteen, beginning to stand on his feet. He showed his complete independence by engaging himself to an apothecary by the name of Smith at the notorious Limehouse Docks in the east end of London. Leading the life of an apothecary's assistant combined with attendance at Guy's and St. Thomas's Hospitals as a student and dresser proved very arduous work. These institutions, situated opposite one another in St. Thomas's Street, were closely linked. For many years they were called the United Hospitals, and prior to 1825, when quarrels arose which ended in the formation of a separate medical school at Guy's, the lectures in surgery and anatomy were given in the lecture theatre at St. Thomas's (R. C. Brock, *Life and Work of Astley Cooper*). William Morgan was also unfortunate in his choice of master, for the man turned out to be a complete scoundrel. After a long day's toil among the dock community, the youthful apprentice was forced to rest under the counter of the shop—this was his only bed. To add insult to injury he had to submit to the cruel behaviour of an employer who treated him "no better than a dog". He endured this for exactly three months, at the end of which time his anger reached boiling point. In a fit of teenage temper he turned on his boss, and with his powerful hands laid him in the kennel close at hand. On the following day his uncle, Dr. Price, found him a place with another apothecary, a Mr. Bradney of Cannon Street, at an agreed fee of sixteen pounds per annum. During the following winter he found it necessary to take rooms nearer the hospitals. We know that he lodged at a Mrs. Kent's, haberdasher, St. Margaret's Hill, Southwark. His stay at Mr. Bradney's was completely successful and he remained there to the end of his medical training. He was a very able and industrious student, his lecture notes being written in exquisite handwriting. The great Cline was a contemporary of his, yet the eminent surgeon under whom they worked regarded William Morgan as his best pupil. Cline pursued a very successful career as an operator, and along with Blizard, Abernethy, and Astley Cooper were instrumental in large measure in making England famous as a centre of surgery in the early nineteenth century (A. E. Clark-Kennedy, *The London*, vol. I, London, 1962, p. 207).

In 1772, owing to his father's death, William Morgan, who was barely twenty-one at the time, was forced to return from Newington Green, the home of Dr. Price, to take over the well-established practice in Bridgend. By doing this he carried out his father's wishes, and at the same time became a comfort to his mother and family. He had been extremely happy at his uncle's residence. He knew all this was to change and suddenly became acutely aware and mindful of the trials and tribulations which were going to confront him as a beginner in medicine. Several difficulties stood in his way. He had ability but this was neutralised by his lack of clinical experience. He was handicapped by a club-foot which was an objectionable deformity in the eyes of some of his more squeamish and sensitive patients. Moreover, he had a formidable professional rival in the person of Dr. Jenkin Williams—a tall, handsome, gaily-dressed medico whose father, a successful farmer at Stormy, claimed descent from the same family as Oliver Cromwell. Even prior to the death of Wm. Morgan II he had taken a keen interest in

Catherine (Kitty), William's sister, though at that time she had been admonished by her father for taking a liking to this "young coxcomb with a fine gold-laced hat". This did not deter the amorous Kitty, for in 1773 she married Jenkin. Their son Dr. Morgan Williams was the father of Caroline, the gifted writer to whose work we have already alluded. After the marriage William Morgan was in a position to give up the battle for patients, relinquishing his practice to his newly acquired brother-in-law. With this important matter settled he then travelled hopefully back to London to seek succour and advice from Dr. Price who by this time had still further enhanced his reputation on monetary matters. Through his written works he was now famous not only at home but also in France, America, and other countries overseas. Price was on intimate terms with some of the best thinkers and intellectuals of the time, including such personalities as Benjamin Franklin, Hume, Lord Shelburne, Joseph Priestley, Henry Cline, and his neighbour, the banker-poet Samuel Rogers. Soon William Morgan was himself moving in these circles.

Towards the end of 1773, John Edwards, Actuary of the Equitable Society, died. The General Court of the Society then elected John Pocock as his successor. On 17 April 1774, through the tremendous influence and sway of Dr. Price, William Morgan was appointed Assistant Actuary. This occurrence must be regarded as a milestone in Morgan's career, for in accepting this post he was to turn his back on and forsake the actual practice of clinical medicine for ever. He himself says that he had little knowledge of arithmetic and algebra when he started, but with hard work and his uncle as mentor he soon grasped the fundamental principles of life-assurance mathematics. Yet he was in a position to utilise his medical knowledge to full advantage in this line of business. Although the Equitable was quite alive to the financial blunder of accepting new members with a poor prognosis, a medical referee was not appointed until the middle of the nineteenth century. For the purpose of turning down poor-risk cases they must have depended on the medical advice given by Morgan and the other doctors in the Court of Directors. John Pocock did not remain in office for very long. In January 1775 he passed away, leaving William Morgan to step into his shoes. Shortly afterwards Morgan was promoted to the position of Actuary, thus offering ample proof of the phenomenal progress he had made during his short period of employment as Assistant. Little did he realise then that he was going to be given the strength to serve this Society for over half a century. Still less could he have imagined that under his shrewd management the Equitable during his term as Actuary was going to become the wealthiest corporation of the world. His initial remuneration comprised a house at the Society's offices in Chatham Place, Blackfriars, and a salary of £120 a year.

In the meantime his brother George Cadogan Morgan had arrived on the scene, staying at Newington Green where he started preparing himself for the dissenting ministry at the Hoxton Academy. Dr. Price and his two talented nephews were thus brought together in an intimate intellectual contact. Their interests covered a wide field which included Unitarian beliefs, advanced radical politics, science and mathematics. Both William and George were engaged in scientific pursuits and conducted experiments on electricity. We shall refer to some important ones by the former very shortly. Electricity was regarded as a serious study by men like Franklin, Priestley and William Morgan, but it had also became a fashionable pastime and novelty in the hands of some miscreants. It is said that the lecherous Louis XV witnessed the administration of an electric shock to a line of monks a mile long and was convulsed with sadistic laughter when they all leapt into the air like galvanised frogs. John Wesley became a staunch advocate of electricity as a therapeutic agent, and he strongly advised intense and prolonged electric shocks for a wide variety of maladies which included malaria and hysteria. To the modern doctor, however, such usage must be regarded as savouring of quackery (J. H. Plumb, *England in the Eighteenth Century*, pp. 103-4).

In 1779 Morgan published his first statistical work entitled *The Doctrine of Annuities and Assurances*, a work which included an introduction and essay by the renowned Dr. Price, who is said to have encouraged his nephew to undertake this task. Morgan must also have come under the magic spell of Joseph Priestley, whose name is coupled with that of Scheele, the Swedish apothecary, in the isolation of oxygen. When Scheele's German treatise *On Air and Fire* appeared in 1777, Priestley promptly arranged for its translation into English, and this was completed in 1780. We learn that Morgan procured a copy which he signed and dated. This must have aroused his curiosity in the subject for a year later his own experimental observations came into print under the title *An Examination of Dr. Crawford's Theory of Heat and Combustion.*

Morgan's first paper to the Royal Society, read on his behalf by Dr. Price (*Philosophical Transactions*, lxxv, p. 272), gave an account of some classical "Electrical experiments made in order to ascertain the non-conducting Power of a perfect vacuum, &c.", the importance of which is recorded in an article by J. G. Anderson entitled "William Morgan and X-Rays", (*Transactions of the Faculty of Actuaries*, vol. xvii, p. 219). In essence his apparatus consisted of a glass tube sealed at one end, which was inverted over mercury. The sealed end was coated for about five inches with tinfoil for the purpose of electrical connection. Morgan mentions the elaborate precautions which he took to free his apparatus and mercury from air by careful and prolonged boiling. Having obtained an excellent vacuum in this way, he found he could not obtain an electrical discharge through the tube when the tinfoil was connected to the electrical machine. Upon admitting a very minute quantity of air, the glass glowed with a green colour. If more air was admitted gradually, the colour of the electric light changed from green to blue, from blue to indigo, and soon to violet and purple. To use the words of V. E. Pullin and W. J. Wiltshire (*X-rays Past and Present*), Morgan had succeeded in producing a Coolidge vacuum, which is practically a non-conductor. On allowing a little air to enter his tube he produced the ordinary phenomena of an X-ray tube. The gas became split up into ions or charged atoms. These bombarded the glass walls and so produced a fluorescence in the glass and feeble X-rays.

The study of the flourescent tube was continued by famous scientists over the next century but it was not until 1895 that Röntgen observed the effects of X-rays outside the tubes. The tubes he used did not differ in principle from the apparatus used by Morgan. Röntgen's discovery of X-rays led to the study of radiation. It follows that the early work of William Morgan is of great historical importance. In a book entitled *British Scientists* by Sir Richard Gregory, Bart., F.R.S., (1941), "Dr. Morgan, a native of Glamorgan", is heralded as the man who, in all probability, was the first experimenter with X-rays.

William Morgan lived at Chatham Place for seven years, during which time his sister Nancy acted as housekeeper. It was from this residence that she witnessed the Gordon Riots in June 1780. At one moment it looked as if the Equitable Assurance office was going to be attacked by the mob, but fortunately no assault was made on the premises.   In 1781 she returned to Wales, because in that year William married a prudent and capable lady by the name of Susan Woodhouse, the daughter of a London merchant.   In the early years of his marriage William Morgan built one of the first houses on Stamford Hill, then quite a rural area, not far from the residence of his brother George at Southgate.   The original Rothschild was his next door neighbour.   A quickset hedge was the only boundary separating these two brilliant financiers, who on the whole were very good friends.   Sometimes, however, relations became strained, and it is said that on these occasions biting remarks and vitriolic exchanges could be heard through the slight barrier that divided them.   The house at Stamford Hill became the central meeting place for all the family and their friends.   During those years of anxiety in the radical movement many ardent and advanced reformers like John Horne Tooke, Sir Francis Burdett and Tom Paine would gather there.   In his unrestrained and vigorous political writings William Morgan had already expressed his strong disapproval of William Pitt's policy, so much so that Pitt hinted that it would be to William Morgan's advantage if he would wield his quill on the side of the Government (*Transactions of the Faculty of Actuaries*, vol. xiv, p. 17).

Sunday evenings at Stamford Hill were lively and memorable affairs.   After the shutters were drawn as a precautionary step against possible political enemies, the music would begin.   One of the highlights of such soirèes was a rendering of John Taylor's revolutionary refrain by Miss Amelia Alderson, who later became Mrs. Opie.   The words of this song, redolent as they are with the spirit of "libertè, egalitè, fraternitè", reflect the mood of this reactionary group:—

"The trumpet of Liberty sounds through the world,
And the Universe starts at the sound,
Her standard Philosophy's hand hath unfurled,
And the nations are thronging around".
Chorus :   "Fall, Tyrants, fall, fall, fall!
These are the days of liberty!
Fall, Tyrants, fall".

illiam Morgan, F.R.S.

Mezzotint by C. Turner after Lawrence

By permission of the National Museum of Wales

Richard Price, D.D., F.R.S.

The coming of hostilities in 1793 made conditions exceedingly difficult for reformers like William Morgan and his friends as they were now in danger of prosecution, their views being diametrically opposed to those of the Government and thus damaging to the war effort. In the previous year Paine was indicted for high treason, and even Morgan received a warning from the authorities. One of the reasons why he did not publish his book *Works of Dr. Price. With Memoirs of his Life* until 1816 was that he was in grave peril of political persecution.

Leaving politics with all their vicissitudes, we shall now examine his life and work as an Actuary. At the time of his installation as Assistant, the gross assets of the Society amounted to nearly £33,000, the total liabilities being estimated at about £22,000, leaving a reserve of £11,000. These figures were produced by Dr. Price from rather scant data. One of Morgan's major initial tasks was to streamline the accounting system of the Equitable, because though the Society had accrued sufficient records under Edwards, the previous "Actuary", it had not invented a method of presenting financial statements in a digestible form for easy assimilation by the directors. It was partly on the strength of these exacting and time-consuming computations that Morgan helped to establish himself as a specialist and adviser on important matters relating to annuities, premiums, and reversionary interests. It must be emphasised that he was at the helm of a life assurance company with very little tradition or pattern to copy, whilst *pari passu* he was making rapid strides in the study of life contingencies, especially in relation to survivorships. In other words, as each day passed by he was actively evolving and organising the concepts of a new science. The directors and members reacted quickly in recognising the scintillating brilliance of their new Actuary, and we note that in 1776 they responded by voting him a gratuity of one hundred guineas as a token of their esteem for his "extra-ordinary diligence". More gifts of this kind followed as the years advanced, and it is recorded that in 1817 he received a further present of £1,000 together with a silver vase. It was on this occasion that Sir Thomas Lawrence, R.A., was invited to paint a portrait of Morgan—a portrait which now adorns a wall in the board-room of the main office at London. It has been said that for many years he was the only true actuary available in the country; and when, in the nineteenth century, other mathematicians could have been consulted, they were eclipsed by his dominant personality and his standing in the insurance world. Despite his religious and political leanings he was a financial expert on questions affecting ecclesiastic property and enjoyed a close friendship with Bishop Watson of Llandaff. In 1825 and 1827 he was examined before a Select Committee of the House of Commons on Friendly Societies. He was outspoken in his condemnation of some of the tables used by these organisations. He despised the methods by which some of their members were enrolled in taverns, hostelries of this type often acting as headquarters.

Dr. Price had already given a lead by constructing tables relating to expectation of life based on the bills of mortality at Northampton. Mortality tables, according to Wolf, claim to show how many, out of a given number of persons born, live to complete each year of age, and hence, how the deaths occuring in a community are distributed among the various age-groups of the population. We now know that the Northampton table was constructed on an unsound basis, but because it erred on the safe side when used in connection with insurance contracts, it helped to swell the coffers of the Equitable. The term "expectation of life" denotes the average number of years which the persons of a specified age, taken one with another, will live according to a given mortality table. Modern statisticians prefer to utilise the phrases "mean duration of life" and "the average duration of life" rather than "expectation of life". In 1738 William Morgan read a paper before the Royal Society embodying ways and means by which premiums should be calculated and exhibited life-tables showing the values by the Northampton and Wargentin's tables compared with approximations then in use. This paper was followed in 1789, 1791, and 1800 by others in which he demonstrated solutions to new problems. These researches were uniquely fresh in their approach and content, though, as might be expected in original studies, there were faults in some of his findings. The high quality of these mathematical investigations did not pass unnoticed by the Royal Society. He was awarded the much-coveted Copley medal in 1789 and was elected as a Fellow in 1790. He served twice on the Council from 1798 to 1800—and again from 1810 to 1812.

From the very beginning William Morgan insisted upon having up-to-date valuations before yielding to the members in their persistent clamourings for bigger and more frequent bonuses. Time and time again Morgan had his whole work cut out in trying to placate and convince them at Court meetings that it was uneconomic to distribute excessively large profits without creating a substantial reserve fund in order to guard against risks in later life and to meet claims arising in future years. It is manifest from the glib remarks still made concerning the astronomical funds of insurance companies that this essential axiom is insufficiently understood even today. After all, members participate in order to provide security for their heirs and dependents. It was Edward Rowe Mores, one of the founders, who selected the motto "Sic nos non nobis" for the Equitable. At once we see how suggestive and apposite it is in this context. M. E. Ogborn sums it up succinctly by saying that "a mutual life assurance society is a continuing business. Ample funds are necessary for the credit and stability of the office and each generation of members comes into a heritage from the past; so in its turn, each generation should endeavour to pass on that heritage unimpaired to the generations that succeed it".[1] Only in this way can the "legacy" be transmitted. The Equitable derived its profits from investments; also in the earlier years from highly-rated premiums. Other companies, in the nineteenth century, used to weight their premiums deliberately, and by so doing enhanced their popularity because this placed them in an easy position to give out bonuses to their members. In 1800, after making another appraisement, Morgan recommended the adoption of the following bye-laws: (i) that valuations be made decennially (ii) that no share-out should be distributed without a valuation, and (iii) that the amount of new additional dividends should not exceed two-thirds of the clear surplus, the remaining one-third being placed in the reserve. These were designed to strike a reasonable balance between the claims of the members and the needs of the Society.

In 1816 he embarked on a very timid uninspiring policy. He proposed to limit the number of members sharing in the bonuses to five thousand, so that any new applicant accepted above this figure was not granted any share-out till an old member died or surrendered his insurance or was forced to let it lapse. He arrived at this decision because he could not or did not see how the premiums

1 The author is indebted to Mr. M. E. Ogborn for permission to make this quotation.

charged could yield the old bonus, and the enrolment of new members could only worsen the situation. He knew only too well that Britain was weakened financially by the Napoleonic Wars. This policy of non-expansion was wrong, for it resulted in a loss in membership and consequently a forfeiture of fresh business. This action virtually caused a "freeze" in the activities of the Society, the impact of which was noticeable for many years after his death. During the period of his leadership he had to resist stubbornly perennial demands for more frequent emoluments and recommendations for smaller reserves. In these affrays he must have received tremendous help and support from his two sons, William IV and Arthur. The former had been a member of the staff since 1809, and in 1817 was promoted Assistant Actuary. Unfortunately, he did not hold this position for long as he was suffering from pulmonary tuberculosis, to which disease he succumbed two years later. William Morgan then arranged for his younger son Arthur to be appointed as Clerk to the Equitable. In 1824 Arthur Morgan became Joint Actuary, and, when his father retired in 1830, Actuary to the Society. Father and son were Actuaries for over ninety-five years—quite an unbeatable record. Like his father, Arthur was made a Fellow of the Royal Society, an honour granted in large measure for his tabulation of the Equitable's mortality experience. He continued as Actuary until his death in 1870. This bond with the Society did not finish here because Arthur's nephew, William Morgan V, son of John Morgan, a surgeon at Guy's, was a junior member of the staff, and on Arthur's demise he became Assistant Actuary, a post he held until his retirement in 1892. Thus, after one hundred and eighteen years of faithful and efficient service, the tie between this extraordinary family and the Equitable was at last severed.

The results of the decennial valuation of 1829 revealed a surplus of over £5,000,000. How magnificently these millions compare with the meagre £11,000 surplus mentioned earlier for the year ending 1773! Throughout the greater part of his life William Morgan was the only practising professional Actuary as we understand the term today, and in this special field of knowledge he had no opponents of any stature. As he neared the end of his career, however, his theories were subjected to a continual bombardment of cruel criticism from expert mathematicians like Baily,

Babbage, and Augustus de Morgan. He owed his shaky survival from these fierce struggles to his greater practical experience—a stored experience which was amply recognised by his friend the President of the Equitable, Sir Charles Morgan, Bart.[2] The grateful baronet was anxious for William to continue as Actuary for the remainder of his life; but he declined, knowing that his physical and mental powers were waning. On retirement he was granted a handsome pension equal to his salary of £2,000 a year for life—an enormous income for those days. This he enjoyed for three years only, for on 4 May 1833 this grand old octogenarian fell a victim of the current influenza pandemic. It is recorded that his own assurances for £2,500 had matured to the impressive sum of nearly £7,500 with profits at death—"Sic nos non nobis".

William Morgan remained a fervent Welshman to his dying day despite the fact that he lived in the metropolis for over sixty years. Even as an old man he was able to demonstrate his bilingual skill by spontaneously turning the words of a Welsh tune into fine English verse with absolute ease. In his role as Actuary of the Equitable he undoubtedly rubbed shoulders with many of the leading personalities of the day. He could have revelled in high society but sought no greater pleasure than the intimate company of his own family. He owned property at Ogmore-by-Sea, now the site of Craigyreos Hotel, which he used to visit regularly in the summer months. This year the Equitable Society is opening up a new branch in Cardiff. For his admirers this office will serve as a constant and tangible reminder of a cultivated, humorous, and versatile Celt who as a young physician returned to the big city, not to advance his knowledge of medicine like so many of his countrymen have done, but to study the mysteries of mathematics and emerge triumphantly as Britain's first Actuary.

2   Sir Charles Morgan (originally Sir Charles Gould) was left the entire Tredegar estates by his brother-in-law, John Morgan, in 1792.

Bibliographical Note

A few of the sources cited in the body of the article call for further mention. J. G. Anderson's article "William Morgan and X-rays" (*Transactions of the Faculty of Actuaries,* vol. 17, 1945), deals in a most authoritative manner with electrical experiments, while Sir William Elderton's article on "William Morgan, F.R.S. (1750-1833)" in the same journal (vol. 14, 1932) forms an admirable introduction to Morgan's actuarial work.

The late Sir William Elderton, who was Actuary to the Equitable Society from 1913-1942, also contributed to the *Genealogist's Magazine* (vol. 12, 1957) an important article under the title "Some Family Connections of William Morgan (1750-1833), F.R.S". Unfortunately, considerations of space do not permit us to narrate how such distinguished families as the Coffins of Bridgend and Llandaff, the Williamses of Coed-y-Mwstwr, the Vachells of Cardiff and the Traverses of London were connected with William Morgan. For information on these connections we advise the reader to turn first of all to H. J. Randall's *Bridgend* and afterwards to Sir William Elderton's outstanding genealogical essay.

Lists of Morgan's own publications are contained in Elderton's first article and in the biographies appearing in the *Dictionary of National Biography* and I. Foulkes' *Geirlyfr Bywgraffiadol o Enwogion Cymru etc.* (Liverpool, 1870). It is interesting to note that Morgan contributed articles on life-assurance and kindred topics to the monumental encyclopaedia brought out by his fellow Welshman and contemporary, Abraham Rees—*The New Cyclopaedia or Universal Dictionary* (45 volumes, 1802-1820). A most useful introduction to the whole question of life-assurance is to be found in the relevant articles of the *Encyclopaedia Britannica.* A. Wolf's *History of Science, Technology and Philosophy in the eighteenth century* (London, 1938) treats fully the main scientific advances made in William Morgan's day.

THE MORGAN FAMILY TREE

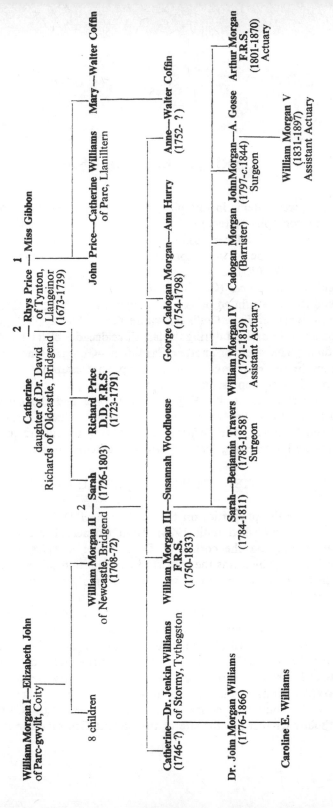

CARDIFF BEFORE 1890

THE twelve items in this pictorial inset are a selection from the photographs preserved at the Central Library, Cardiff, and are reproduced by kind permission of Mr. J. E. Thomas, F.L.A., City Librarian. Some of them appear in such works as John Hobson Matthews' *Cardiff Records* (6 vols., Cardiff, 1898-1911) and S. W. Allen's *Reminiscences* (Cardiff, 1918), whereas others are now being reproduced in a printed book for the first time. Nine of the prints are the work of J. S. Collings, whose family had a photographic business in Bute Street during the last three decades of the nineteenth century. The work of another Cardiffian—George Henry Wills, a shipowner and shipbroker who took up photographic work as a hobby—is also represented; but the pioneers to whom we owe the earliest items of all—High Street *c.* 1865 and the *Cowbridge Arms c.* 1870—are unknown. The notes which follow are necessarily brief, their purpose being merely to outline the most salient and interesting features which the items present.

SOUTH-EAST VIEW FROM THE CASTLE CLOCK TOWER *c.* 1871.

Notice the properties on the north side of Duke Street, which were not demolished until 1923; High Corner House (the Bute Estate Office) on the corner of Duke Street and Castle Street; Angel Street, which was the westward continuation of Duke Street; Castle Street, which extended from High Corner House to the Castle gate and also in a westerly direction alongside the boundary wall of Castle. Under the Cardiff Improvement Act of 1875 the buildings on the north side of Angel Street and the south side of Castle Street were demolished, the resulting thoroughfare being thenceforward known as Castle Street. Also demolished were the buildings in Broad Street, notably the two inns—the *Cardiff Arms* and the *Cowbridge Arms*—which are dealt with on a later page. Other noteworthy buildings appearing in the view are Zion Calvinistic Methodist Chapel (on the site of the present Central Library) with

Photograph by J. S. Collings

S.E. view from the Castle Clock Tower, c. **1871**

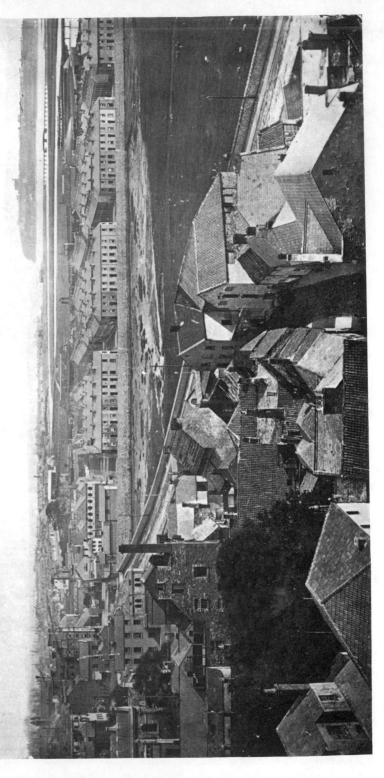

S. view from the Castle Clock Tower, c. 1871

Photograph by J. S. Collings

W. view from the Castle Clock Tower, c. 1871

Photograph by J. S. Collings

High Street, *c.* 1865

Houses and Business Premises in High Street, 1874

Photograph by J. S. Collings

St. Mary Street and High Street, 1881

Photograph by J. S. Collings

Old Houses in St. Mary Street, 1881

Photograph by J. S. Collings

Cardiff Arms Hotel, *c.* **1878**

Photograph by J. S. Collings

Broad Street and Angel Street (now Castle Street) from the West, *c.* **1870**

Spital Cottages, Crockherbtown, 1883

Old Taff Vale Railway Station, 1886

houses immediately adjoining it; premises on the east side of High Street which are still standing, e.g. those lately occupied by Samuel Hall Ltd., and those still used as offices by Stephenson and Alexander; and lastly the old *Angel Inn*, the front façade of which, despite rebuilding, still presents very much the same appearance Ceasing to be an Inn after the present *Angel Hotel* was built and High Corner House demolished, it became the Bute Estate Office. It now houses the offices of Western Ground Rents Ltd. and various other firms and companies.

SOUTH VIEW FROM CASTLE CLOCK TOWER c. 1871.

Womanby Street is in the foreground, while in the centre is Cardiff Arms Park as it was before any building has been erected on the west side of Westgate Street. Beyond the Park are Temperance Town, the Railway Station, and the industrial training ship *Havannah* (in the river below Penarth Road Bridge). In the background on the right, near the mouth of the river, is the bridge which was removed after the construction of the present Clarence Bridge in the years 1889-90. The flooded portion of the Park is the part now occupied by the General Post Office building which was erected in 1896.

WEST VIEW FROM THE CASTLE CLOCK TOWER c. 1871.

Houses in Mark Street are in the course of construction. In the background is St. John's Church, Canton, and Severn Road, one of Canton's earliest streets. The nave of St. John's was built in 1853, the aisles were added in 1857, but the tower, spire, chancel and vestry were not constructed until 1870. Also noteworthy are the houses in what is now Cathedral Road (built before the street as a whole had been planned) and the remains of an older bridge a few yards north of the existing one. Remains of this older bridge, though not so conspicuous, can still be seen. The existing bridge, built in 1859 by Daniel Thomas, father of Sir Alfred Thomas (Lord Pontypridd), was widened in 1877 and again in 1930-31.

HIGH STREET, APRIL 1872.

A view of High Street, with part of St. Mary Street in the distance. The triumphal arch had been erected for the occasion of the wedding of the third Marquess of Bute (John Patrick Crichton-

Stuart), who married the Hon. Guendolen Mary Anne, eldest daughter of Edward, first Lord Howard of Glossop, at Brompton Oratory, London, on 16 April 1872. A comparison of this view with the views on the opposite page and with the street as it stands today is of great interest. The statue, which is that of the second Marquess of Bute, was removed in 1879 to a spot near its present site at the south end of St. Mary Street. Cardiff's first horse tram service—from this statue to the Docks—started in 1872.

HIGH STREET *c*. 1865.

Notice the old Brecon Bank in the centre of the view, and High Corner House facing High Street. The Brecon Bank was taken over by Lloyds Bank in 1890. The premises to the south of the Bank are described under the next item.

HOUSES AND BUSINESS PREMISES IN HIGH STREET, 1874.

These houses and business premises include the old *Sugar Loaf Inn* (No. 25), the door at the side of which gave access to a court of small tenements. When the view was taken all these properties were due for demolition. The business premises which succeeded them now form the block of offices etc. fronting the Castle Arcade. A small portion of the Brecon Bank is visible on the right of the view.

ST. MARY STREET AND HIGH STREET, 1881.

Immediately to the right of Ashton and Ward's fish shop is the entrance to Landore Court, which could also be approached from Westgate Street. Next in order to the right, and awaiting demolition, are two business premises, the first of which had been in the occupation of newsagent and bookseller Philemon Thomas (see Stewart Williams, *Saints and Sailing Ships*, Barry, 1962, p. 41). After these come the Town Hall, the Post Office, and the newly erected National Provincial Bank building, which is still standing. After the demolition of Philemon Thomas's shop and the old *Bath Arms* adjoining, the London and Provincial Bank (later merged with Barclays) erected the premises which now occupy the site. The Town Hall and Post Office have been replaced by the C.W.S. building.

OLD HOUSES IN ST. MARY STREET, 1881.

These old houses were on the site of the present Market Buildings. When the view was taken, they were being used temporarily as an office in connection with a prize drawing scheme to aid the funds of Cardiff Infirmary. Several members of the Committee administering the scheme are in the group of people assembled outside the houses. The names of twelve persons in the group are given in *Cardiff Records*, vol. 6, p. cxxviii, tenth from the left being S. W. Allen, the engineer who by means of his book *Reminiscences* safeguarded for posterity a considerable amount of invaluable information on nineteenth century Cardiff. To the left of the houses can be seen part of the old Police Station—the old County gaol which once occupied the same site was purchased by Cardiff Corporation in 1833 for £2,000. To the right of the houses is the entrance to the market (erected in 1835 and since rebuilt).

THE CARDIFF ARMS INN c. 1878.

The *Cardiff Arms*, one of Cardiff's leading hostelries, was demolished in 1878, when the road was widened to the line of the building shown on the left of the photograph. Adjacent to this building the *Angel Hotel*, which superseded both the *Cardiff Arms* and the *Angel Inn*, was erected. The *Cardiff Arms* stood in Broad Street, a short thoroughfare which ran at right angles to both Angel Street and Castle Street. Facing it across the street and extending from the corner of Angel Street to the corner of Castle Street was the *Cowbridge Arms*. By 1851, *i.e.* soon after the straigthening of the river Taff which had previously flown at the rear of the *Cardiff Arms*, the enlarged park had taken its name from the adjoining inn.

THE COWBRIDGE ARMS c. 1870.

Like the *Cardiff Arms*, the *Cowbridge Arms* was demolished in 1878. According to *Cardiff Records*, vol. 6, p. cxxiv, it was one of the favourite inns resorted to by farmers, the open space in front being crowded with carts and traps on market days and the horses being stabled in the *Cardiff Arms* yard close by.

SPITAL COTTAGES, CROCKHERBTOWN, 1883.

These cottages stood in Crockherbtown (now Queen Street)

immediately to the west of the present *Alexandra Hotel*. The Spital (or Spitle) which used to stand nearby was a medieval leper hospital which became private property after the Restoration (see William Rees, *Cardiff : A history of the City*, pp. 164-5). The old Infirmary (subsequently the first University College building) in Newport Road, the Taff Vale Railway Station and the present Gaol appear to have been built on former Spital land. The cottages have been replaced by the present Spital Buildings.

TAFF VALE RAILWAY STATION, 1886.

The photograph shows the first "Queen Street" station, which probably dated back to the opening of the Taff Vale Railway in 1840. The station was rebuilt in 1887.

OBSERVATIONS ON THE POPULATION CHANGES IN GLAMORGAN, 1800-1900

by

MOELWYN I. WILLIAMS, M.A.

THE outstanding features of the social history of Glamorgan during the nineteenth century were the phenomenal changes that occurred in the size, distribution and structure of its population. These changes may be said to have taken place in two stages, the first extending from about 1760 to 1850, and the second from about 1850 to 1921. The first stage coincided with the growth and development of the Glamorgan iron works, whilst the second stage coincided with the vigorous exploitation of local coal deposits, more especially after 1871.

In 1800, the population of Glamorgan remained fairly evenly distributed over the whole county. The lowland regions of the Vale and the Gower peninsula, with an average density of about 50 to 100 persons per square mile, were in fact much more populous than the hill districts of the coalfields where there were still extensive areas with a density of only about 20 to 30 persons per square mile. The most populous area at this time was naturally centred around the iron works at Dowlais and the Merthyr Tydfil area where, by 1850, the Guests, the Crawshays, the Hills and the Homfrays had established a "mineral kingdom" which extended from Hirwaun to Blaenavon.[1] Similarly, in the south-west of the county, the copper smelting works of the Neath and Swansea districts had also attracted their share of the population. The census returns for 1801 revealed that the population of Glamorgan then stood at 70,879, of which 7,700 persons, or nearly one-tenth of the total for the whole county, resided in the Merthyr area, 6,821 in Swansea, and 1,870 in Cardiff. By 1841 Merthyr had a population figure far exceeding the combined total for Swansea and Cardiff.

The first stage in the development of the mineral resources of Glamorgan, therefore, set in motion a number of forces which

1 J. F. Rees. "How South Wales became industrialised". *Studies in Welsh History*, ch. IX, pp. 130-48.

eventually revolutionised the economic and social life of the county. Long before 1800, observers had noted that the iron works in Merthyr, as well as the copper smelting works at Swansea and Neath, were economic forces which were making positive inroads into the old agricultural-pastoral economy.   Although it is true to say that in 1800 the majority of the people of Glamorgan still earned their living from the land, it was, nevertheless, becoming increasingly evident that alternative forms of employment were already attracting workers away from agriculture and rural life.   It was observed, for instance, that "the price of provisions . . . has of late years been very high owing to the increased demand of the manufacturing districts. . . The price of labour is equally enhanced from the same cause".

In 1814 the demand for labour in the manufacturing districts of Glamorgan was said to have been so great that in the Vale "every man knows that in case of disagreement with his employer, he has a probable recourse at the various 'works' where high wages and constant employment hold out a strong temptation to exorbitance in negotiating terms with individuals who are compelled, with slender purses, to bid against the wealth of Merthyr Tydvil and Swansea". This new competitive element which had already entered the labour market of Glamorgan was undoubtedly a matter of great concern to all employers of labour, and strong action was often considered necessary to keep wages in check.   For instance, in 1806 "five rope-makers in the employ of Messrs Grove & Co. of Swansea were committed to Cardiff for three months for conspiracy to rise wages"   (*The Cambrian*, 18 July 1806).

At the beginning of the nineteenth century the people of Glamorgan were obviously becoming directly concerned with wages and conditions of employment in industries other than agriculture. Likewise, employers of labour in the agricultural areas of the county were becoming aware of a degree of instability in what had once been a constant and reliable labour supply in the countryside.   Various remedial measures were consequently taken in an attempt to stem the flow of workers away from agriculture.

It is not without significance, therefore, that in 1816 the Glamorganshire Agricultural Society (founded in 1772) extended its awards, and began to offer premiums to farm servants in order to encourage thrift and long service.   Again, in 1819 the following premiums were offered :

(a) To the labourer in husbandry by whom the greatest number of children have been brought up to at least seven years of age without Parish Relief, 4 guineas; for the second greatest number, 3 guineas; and to the third and fourth greatest, 2 guineas and 1 guinea respectively.

(b) To men servants in husbandry who shall have received wages for the greatest number of years' service (not less than seven) uninterruptedly performed from the age of sixteen years in the same family and shall produce satisfactory certificates from their employers of their continued good behaviour; to the first, 3 guineas; to the second, 2 guineas.

(c) To woman servants in husbandry, under similar circumstances and conditions; to the first, 3 guineas; to the second, 2 guineas.

(d) To four labourers in husbandry, having been married, who shall have continued the greatest number of years (not less than seven) in constant employ as such on the same farm or with the same master . . . to the first, 3 guineas; to the second, 3 guineas; to the third, 2 guineas; and to the fourth, 1 guinea.

The premiums were not easily won.   The awards agreed to by the Society at a meeting held on 18 November 1836 at the *Bear Inn*, Cowbridge, were as follows :

1. *Bringing up a family*

To William Rees of Colwinston, having had born to him 12 children of whom he had brought up eight without Parish Relief—£4.

To Richard Deere of Llanmaes, having had born to him seven children all of whom he brought up without Parish Relief —£3.

2. *Length of servitude*

To Richard Evans of Ystradyfodwg, having continued 18 years in the same family from the age of 14—£2.

To Hopkin Hopkin of Coychurch, having continued seven years in the same family from the age of 14—£1.

To James Richards of Roath, having been married and continued in constant employ on the same farm . . . 32 years without Parish Relief—£4.

Moreover, the Bridgend Labourers' Friend Society (which by 1841 embraced the Hundreds of Newcastle and Ogmore) also awarded prizes for long and uninterrupted service on the same farm. According to the rules of this Society, candidates for prizes for "long and faithful service" must have served for at least three to five years, and had to be under 31 years of age.

It is also interesting to observe that the upward trend in agricultural wages eventually resulted in the abandonment of many old harvest customs which, while they continued, were of immense economic benefit to farm workers in the countryside. One of these customs was linked with the local practice of hand-reaping corn crops in the Vale. This method was severely criticised by contemporary observers, for its only merit was that it produced the most "tidy sheaf"; but it did not leave the "cleanest stubble". At harvest time, the usual practice in Glamorgan was for the farmer to let his wheat to be hand-reaped by the acre, "with victuals and beer". Each reaper then claimed the right "by immemorial usage" for his next of kin to glean in the field while the reapers were at work. But in certain areas, as in the Penmark and Llantwit Major districts, if the reaper had no family or next-of-kin, he would then lease his field to other gleaners at so much per acre. In the late eighteenth century the reaper (i.e. the lessor) would get 6d. per acre from the gleaners; in 1802 he got 1/-, and in 1811 the price had advanced to 2/6d. per acre. By the 1830's the price at which wheat fields were "leased" to gleaners was dictated "by the conscience of the reaper" in leaving a good share of the crop behind. In this way it was estimated that the local farmers often lost up to 30/- per acre. As the wage rates continued to rise, it is not surprising that ultimately "the gates in many places became locked against gleaners until the last sheaf was out of the field and the 'hell-rakes' had collected nearly the whole of the straggling ears". Nor is it surprising that by 1835 the custom of leasing in the Vale had been practically abolished by the introduction of reapers from other counties. The ramifications of the upward trend in wages which accompanied the early impact of industrialisation were many.

By the end of the first stage of industrial development in Glamorgan, the population had risen from 70,879 in 1801 to 231,849 in 1851. It has already been pointed out that the increases during this period had coincided with the rapid extension of the iron industry which had made necessary the building of local canals and railways. In 1791, for example, the Glamorganshire Canal from Merthyr to Cardiff was opened, as well as the Neath Canal. These were to be followed by the Swansea Canal in 1798, and the Llansamlet Canal in 1803. Moreover, in 1841 the Taff Vale Railway was opened, and by 1851 the South Wales Railway, which connected Chepstow and Swansea, had been completed. All these undertakings tended to push up wages and drew additional numbers of workers away from the land.

The pace at which the population of Glamorgan grew during the second phase of industrial development may be illustrated by means of the following table :

Year			1851	1901	1911
Population			231,849	859,931	1,120,910

It will be seen that the figures for 1911 are almost five times those for 1851, and in fact represent almost half the total of 2,420,921 for the whole of Wales. This period was dominated by the exploitation of the Glamorgan coalfield. The change of emphasis from iron to coal production is reflected in the population figures for Cardiff when compared with those for Merthyr and Swansea :

			1801	1841	1861	1901
Cardiff			1,870	10,077	32,954	164,333
Swansea			6,821	19,115	33,972	94,537
Merthyr			7,700	34,977	49,794	69,228

No less dramatic was the rise in the population of Barry which stood at about 100 in 1881, but by 1891 it had risen to 13,000, and by 1921 it had reached 38,900. Even more striking, perhaps, were the increases in the population figures for the parish of Ystradyfodwg. This was once a fairly rich pastoral region noted for its cattle and sheep rearing. In 1836 it was still unspoiled, and its wild natural beauty attracted the eye of many contemporary tourists.[2] Even as late as 1861 the population of the area did not exceed 4,000, but by 1871 this figure had increased to 16,925, and by 1921 it had reached the incredible total of 162,717—a figure which represented a population density of about 23,680 persons per square mile of the built-up area of the Rhondda Valley.

2 See Appendix, which is a quotation from the observations made by a traveller on a journey through the Rhondda Valley in 1836.

The period from about 1860 to 1911 witnessed a vigorous, if not ruthless, exploitation of the coalfields of the Blaenau, as well as an acceleration in the building of new railways and docks.   It was during these years that a major part of the economy of the county was being geared to the export trade in coal.   High rates of wages in the "works", together with the prospects of a higher standard of living with shorter working hours, had already brought thousands of workers into Glamorgan from other counties.   The volume of immigration between 1861 and 1911 assumed striking proportions, as the following statistics show :

Year	1861	1871	1881	1891	1901	1911
Total population of Glamorgan	317,752	397,859	511,433	687,218	859,931	1,120,910
Number born in other counties	116,812	117,904	180,794	260,684	297,833	390,941

But whilst the movement of workers into Glamorgan from other counties continued, there was at the same time some degree of redistribution of population taking place locally.   Early in the 'sixties workers from the iron works at Merthyr were already moving in small but significant numbers to the coal pits of the Rhondda.   After about 1870 the sinking of more and deeper pits created a bigger demand for labour which was partly met by gangs of workers moving away from the iron works.   At the same time the movement of agricultural workers away from the land continued, and these movements seem to have assumed a fairly clear pattern, as may be gathered from a brief examination of the population movements in the Vale of Glamorgan.

Despite the upward trend in agricultural wages and other incentives which were offered in an attempt to keep men on the land, the indigenous labourers still moved towards the relatively higher wages obtainable in the non-agricultural occupations.   The consequent local labour shortages were made good by immigrant labourers from elsewhere who were themselves attracted, initially, by the relatively high agricultural wages in the Vale.   In 1867 an official report stated that wages in the Vale were high—12s. a week appears to be the lowest pay for an ordinary agricultural labourer.

In the neighbourhood of Bridgend, wages were about 12*s*. to 15*s*. per week for ordinary labourers. The rates prevailing in other parishes were as follows :

Parish			*Wages paid to males in 1867 per week*
Bonvilston	....	....	12*s*. to 15*s*.
Llanmaes	....	....	10*s*. to 12*s*. in winter.
			12*s*. to 15*s*. in summer.
Penmark	....	....	12*s*. to 15*s*.
Peterston	....	....	12*s*. (regular), 2*s*. 6*d*. per day (irregular)
St. Fagan's	....	....	12*s*. to 16*s*.
Llanilltern	....	....	15*s*. to 20*s*. in harvest time

In addition to cash payments, agricultural workers received "real" wages in the form of "daily board in the farm house", "house rent free", potato ground and the right to buy butter and cheese (and sometimes corn) at a fixed price.

It should be observed at this point that in the 1860's the average weekly wage paid to farm workers in Somerset was 10*s*.; in Devon 9*s*. 2*d*.; in Dorset 9*s*. 4*d*.; in Wiltshire 9*s*. Agricultural wages in the Vale of Glamorgan were still in advance of those prevailing in adjacent Welsh and English counties. By the 1890's the disparity became more conspicuous, as the following table illustrates :

Average earnings of agricultural labourers in 1898 (including value of allowances in kind) [3]

County				Average rates
Glamorgan	....	....	....	19*s*. 1*d*.
Somerset	....	....	....	15*s*. 10*d*.
Devon	....	....	....	16*s*. 7*d*.
Cornwall	....	....	....	16*s*. 7*d*.
Gloucester	....	....	....	15*s*. 1*d*.
Wiltshire	....	....	....	15*s*. 0*d*.
Carmarthen	....	....	....	16*s*. 7*d*.
Cardigan	....	....	....	14*s*. 9*d*.
Brecon	....	....	....	16*s*. 8*d*.

The last decade of the century witnessed an intensification of work in the coalfields of the county, and this resulted in a further movement of indigenous workers away from the Vale. Meanwhile the relatively high rates of agricultural wages in the Vale had attracted so many farm workers from the neighbouring counties of England that by 1893 it was officially stated that "labourers from Wiltshire, Somerset and Devon, from Hereford and the Cirencester district of Gloucestershire have almost everywhere superseded the

3   Brinley Thomas. "The migration of labour into the Glamorganshire coal-fields, 1861-1911". *Economica*, X, 1930, pp. 275-94.

indigenous Welsh labourer in the Vale of Glamorgan, excepting along the seaboard in parts that are remotest from railway communication". But even the newcomers did not remain very long on the farms "for higher wages and shorter hours almost invariably succeeded in attracting them to the mineral districts, so that other labourers have to be continually drafted from the same English counties to replace them".

It would be quite erroneous, however, to conclude that there was a continuous efflux of persons from all parishes of the Vale to the industrial areas of the uplands. It would be more correct to argue that towards the end of the century there was a general movement of workers away from agricultural occupations within the Vale rather than from the respective parishes of the Vale itself. For instance, the construction of the railway from Llantrisant to Cowbridge (opened in 1865 and extended to Aberthaw in 1892), together with the building of the Vale of Glamorgan Railway from Bridgend to Barry (1888), whilst attracting workers away from the local farms, did not actually take them away from the Vale. In fact there were temporary increases of population during this period in some parishes where normally a decrease would be expected. Some interesting examples of these trends may be seen in the hamlets and parishes represented in the following table :

Parish or Hamlet	1851	1861	1871
Lower Coyty (sic).....	1,779	2,174	2,761
Higher Newcastle	822	1,357	2,524
Newton Nottage	959	1,082	1,455
Upper Tythegston	1,027	1,572	1,390
Pyle	991	1,192	882

The increase of population in Lower Coity, Higher Newcastle and Upper Tythegston between 1851 and 1861 was attributed "to the extension of collieries, and of coke and iron works". Between 1861 and 1871 the population in the two former parishes continued to increase due "to the influx of labourers from the surrounding agricultural districts in consequence of the flourishing condition of the iron works and collieries at which constant employment at a higher rate of wages are obtained". During the same decade there was a reversal in the population figures for the hamlet of Upper Tythegston, which was attributed to "the closing of the Cefn iron works and to migration to America and Australia". The increase of population in Newton Nottage between 1861 and 1871 was undoubtedly due "to the building of new docks and to the opening of a new line of railway at Porthcawl where a large export coal trade was carried on". In contradistinction, the decrease in the population of Pyle during the same decade was said to have been due "to the removal of many colliers to the Ogmore Valley where new pits had been opened".

The only instances of emigration from the Vale to overseas lands were from Welsh St. Donat's and Upper Tythegston where decreases in population were attributed partly to "emigration". It is also recorded that the parish of St. Bride's Major, in the south-west corner of the Vale, had lost a high proportion of its inhabitants between 1845 and 1853, but in this instance the movement was associated with the Mormon exodus from Wales to the Salt Lake City. With the exception of isolated emigrants to overseas countries, the movement of persons out of the Vale formed part of the general redistribution of the population within the county.

Taking a general view of the population changes in the Vale during the second half of the nineteenth century we will find that there were three groups of parishes, namely (a) those whose population decreased steadily throughout the period; (b) those in which the population at first decreased and then increased consequent on the development of local industrial or commercial undertakings; (c) those where the population decreased and later increased by the process of incorporating rural territory into urban.

The nineteenth century was obviously a period of tremendous economic and social change during which Glamorgan became an industrialised county with the majority of its population dependent on non-agricultural occupations as a means of livelihood. The degree of change which had ultimately taken place in the structure of the population of the county by 1891 may be gathered from the following figures :

Proportion per cent of the population engaged in each class of occupation in 1891

Agricultural	Professional	Domestic	Commercial	Industrial	Unoccupied
2.2	3.0	6.3	6.7	41.1	40.7

The general movement of labourers away from agriculture may

be illustrated by comparing the size of the "agricultural labourers" class with that of the "general labourers" class for the years 1851 to 1891 :

Year	Agricultural labourers	General labourers
1851	9,174	9,130
1861	7,019	10,483
1871	5,385	14,208
1881	4,770	14,990
1891	4,235	20,645

The same trend is revealed if we examine the figures for the total number of persons employed in agriculture at the several decennial points between 1851 and 1891 as shown in the following table :

Number of persons employed in agriculture in Glamorgan, 1851-1891

1851	15,005
1861	12,565
1871	10,634
1881	9,717
1891	9,982

In the foregoing paragraphs an attempt has been made to show that so long as agriculture remained the basis of the material life of the county, the population remained fairly stable. It was during this period of relative social stability, however, that the Welsh language prospered. Except for those regions along the Glamorgan coastline, where trade and social intercourse with the West of England had resulted in widespread anglicisation, it may be averred that in 1800 Welsh was still the everyday language of the vast majority of the 70,879 persons who inhabited the interior of the county.

Nevertheless, during the first decades of the nineteenth century the stage was already set for the inter-play of those economic and social forces which were inherent in the industrial development of Glamorgan, and which were later to place the Welsh language at a discount. It has been emphasised that higher wages, shorter working hours, and the prospects of a higher standard of living, were the factors with which ordinary men and women were showing an increasing concern. Consequently thousands of workers gravitated towards the non-agricultural occupations in the works, at the docks, in the towns, and on the railways. This movement away from agriculture and agricultural life resulted in the ultimate break-up of the "old order" in which men's economic, social and mental activities were governed mainly by the requirements of the cultivation of the land and the distribution of its products.

By 1900, the redistribution of population within the Vale of Glamorgan, together with the immigration of large numbers of farm workers from the West of England, had resulted in the disappearance of much of the traditional pattern of social and cultural activities in this lowland region. Broadly speaking the "old order" had lost its viability within the vortex of industrialisation. But if the traditional Welsh "way of life" had been permanently undermined in the rural areas of Glamorgan, a new pattern of living, with its own peculiar Welsh characteristics, had emerged in its industrial valleys, despite the large concentrations of English immigrants who had settled there between 1851 and 1911. This new "way of life" which had superseded a previous traditional Welsh "way of life" is by today regarded as the "traditional" way of life of the Rhondda and other industrial regions of Glamorgan— a way of life which many modern Welsh and Anglo-Welsh writers have tried to portray (sometimes quite wrongly) in works of travel, fiction and drama.

The emergence of a new "Welsh way of life" in Glamorgan during the period of its industrialisation was undoubtedly due to the concentration of thousands of Welsh-speaking Welshmen from all parts of Wales who had been lured into industrial jobs by the same considerations as prompted many of the indigenous agricultural workers to leave the local farms. The pattern of settlement in the mining valleys gave rise to a closely-knit community whose members shared common dangers and common interests. This social setting was undoubtedly a major factor making it possible for Welsh to become the language of everyday conversation, and a medium for intellectual activity. One authority has argued that "the Welsh language was saved by the redistribution of a growing population brought about by industrialism".[4] The statistical evidence with which this argument is supported is convincing, yet the concentration of large numbers of Welsh-speaking Welshmen in the industrial centres would not in itself be sufficient to account for the survival of the Welsh language if it were not accompanied by a natural or unsophisticated attitude on the part of the Welsh

4 Brinley Thomas. "Wales and the Atlantic economy". *Scottish Journal of Political Economy*, VI, 1959, pp. 169-92.

people toward their mother tongue. Such an attitude was nurtured and sustained by the deep-rooted influences of Welsh Non-conformity, and more especially through its main agency, the Welsh Sunday School, which contributed much towards retarding the anglicising[5] influences of the 1870 Elementary Education Act throughout the industrial areas of the county.

During the last quarter of a century there have been further changes in the size, distribution and structure of the population of Glamorgan which have resulted in a pattern of social life that is twice removed from that which was dominated by the rural setting of Glamorgan in 1800.

5   For a full discussion on this topic see : J. Parry Lewis. "The anglicisation of Glamorgan". *Morgannwg*, IV, 1960, pp. 28-49.

APPENDIX

"A tourist", describing his journey through the parish of Ystradyfodwg in 1836 wrote thus : "The journey from Newbridge along the banks of the Rhondda Fawr to Ystradyfodwg must be performed on horseback, as the road is not very convenient for carriages. The attention of the traveller will be arrested by several waterfalls during his progress through the valley, and on his arrival at a place called Dinas, the mountain scenery of Ystradyfodwg will burst into his view . . . Not far from Dinas there is a small group of cottages called Pandy, and here we observed a narrow lane leading to the mountains on the left of the road. A digression of half a mile in this direction will amply repay the traveller for his trouble . . . There are no good Inns to be found in these *fairy* regions, and a traveller who cannot make a dinner on eggs and bacon must quietly resign himself to his fate and pass the day in fasting . . . We diverged accordingly near a farm house called Ty Newydd and proceeded for about half a mile amidst the wildest and most magnificent scenery".

THE MOUNTAINS OF GLAMORGAN

The mountains of Glamorgan
Look down towards the sea :
Their songs are clear as any bell
In melodies that rise and swell ;
And steadfastly they sentinel,
A Vale of mystery.

The mountains of Glamorgan
Are wondrous in the Spring :
I think our dead folk gather there
To bless this land in song and prayer,
For every grove and woodland lair
Grows loud with whispering.

When I have reached my journey's end
And I am dead, and free,
I pray that God will let me go
To wander with them, to and fro,
Along those singing hills I know
That look towards the sea.

A. G. PRYS-JONES.

CHRISTIAN ORIGINS IN GLAMORGAN

by

R. W. D. FENN, M.A., F.S.A.(SCOT.)

THE origins of organised Christianity in Glamorgan, like those of the rest of Wales, belong to the Dark Ages, "dark not because we have any right to assume that they were morally or theologically debased but because little genuine light can be thrown upon them and specialist historians, as they move about them, collide often and sometimes resoundingly".[1] The beginnings of the Church in Wales are still a huge dim field in which the student has to peer about with such particular light as he can find, always being ready, on further enlightenment, to admit he has mistaken his way.

I

Unlike England, where Christianity was sufficiently organised by A.D. 314 to send the Bishops of York, London and the mysterious Londinensium or Lindensium to represent it at the Council of Arles, there is no evidence for Wales of any organised Christianity during the Roman occupation, which ended to all intents and purposes in 383 when Magnus Maximus led his forces out of Britain in his unsuccessful attempt to make himself master of the Empire. Magnus Maximus, a distinguished soldier of Spanish origin, was a Christian who married a wife associated with Caernarvon, called Elen or Helen whom Welsh history conveniently confused with the more famous Empress Helena, wife of Constantine the Great. But Magnus Maximus's Christianity, like the earlier martyrdoms of Julian and Aaron at Caerleon at the beginning of the fourth century, is evidence, not for a rudimentary Church in Wales, but of isolated Christians scattered over the countryside who were not necessarily even natives but were, instead, foreigners connected either directly or indirectly with the Roman occupation.

1 Dr. Edward Williamson. "The origins of the Church in Wales" (*Welsh Church Congress Handbook*, 1953).

122

It seems that Erging, a district in southern Herefordshire bounded by the Wye, the Monnow and the Black Mountains was the cradle of the Welsh Church, at least in south-east Wales. Both the name Erging and its English equivalent of Archenfield are derived from the name of the local Roman capital and mining town, Ariconium. However, though Welsh Christianity began to emerge from this region in the early fifth century it was not a survival from the few individual Christians who may have lived thereabouts in Roman times. No Christian remains of the Roman period have been found there, and the pagan revival initiated by Julian the Apostate in the 360's saw a splendid temple built to Nodens, the Hunter God, not far away, near Lydney, and other signs of a pagan revival have been found in the Forest of Dean area.

It was Erging's strategic and economic position rather than its connection with the past that made it the centre of early Welsh Christianity. It had, for example, good connections by road not only with the rest of Wales, but with southern England as well, where there was sufficient Christianity to foster an outbreak of Pelagianism which St. Germanus and St. Lupus suppressed on their visit in 429. Moreover, after the withdrawal of Roman troops from Britain there was a general movement westwards, from south and south east England, of Christians who were fleeing from the raids and conquests of the pagan Saxons, and it was inevitable that some of these Christian exiles made their way to Erging amongst other places. Another contributory factor in making Erging a centre of Christian growth was the revival of trade and commerce which the fifth century saw between Wales and Gaul and beyond. Traders using the western approaches came to mining centres like Erging and brought Christianity amongst their wares. Christianity was now the official religion of the decaying Roman Empire and found in Erging, perhaps the most Christianised part of Wales, not only more fertile ground in which to grow than elsewhere, but also a useful road system for its new converts to use on their missionary journeys into the rest of Wales.

At the end of the fourth century Elen was amongst these Christian missionaries and traders. When her husband Magnus Maximus held his Imperial court at Treves they had both been in close contact with St. Martin, whose monasticism at Tours, like that at Lerins, became the inspiration of the monastic organisation of the

Welsh Church. When Magnus Maximus was killed in 388 Elen and her "children" Constantine (whom in another Welsh historical confusion has been identified with Constantine the Great) and Peblig returned to Wales, their arrival in the vicinity of Erging from the Bristol Channel being commemorated by the dedications at Llanelen and Llangystennin (Welsh Bicknor).

The penetration of Christianity in the early fifth century from south-east Wales as far west as Bletherston in Pembrokeshire, another Elen dedication, is represented in Glamorgan in only two places ; the defunct Llanelen near Llanrhidian and Cosmeston, near Llandough juxta Cardiff, a place name which in all probability honours Elen's son Constantine. The weakness of Christianity in the County at this period is illustrated by the paucity of these early dedications.

II

The Venerable Bede in his *Ecclesiastical History of the English People*, written in the early eighth century, has a story of how Lucius, King of Britain, wrote a letter in 156 A.D. to Pope Eleutherius asking for Christian instruction for himself and his people.

The twelfth century *Book of Llandaff* in a much later and more developed version of the story relates that King Lucius sent Elfan and Medwy to Rome as his ambassadors, and in still later versions Elfan and Medwy, together with Dyfan and Fagan, were sent by the Pope to convert Britain and to instruct King Lucius.

King Lucius has been identified with Lleurwg, the former patron of St. Mellons, Monmouthshire, near the now extinct dedication of Llanfedw which may have commemorated St. Medwy. St. Fagan and St. Dyfan have dedications not far away in Glamorgan and St. Elfan alone lacks a church. If only the legend were true this group of dedications would be evidence for the existence of Christianity on the Monmouthshire and Glamorgan borders in the middle of the second century A.D. Unfortunately, good reasons compel the rejection of this legend as an extravagance of fiction, for the Lucius who wrote to the Pope was more probably Lucius, king of Edessa in Mesopotamia, than king of Britain where there is no record of any king with such an un-British name. Moreover, the letter, it is alleged, was written in 156 A.D. to Pope Eleutherius, who, in fact, became Pope twenty-one years later in 177 A.D.

In fact, these dedications in the vicinity of the Glamorgan and Monmouthshire border belong to a later period in the ecclesiastical history of the area, when during the fifth century the Irish pirates who had raided Wales constantly during the Roman occupation were succeeded by Irish saints who evangelised and settled in the region.

Amongst these Irish missionaries who entered Wales by sailing up the Bristol Channel was St. Tathan (alias St. Meuthius) who at the end of the fifth century or at the beginning of the sixth, settled at Caerwent on land given him by the local ruler, whereon he established a famous school and near which archaeologists have unearthed a post-Roman chapel thought to be connected with him. He is commemorated in Glamorgan at St. Athan and Llanmeuthin, (Llanvithyn), near Llancarfan, two places which are not far from the dedications to St. Lythan, St. Dyfan and St. Fagan (who has been identified with the wandering Irish scholar Bachan and who shared with St. Tathan the distinction of having been one of St. Cadoc's teachers). The proximity of this complex of dedications to St. Fagan and his legendary second century companions to St. Athan suggests that they really commemorate the local activities of a group of missionaries who worked their way westward into Glamorgan from Monmouthshire either as St. Tathan's contemporaries or as disciples of his who came from his principal monastery at Caerwent.

Other Irish missionaries landed on the western peninsulas and travelled inland along the old Roman roads and their journeys are mapped by the Ogham stones they left in their wake. One of these travellers was St. Brynach, who, though his main sphere of influence was in north Pembrokeshire where Nevern is his principal church, has a Llanfrynach to represent him both in Glamorgan and Breconshire.[2] Welsh hagiography portrays him as the "soul friend" or spiritual director of Brychan, king of Brycheiniog, the legendary father of a prodigious number of saints, some of whom, like St. Gwladus at Capel Gwladus, St. Tudfil at Merthyr Tudfil and Llyswyrny (Llysworney) and St. Cein at Llangeinor, have dedications in Glamorgan. Along with the dedication to St. Brynach these churches in the County are part of a considerable missionary movement which, centred in Brycheiniog in the early sixth century, reached out beyond South Wales over the Bristol Channel into Somerset, Devon and Cornwall.

2 Stewart Williams, *Saints and Sailing Ships*, p. 112.

III

The movements of Christianity into Glamorgan from Erging and Monmouthshire in the east and Breconshire from the north were unified in the person of St. Cadoc of Llancarfan. In the second half of the fifth century the land between the Tawe and the Usk was conquered by Glywys, whose name suggests that he originated in the region of what is known today as Gloucestershire. One of his sons, Gwynllyw, married Gwladus, a daughter of Brychan Brycheiniog and their first child, born about the year 500, was St. Cadoc. Gwynllyw, who on his father's death ruled from the Rhymney to the Usk and is the founder of St. Woolos' Cathedral, Newport, sent his son to St. Tathan at Caerwent for his education, where he learned the basis of the monastic life.

St. Cadoc's influence and prestige were strengthened by his connections with the ruling dynasties of south east Wales. He founded his principal monastery at Llancarfan on land given him by an uncle, the local ruler, and the strength of his dedications in Monmouthshire, Glamorgan and Breconshire is partly due to his family ties with the rulers of those parts. With such patronage it was inevitable that Llancarfan should become, under St. Cadoc, the most important monastery in Glamorgan, attracting to itself such distinguished visitors as St. Finnian of Clonnard and St. Gildas, the Jeremiah of Wales.

The primacy of St. Cadoc in Glamorgan is illustrated by the number of dedications he has in the County, and his disciples, like Cynwyd (Llangynwyd), Barrwg (Barry Island), Cynfwr (Llangynfwr, near Bishopston and now defunct) and Edeyrn (Llanedeyrn) consolidated his influence. His dedications at Cadoxton-juxta-Neath, Cheriton and Port Eynon represent the strengthening of the Christian Church in west Glamorgan and in this St. Cadoc was helped by his friendship with St. Gildas and by members of his own family.

St. Gildas has a prominent place in the *Life of St. Cadoc* and whatever the historical value of the individual incidents related therein about the two men, the tradition which associated them together is well established. St. Gildas in his writing made a considerable impact upon the pastoral theology and monastic organisation of the Celtic Church in Wales, and his connection with Glamorgan as a whole, quite apart from his visits to Llancarfan, is commemorated by the group of dedications in Gower at Llangenydd, Llanmadoc and Rhosili to the "Sons of Gildas" all of which are near the Cadoc dedications at Cheriton and Port Eynon and emphasise the link with that saint.

The sons and the children of the saints frequently appear in Welsh hagiography, though from the point of view of history their relationship was that of master and disciple rather than father and son. The "Sons of Gildas" settled in Gower where Merchguin, another of St. Cadoc's many uncles, was the ruler. The association between their master and the founder of Llancarfan together with the proximity of their churches to St. Cadoc's Gower dedications suggests that the settling of the Sons of Gildas in that part of the County was a feature of St. Cadoc's policy for the religious growth of west Glamorgan.

Whilst the Sons of Gildas were working in the Gower peninsula, two other saints, St. Tudwg (Tythegston) and St. Cewydd (Llangewydd, a defunct dedication in Newcastle parish) arrived in the County. St. Cewydd is a Celtic counterpart to St. Swithun, and like the Sons of Gildas, came from north Wales and shares with them and St. Tudwg a place in the history of the Church in Glamorgan in the first half of the sixth century.

St. Cadoc was amongst the many Welsh saints who fled to Brittany to escape the Yellow Plague in 547 and when he returned he was confronted by the same challenge of Church reconstruction and reorganisation which then faced all the ecclesiastical leaders of Wales, amongst whom St. David was emerging as the up and coming young man. It was not long, however, before even heavier responsibilities fell upon the Abbot of Llancarfan. The *Life of St. Cadoc* relates the tradition that before his retirement from Llancarfan St. Cadoc ruled Glamorgan as an abbot-king. Abbot-kings were more common in the Irish Church than in the Church in Wales, but St. Cadoc had strong connections with Ireland on his mother's side, and was a frequent visitor there. The monastery he founded upon the banks of the Liffey maintained its contacts with Llancarfan down to the Norman conquest of Wales and a not very early Irish tradition associates him, alongside St. David and St. Docco, with the introduction into Ireland of some sixth century liturgical reforms.

St. Cadoc's reign in Glamorgan as an abbot-king was the

prelude to a period of political instability which overtook the County in the second half of the sixth century. His claim to the throne was probably as the senior surviving member in Glamorgan of the house of Glywys. Unfortunately his reign did not solve the kingdom's political problems and towards the end of his life he abdicated, retiring at the same time from Llancarfan to the mysterious Beneventum which may well be Banwell in Somerset. Not long after St. Cadoc's departure from Glamorgan to Beneventum where he died, his kinsman, St. Beuno, fled from south Wales to Berriew in Montgomeryshire and in about the year 570 there appeared in Glamorgan (in the person of its conqueror, Meurig ap Tewdrig) a new dynasty from south-east Wales.

IV

The biggest obstacle to the consolidation of Meurig ap Tewdrig's dynasty in Glamorgan was the memory of St. Cadoc and the prestige it gave to the deposed house of Glywys. To some extent Meurig ap Tewdrig was able to counteract these traditions and connections with the past, personified in St. Cadoc, by establishing traditions and connections of his own in Glamorgan. In this he was fortunate in having the assistance of the disciples of St. Illtud and St. Teilo.

When St. Teilo, a west Wales saint, died at Llandeilo Fawr in about the year 569, there arose the immediate problem of his successor. In Welsh monasteries the abbacy was often an hereditary office, and had not complications arisen, St. Teilo's nephew, St. Oudoceus, would have had a good claim to follow his uncle as abbot. But St. Teilo was not a native of Llandeilo where he had built his principal monastery because of its strategic site, and Welsh Tribal Law insisted upon a local man being his successor. This happened at Llanelwy (St. Asaph) in north Wales when St. Asaph, a local tribesman, followed St. Centigern who had returned to Glasgow. Consequently, St. Oudoceus had to forego his claim to the Llandeilo abbot-bishopric and with his followers find a new home.

The changes at Llandeilo coincided with the greater political changes in Glamorgan and St. Oudoceus was able to hitch his wagon to the rising star of Meurig ap Tewdrig who saw in him just the traditions and connections with the past he needed to establish his dynasty firmly and to counteract the loyalties which still survived for the memory of St. Cadoc and the house of Glywys. St. Oudoceus

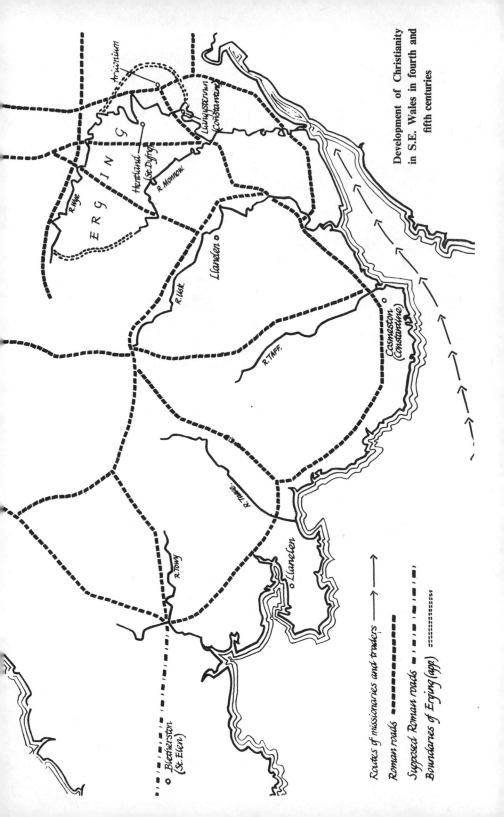

Development of Christianity
in S.E. Wales in fourth and
fifth centuries

Ariconium

Llanvyssurium
Constantius

Hentland
(St. Dyfrig)

E R G I N G

R. Wye

R. Monnow

R. Usk

Llandeen

R. Taff

Cosmeston
(Constantine)

R. Rumnea

R. Tawy

Llandeen

Bicchurston
(St. Elen)

Routes of missionaries and traders ⟶
Roman roads ▰▰▰▰▰▰
Supposed Roman roads ▰ ▪ ▰ ▪ ▰ ▪ ▰
Boundaries of Erging (app.) ═══════

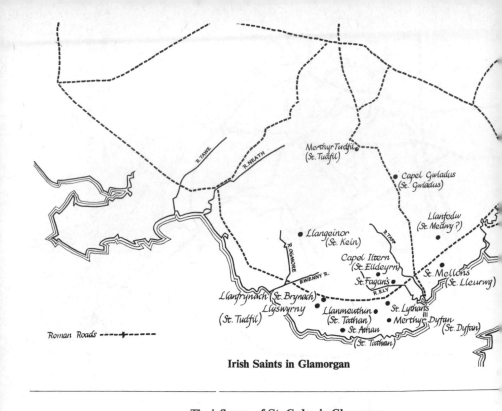

Irish Saints in Glamorgan

The following labels appear on the map:

Merthyr Tudful (St. Tudful)
Capel Gwladus (St. Gwladus)
Llanfodw (St. Medwy ?)
Llangeinor (St. Kein)
Capel Iltern (St. Elldeyrn)
St. Mellons (St. Lleurwg)
St. Fagan's
Llanfrynach (St. Brynach)
Llyswyrny
Llanmeuthin (St. Tathan)
St. Lythans
Merthyr Dyfan (St. Dyfan)
(St. Tudful)
St. Athan
(St. Tathan)
R. TAWE
R. NEATH
R. OGMORE
EWENNY R.
R. TAFF
R. ELY

Roman Roads ----+----

The influence of St. Cadoc in Glamorgan

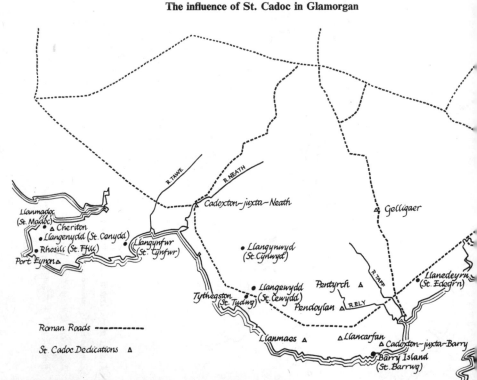

The following labels appear on the map:

Llanmadoc (St. Madoc)
Cheriton
Llangenydd (St. Cenydd)
Rhosili (St. Ffili)
Port Eynon
Llangynfwr (St. Cynfwr)
Cadoxton-juxta-Neath
Gelligaer
Llangynwyd (St. Cynwyd)
Llangewydd (St. Cewydd)
Tythegston (St. Tudwg)
Pentyrch
Pendoylan
Llanedeyrn (St. Edeyrn)
Llanmaes
Llancarfan
Cadoxton-juxta-Barry
Barry Island (St. Barrwg)
R. TAWE
R. NEATH
R. TAFF
R. ELY

Roman Roads ----------
St. Cadoc Dedications △

settled at Llandaff and the Teilo dedications at Llandeilo Talybont, Bishopston, Caswell and Merthyr Mawr commemorate the move from Llandeilo Fawr. Under the patronage of Meurig ap Tewdrig the new monastery, sited on the banks of the Taff, then navigable, and near the Roman road from Neath to Bassaleg, became the new and lasting home of St. Teilo's traditions and for centuries exercised the right of providing the Celtic Church in Glamorgan with its bishops.

Whilst St. Oudoceus was establishing the traditions of St. Teilo at Llandaff, the traditions of St. Illtud were being established at Llantwit Major. St. Illtud, a contemporary of St. Dyfrig, had his principal monastery in west Wales, probably on Caldey Island, and it was from here that his influence "turned Wales into a monastery". During the Yellow Plague of 547 the monks of the now dead Illtud went for safety to Brittany. But instead of returning to Pembrokeshire, they travelled eastwards into Glamorgan to settle at Llantwit Major, and the Illtud dedications at Pembrey, Ilston, Oxwich, Llantwit-juxta-Neath and Newcastle mark their route from Caldey. Llantwit Major, like Llandaff, enjoyed royal patronage and for a while became the burial place of the kings of Glamorgan. It appears that St. Illtud's monks were accompanied to Glamorgan by several of his disciples and associates, some of whom were Bretons, represented by St. Canna at Llangan, St. Crallo at Coychurch, St. Isan at Llanishen, St. Tyfodwg at Llandyfodwg, Ystradyfodwg and Llantrisant, St. Gwynno at Llanwonno and Llantrisant and St. Cerig at Porthkerry. Yet despite these developments in the religious history of Glamorgan in the late sixth century, Llancarfan remained pre-eminent in the County and when the Normans arrived six hundred years later they found its declining community far more alive to the contemporary situation than its rival at Llantwit Major.

V

Celtic Wales was a tribal country and consequently its Church was also tribal. Knowing nothing of parish and dioceses in the modern sense, tribal divisions were served by "mother churches" like Llancarfan and Llantwit Major which had defined spheres of influence corresponding with the political unit in which they were situated. These "mother churches" were monastic and were ruled by an abbot and chapter which was usually a family affair and the abbacy hereditary. The monks were neither invariably celibate nor in orders and the abbot himself could be a layman. On the other hand, their numbers in some monasteries were very large and scholars, for example, accept the figure of three thousand monks quoted for the monastery of St. Deiniol at Bangor on Dee. Within the monastic "llan" or enclosure the members of the monastery lived, as an ecclesiastical tribe, in cells with their families and did not share the common table and roof which was so prominent a feature of later monasticism. Learning and scholarship had an honoured place in the routine of the Celtic monastery and Llancarfan and Llantwit Major were famous for the schools attached to them, though, unlike their Irish counterparts, they produced no manuscripts of comparable beauty to the *Book of Kells*, and the schools of sculpture at Llantwit and Margam belong to a later period.

The poverty of Wales determined the rudimentary character of its architecture. Even the monasteries were simple buildings of wattle and slime and the churches were so small that during services the greater part of the congregation stood without as was still the custom in parts of western Ireland at the beginning of this century.

The extent of the territorial jurisdiction of the bishops in Glamorgan was co-terminous with the boundaries of the kingdom they served and would fluctuate with its fortunes. Politically, the Church was subordinate to the authority of the king and it could not hold lands without his consent and its rights of granting sanctuary were limited. On the other hand, the Church had complete spiritual independence and the bishop, who had the sanction of excommunication over the king, protected the rights and privileges of the clergy.

The most distinctive characteristics, however, of the Celtic Church in Wales were its liturgy, its method of calculating Easter and its tonsure. The sacraments of Baptism and Confirmation were administered together in infancy by a priest who used oil which had been consecrated by the bishop. The method of calculating the date for celebrating Easter in Wales had been settled at the Council of Arles in 314, which had been attended by three British bishops. But when the system was subsequently modified elsewhere, Celtic conservatism resulted in Good Friday and Easter being celebrated on occasion in Wales on different dates from the rest of the Church.

The tonsure worn by Celtic monks in Wales was unique, for they shaved neither the whole nor the crown, but instead they removed a semi-circle of hair from the front of their heads.

These idiosyncracies are the by-products of the facility with which the Celtic Church accommodated the Welsh political and social systems to its own needs. The monastic ideal appealed to the Celtic imagination and the conception of the monastic tribe living alongside the secular tribe was the foundation of that vigorous piety and learning which was the glory of the Church in Wales when St. Augustine's mission to Kent was still in its infancy.

1—THE CHILDREN OF BRYCHAN AND THE DYNASTY OF GLYWYS IN GLAMORGAN

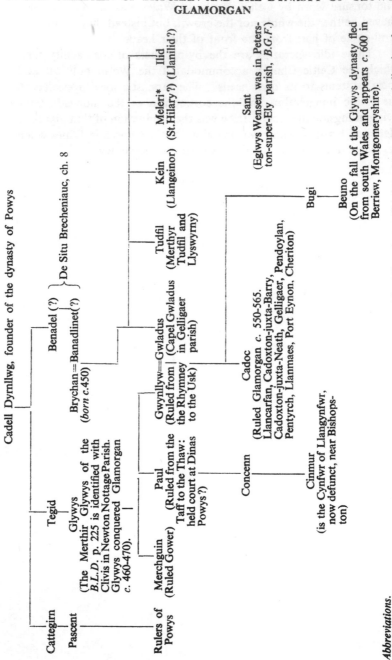

Note.—*St. Hilary is usually classed as a Norman dedication, but Meleri, according to Egerton Philimore (quoted by *B.G.F.*) is derived from Hilaria with the common honorific prefix Mo.

Abbreviations.
B.L.D. The Text of the Book of Llan Dav.
Edited by J. Gwenogvryn Evans and John Rhys. 1893.
B.G.F. S. Baring Gould and J. Fisher. *Lives of the British Saints.*

II—IRISH SAINTS IN GLAMORGAN

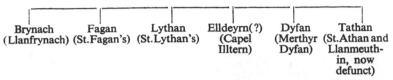

Brynach	Fagan	Lythan	Elldeyrn(?)	Dyfan	Tathan
(Llanfrynach)	(St.Fagan's)	(St.Lythan's)	(Capel Illtern)	(Merthyr Dyfan)	(St.Athan and Llanmeuthin, now defunct)

Note. 1. The Elldeyrn of Capel Illtern is an unknown saint and included in this group because of proximity to the dedications of the other saints in the group.

III—DISCIPLES OF ST. CADOC OF LLANCARFAN IN GLAMORGAN

Cadoc *c.* 500-565

Cynwyd	Barrwg	Cynfwr	Edeyrn
(the Cynwyt of the Vita Cadoci, ch.49. Llangynwyd)	(alias Finnian, the revived dedication of Barry Island)	(Cinmur of the *B.L.D.* and the Vita Cadoci. Llangynfwr nr.Bishopston, now defunct)	(Vita Cadoci, ch. 55. Llanedeyrn)

Notes. 1. St. Docco (Llandough near Cardiff and Llandough near Cowbridge) and St. Gildas (who has no Glamorgan dedications but who is represented in Gower by his "sons") belong to this period as St. Cadoc's contemporaries.

2. Perhaps Cyfelach (Llangyfelach) belongs to this group. His dedication was later replaced by that of St. David when St. Cadoc's influence in Glamorgan was eclipsed after *c.* 600.

IV—THE "SONS OF GILDAS" IN GLAMORGAN

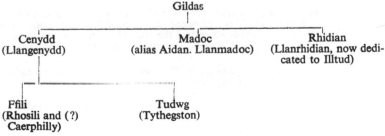

Gildas

Cenydd	Madoc	Rhidian
(Llangenydd)	(alias Aidan. Llanmadoc)	(Llanrhidian, now dedicated to Illtud)

Ffili	Tudwg
(Rhosili and (?) Caerphilly)	(Tythegston)

Notes. 1. Tudwg, of whom little is known, has been included in this group simply on the strength of the proximity of his dedications in Brittany to those of Gildas and Cenydd.

2. Rhidian is not a well authenticated saint and he has been superseded by Illtud at Llanrhidian.

3. Cewydd (Llangewydd) belongs to this period, arriving in Glamorgan at the same time as the "Sons of Gildas".

V—THE DISCIPLES OF ST. ILLTUD IN GLAMORGAN

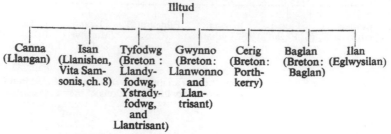

Illtud

| Canna (Llangan) | Isan (Llanishen, Vita Samsonis, ch. 8) | Tyfodwg (Breton : Llandyfodwg, Ystradyfodwg, and Llantrisant) | Gwynno (Breton: Llanwonno and Llantrisant) | Cerig (Breton: Porthkerry) | Baglan (Breton: Baglan) | Ilan (Eglwysilan) |

Notes. 1. Ilan is associated with St. Illtud and was not necessarily his disciple. He appears in the *Life of St. Samson* as an abbot who visited the aged Illtud.

2. Tyfodwg and Gwynno share the dedication at Llantrisant with St. Illtud, thereby implying a connection between the three saints.

3. Curig was a Breton connected with St. Illtud who went to Brittany, perhaps after St. Illtud's death. He was consecrated a bishop in Brittany and has been confused with St. Cyriacus, the boy martyr of Tarsus.

4. *B.G.F.* distinguish the Glamorgan dedication to St. Baglan from the Baglan ab Dingad of Llanfaglan, Caernarvonshire. Medieval tradition is the only authority for connecting him with St. Illtud.

5. The *B.L.D.* gives Eglwys Ilan as Martyrium Ilan. The only authority for associating Ilan, an otherwise unknown saint, with St. Illtud is the appearance of one of his dedications in the centre of a group of dedications to St. Illtud in Brittany.

VI—PLACE-NAME DEDICATIONS IN GLAMORGAN

1. *Llanbleddian :* The church of the wolf. A legend relates how one of Maelgwn Gwynedd's men seized one of St. Brynach's cows. The wolf attending the beast related the theft to his master who thereby retrieved it. Llanbleddian is near a Llanfrynach and adjoins Cowbridge.

2. *Llanfabon :* The medieval life of St. Nectan makes Mabon a daughter of Brychan by Gwladus, but this has no support in the Welsh pedigrees, and it is improbable that the Cornish St. Mabyn is the patron of Llanfabon. Mabon means a boy or a youth, and Llanfabon is simply the Church of the Youth. Mabon is the name of a Celtic Sun deity and this dedication may also embody overtones of the Christianisation of pagan gods, as in the case of St. Bride.

3. *Capel Brithdir :* Brithdir is a place and not a personal name.

4. *Llanilid :* The Ilid of Llanilid probably refers neither to the daughter of Brychan nor to Julitta, mother of Cyriacus, but to a local site, as in the names of Llandovery and Llandaff. The *B.L.D.* and Nennius's *History of the Britons* imply that Ilid represents the name of a district and not a person.

VII—DEDICATIONS TO SAINTS OTHERWISE UNKNOWN

1. Llanguick—Ciwg
2. Llansamlet—Samlet.
3. Llansawel (Briton Ferry)—Sawel.
4. St. Donat's and Welsh St. Donat's—Donat
5. Llansannor—Sannor. The *B.L.D.* calls it the Church of the Thaw, avoiding the problem of the saint's identity.
6. Llanharan—Haran.

VIII—DEDICATIONS TO SAINTS INTRODUCED TO GLAMORGAN AFTER THEIR DEATHS

1. St. Teilo,   Llandaff, with Dyfrig and Oudoceus
   after *c.* 570 : Merthyr Mawr
                 Bishopston
                 Pontarddulais (Llandeilo Talybont)

2. St. Illtud,   Llantwit Major
   after *c.* 570 : Llantrisant
                 Llantwit Vardre
                 Llantrithyd
                 Llantwit-juxta-Neath
                 Newcastle
                 Ilston
                 Oxwich
                 Llanrhidian
                 Oystermouth (?)

3. St. David (and St. Non). In the 10th century, when Gower became part of the kingdom of Deheubarth, of which David was the chief saint, he acquired dedications there as well.
                 Llangyfelach, originally Cyfelach
                 Llanddewi
                 Llanon, defunct, near Ilston. St. Non is St. David's mother.

4. St. Bride, a Celtic dedication introduced by the Normans, in the thirteenth century.
                 St. Bride's Minor
                 St. Bride's Major
                 St. Bride's-super-Ely.

5. Owain of Ystradowen is not necessarily a Celtic dedication at all, but the name of the secular donor of the land upon which the Church was built, and the *B.L.D.* mentions two Owains, both of whom ruled in Glamorgan during the tenth century.

DRUIDISM AT PONTYPRIDD

by

ROY DENNING, F.L.A.

"Primary chief bard am I to Elphin,
And my original country is the region of the summer stars,
Idno and Heinin called me Merddin,
At length every king will call me Taliesin".

From *Hanes Taliesin*, trans. Lady Charlotte Guest.

D RUIDISM at Pontypridd, in spite of local conviction to the contrary, is not older than the beginning of the nineteenth century. It is a romantic fiction traceable to "Iolo Morganwg", perpetuated by his son Taliesin, followed by the celebrated Dr. Price of Llantrisant and the bard "Myfyr Morganwg", finally receiving its apotheosis in the wild fancies of "Morien". The origins and history of this curious phenomenon are investigated in the following pages, and it is hoped that some light will be shed on the manner in which the Druidic tradition became incorporated into the folk-lore of the district.

Lest confusion arise in the mind of the reader, it should be explained that Iolo's version of Druidism had little in common with the fragmentary picture presented by classical authors such as Caesar and Pliny. The autocratic priesthood, with its human sacrifices, transmigration of souls, sacred groves and holy mistletoe, is changed almost beyond recognition in the nineteenth century version. The grave old priest, "sage beneath the spreading oak", has become, in the latter-day Druid, the embodiment of the traditional wisdom of the ages and an adherent of the ancient patriarchal religion, reverencing the sun as the symbol of the Creator, interpreting the cosmic meaning of natural objects such as moving stones, a master of the oldest measures of poetry and a diviner of secret things. Such a man could be no ordinary mortal, and the vein of superiority plainly visible must be significant to the psychologist. The general air of esoteric obscurity is enhanced by the mystic significance given to Glamorgan as the home of Druidism, and to the Welsh language as the medium of the sacred learning.

In order to place Iolo's Druidism in historical perspective some brief outline of the growth of the interpretation of Druidism is now given. It must be made clear at the beginning that "classical" Druidism was stamped out in Britain by the Romans, who saw in it a threat to their system of government. After A.D. 400 nothing is heard of Druidism, the last reference coming from Gaul. Medieval writers are silent on the topic, until, with the revival of classical learning at the Renaissance, scholars began to take an interest in the history of pre-Roman Europe. Prominent in Elizabethan times were Leland, Bale, Holinshed and Camden, followed by John Aubrey and Dr. William Stukeley. Both the latter maintained that Stonehenge and Avebury had been Druidic centres in these islands, but the Rev. Henry Rowlands attempted to prove, in his *Mona Antiqua Restaurata* (1723), that Anglesey had been the chief seat of the Druids.

During the seventeenth century there arose the belief that Druidism was synonymous with the patriarchal religion of Noah and his descendants, and that the Druids had maintained the primitive language of the world in its pure state after the confusion of tongues following the building of the Tower of Babel. This primitive language was sometimes given the name of "Gomerian", and was believed to be a form of Celtic. (One wonders if this is the origin of the tradition that the language of Paradise is Welsh!) The supposed patriarchal connection led to the Druidic religion being described as "arkite", a concept which became extremely complicated with the publication in 1803 of the Rev. G. S. Faber's *Dissertation on the mysteries of the Cabiri*. Faber held that there was an element of sun-worship in the Druidic religion, and he produced the term "helio-arkite" to describe it, an expression which was to occur many times in the writings of Owen Morgan ("Morien"), the Pontypridd historian.

Celtic scholarship was brought to bear upon Druidism during the eighteenth century, when ancient Welsh poems, such as *Hanes Taliesin*, were studied for their Druidic associations. These poems are obscure in the extreme, and although they contain the relics of primitive beliefs, they shed no light on Druidism. *Hanes Taliesin* is believed to be the work of a sixth century poet called Taliesin, but the earliest known version appears in the thirteenth century *Llyfr Taliesin*. It tells, in symbolic manner, the story of the life of the bard, and includes the well-known legend of Gwion Bach, who becomes omniscient by accidentally partaking of the potion of the Cauldron of Inspiration which is being brewed by Caridwen to compensate her son, Afagddu, for his ugliness. Gwion eventually becomes Taliesin, "the radiant-browed".

Outstanding among the interpreters was the Rev. Edward Davies of Bishopston, whose *Mythology and rites of the British Druids*, 1809, attempted to explain the story of Taliesin as a sort of deluge myth, related to the Biblical story of the Ark, and couched in Druidic symbolism. Davies held a poor opinion of Edward Williams (better known as "Iolo Morganwg"), who was his chief contemporary rival in the interpretation of the Druidic mysteries, but it was the latter who was to become the "father" of the cult as practised in Pontypridd.

Iolo Morganwg was a self-educated journeyman mason. His prodigious energy and devotion to research into the history and literature of Glamorgan made him one of the foremost figures in these fields. Though he lived in comparative poverty in a tiny cottage at Flemingston for most of his life, his opinion was respected and cultivated wherever Welsh scholarship was held in regard. Unfortunately, such was his enthusiasm that he was unable to make a distinction between historical events and those which he felt should have happened. Hence his work is full of inaccuracies and downright forgeries, most of the romantic tales of the history of Glamorgan being traceable to Iolo. According to the late Emeritus Professor G. J. Williams (whose death early this year is an irreparable loss to Welsh literature), the idea of Druidism was gaining an increasing hold on the imagination of Iolo during the 1770's (*Iolo Morganwg*, vol. I, Cardiff, 1956, p. 182). He had been interested in the work of the Rev. Henry Rowlands, but such was his concern for the glory of his native county that before long Stonehenge, Avebury and Mona were made to yield pride of place to Glamorgan as the Druidic centre of Britain.

Iolo's authority for his views was based partly upon his own forgeries and partly upon early Welsh poetry, supported by the assertion that he himself was the last of the Druids, having been initiated into the ancient mysteries by Edward Evans of Aberdare, a descendant of the bardic priesthood. Iolo held that Druidism had never died out in Glamorgan, a view which aroused much interest at the time, and further, that primitive Druidism was identical with the patriarchal religion of the Old Testament. He apparently had no difficulty in reconciling his Christian beliefs (he declared that he was a Unitarian) with his Druidic leanings (Elijah Waring, *Recollections and anecdotes of Edward Williams*, 1850, pp. 32-4). Together with Owen Jones, and William Owen Pughe, he was responsible for the publication of *The Myvyrian Archaiology of Wales* (1801), a work which contains many of his forgeries, and which was to influence later "Druidic" thought in no small measure.

The first recorded association of Iolo with Pontypridd is that related by Morien in his *History of Pontypridd and the Rhondda Valleys*, Pontypridd, 1903, pp. 6-7 :—

"Lewis Evans (Lewis y Saer), who died in the eighties, well remembered an Eisteddfod in 1814 (? 1815) being held at the New Inn Hotel, then kept by a bard named Gwilym Morganwg, whose surname was Williams. But what lends additional interest to that gathering is that the celebrated Welsh antiquary, Iolo Morganwg, was there. Lewis told the writer that he saw Iolo Morganwg and Gwilym Morganwg, a banner carried in front of them, walking at the head of a procession over Taav Street and then over the great bridge and on to the Rocking Stone on the Common above. Ancient ceremonies were performed on the great stone by Iolo in the role of Y Gwyddon or Odin, the Archdruid, not the least interesting being sheathing the State Sword of Wales, to convey the valuable lesson, as in Gethsemane, that there is more credit in sheathing the sabre than in drawing it forth among the sons of men. Nowhere else except in Wales is the sublime lesson now taught".

As the Rocking Stone was the centre of the Druidic ceremonies at Pontypridd, some description of it might now be of interest. Y Maen Chwyf (to give the Stone its Welsh name) stands on the edge of a steep cliff to the east of, and overlooking, the Cardiff-Merthyr road. It consists of Pennant sandstone (the common stone of the district) and has a superficial area of about 100 square feet. Its cubic capacity is approximately 250 cubic feet, its weight is about 9½ tons, and it is supported by a natural rock platform. The Stone has been immovable for many years.

Surrounding Y Maen Chwyf is a "serpent" of standing stones, consisting of two concentric circles joined to the north-west by a winding "avenue" of stones culminating in a small circle equipped with two "eyes"—the "head" of the serpent. There is also a rudimentary "tail". Below the eyes is a single small stone set on edge. This is known from old photographs to be the survivor of a group forming the Nod Cyfrin, or Awen (/ɪ\), which is alleged to be a Druidic sacred device. The outer circle of stones surrounding the Rocking Stone has a diameter of about 12 yards, and consists of 28 stones of Pennant sandstone, rough-shaped, and standing on an average about 3 feet high. The inner circle has a diameter of about 8 yards, and consists of 14 stones, also of Pennant sandstone. These stones are much smaller than those of the outer circle, and are sometimes less than one foot in height.

The "avenue", which crosses a small stream, consists of 37 stones (including the "head"). Except for the head the stones are arranged in pairs. The eyes are made of two stones, roughly cubic, fairly well-dressed, each side being perhaps 18 inches in length. These stones are set at an angle of about 120° in the ground, facing north-west, and the face of each stone is inscribed, the right eye having three concentric circles and the left five, spaced at varying intervals. The right eye has an inscription in the alphabet of "Coelbren y Beirdd", of which more later. This inscription lies within the two outer circles, which form a band about 2½ inches wide. The iris is inscribed with the Nod Cyfrin, and is surrounded by half-a-dozen symbols, badly weathered. The left eye has no inscription other than the circles, but a hole a couple of inches deep has been pierced in the centre.

Geological evidence points to the Stone having been placed in its present position as the result of glacial action, and, contrary to legend, it has no archaeological significance. Nevertheless, it was the centre of much activity during the nineteenth century, including several bardic congresses which culminated in one presided over by "Taliesin ab Iolo Morganwg" in 1834 (*Saturday Magazine*, 17 January 1835, p. 24).

Dr. William Price of Llantrisant, who regarded himself as the spiritual heir of the Druids, took a great interest in the Stone when he lived in the Pontypridd area. In 1838 he issued a circular inviting subscriptions towards the cost of erecting a tower near the

Rocking Stone. The tower was to be a Druidic museum, and was to be in the charge of the bard of "Cymdeithas Y Maen Chwyf", which was the local Cymmrodorion Society. A copy of the circular is to be seen in the *Cardiff Times*, 23 June 1888. Dr. Price regarded the Stone as being "infinitely more deserving of that term (temple) than the Temple of Jupiter Ammon in Thebes," but the scheme failed, as appears by a letter which he published in the *Glamorgan, Monmouth and Brecon Gazette and Merthyr Guardian*, 21 September 1839 :—". . . one is tempted to exclaim, *what*, in the sacred name of the most profound ignorance, sways and possesses you (the gentry) to refuse or withold your patronage and protection to that monument of the infant industry and wisdom of your immortal progenitors, *to whom you owe your very existence as a civilized people.*" Dr. Price is alleged to have performed "Druidic" rites at the Rocking Stone, but in his old age he stated that his only activity of this type had been to chant "a song of the primitive Bard to the moon" (*Cardiff Times*, 23 June 1888).

The serpent may derive its inspiration from Dr. Stukeley, for he "brewed the legend of a community of all-powerful priests of an ultimate Phoenician origin, and professing the patriarchal religion of Abraham, who built stone temples in the form of sacred serpents : *Dracontia*, he said these serpent fanes were called, though he had no authority at all in antiquity for the word in a *temple* sense" (T. D. Kendrick, *The Druids*, 1927, p. 10). The Rocking Stone serpent is said to have been erected in about 1860 by Evan Davies, better known as "Myfyr Morganwg", the Pontypridd bard (*Pontypridd Observer*, 4 March 1950), a view which is supported by the following quotation from S. C. Hall, *The Book of South Wales*, 1861, p. 223 :—"It was, however, easy to see that this (the serpent) was a modern creation ; it is the work of an enthusiastic gentleman of the neighbourhood". The only other evidence relating to the date of the serpent is the article in the *Saturday Magazine* quoted above. The accompanying woodcut shows the Stone without the serpent, and there is the explicit statement that "The ground immediately around the Stone is at present a bare sheep-walk".

Myfyr, the supposed erector of the serpent, succeeded Taliesin ab Iolo Morganwg as Archdruid or Gwyddon, a title which was vigorously contested by Dr. Price (T. R. Roberts, *Eminent Welshmen*, Cardiff, 1908, p. 41). Myfyr's Druidism was strongly

influenced by his reading of the *Asiatic Researches* of the Asiatic
Society of Bengal (20 vols., Calcutta, 1788-1836), which work he is
known to have possessed (Morien, *op. cit.*, p. 85) :—

> "Strange to say, he came to the conclusion that Christianity
> is based on the legends relating to the ninth incarnation of
> Vishnoo, the second person in the Hindoo Pantheon Triad.
> He held that the Indian system of religion is Druidism in
> confusion, and that it had gone to India in remote ages, from
> the upper reaches of the Euphrates and Southern Armenia
> (*ibid.*, pp. 85-86).

Evan Davies, to give him his proper name, was born on the
6 January 1801, in the parish of Coychurch. Though he seems
to have had no schooling he devoted his spare time to study, and his
works bear the stamp of wide reading. In *Gogoniant hynafol y
Cymmry* (Pontypridd, 1864), the gist of his teaching is to be found,
and a strange synthesis of Eastern mysticism, classical mythology
and Christianity it is seen to be. He was a gentle soul, highly
respected in his day, but his philosophy was too esoteric to interest
the man-in-the-street. His Druidism looks back to a golden age
when all was purity and light, and he frequently compares this
happy period with the sectarianism, lawlessness and immorality of
his own Christian century. He held "Druidic" services at the
Rocking Stone from about 1853 to 1878 (Morien, *op. cit.*, pp. 89,
92). Though he was a Nonconformist preacher till the age of 34,
he became strongly opposed to the Christian Church (he referred to
the local ministers as "fortune-tellers"), and his feelings were
reciprocated by the clergy. He died in 1888.

Myfyr believed fervently in the authenticity of "Coelbren y
Beirdd", a "Druidic" system of writing, but his trust was misplaced,
for the Coelbren was another invention of the teeming mind of
Iolo. In 1840 Taliesin ab Iolo had published his *Traethawd ar
hynafiaeth ac awdurdodaeth Coelbren y Beirdd*. Here a number of
sources are given for the Coelbren, notably the Glamorgan bard
Llywelyn Sion, but all the relevant literature had been lost, burned
or destroyed, after being fortuitously copied by Iolo. The only
other evidence for the antiquity of the Coelbren comes, not un-
expectedly, from Dr. Price. At an eisteddfod in Merthyr, in the
year 1870, he exhibited a wooden plaque which he described as a

version of Coelbren y Beirdd, claiming that he had found it in Paris
thirty years previously.   It was supposed to bear a song composed
2,600 years before by one Ap Alun, a Welsh prince, who ruled the
whole civilized world of his time.   The song was a prophecy that
one day a man would appear who would interpret the secrets of
the "Coelbren".   Doubtless this remarkable example of ancient
Welsh foreknowledge referred to the Doctor himself.

Dr. Price and his eccentricities of character and dress are too
well known to need relating here.   It should be stated, however,
that in modern medical opinion Dr. Price suffered from paraphrenia,
a form of schizophrenia.   A great deal of his unorthodox behaviour
can be accounted for on this premise.   His Druidism was derived
largely from the *Myvyrian Archaiology* and Davies' *Mythology and
rites of the British Druids*, though, like Iolo, he transferred all Druidic
glory to Glamorgan.   He carried the exaltation of his county to
extreme lengths, as appears in a letter to "Mr. Jones, printer"
(editor of *The Cardiff and Merthyr Guardian*), dated Boulogne,
27 December 1861 :—"All the Greek Books are The Works of the
Primitive Bards, in our own Language!!!!! . . . Homer was born in
The Hamlet of E Van, near Caerphilli and built Caerphilli Castle".
The letter is signed "Arglwyt Deheudir Cymry" (Lord of South
Wales).   The modern view of Dr. Price's affliction receives support
from his contemporaries, as witness a letter from William Thomas of
the Courthouse, Merthyr, to the Marquess of Bute, dated
18 August 1839 :—"The weaver in question (a Chartist agitator)
. . . is occasionally assisted by a person (probably not unknown to
your Lordship) of the name of Doctor Price Nantgarw near Cardiff,
a fit subject in the opinion of most for a Lunatic Asylum".   But the
formidable Doctor was never thus confined, and continued to
provide South Wales with a lively topic of conversation till his
death in 1893.

The best-known adherent of Druidism at Pontypridd was Morien.
He was probably born at Dinas in February, 1836, but he carefully
concealed his age.   For many years he was a reporter for the
Western Mail, and his descriptions of the rescue attempts attending
the Tynewydd Colliery flooding of 1877 kept the country on tenter-
hooks for more than a week. He was a prominent member of
"Clic y Bont", a brilliant gathering of bards and musicians which
used to meet at the Taff Street office of the auctioneer-bard, "Dewi

Haran". Here his reputation was that of "... the irrepressible Morien, who was oftener in the clouds than on solid earth, and always half drunk on Myfyr's Druidism . . ." ("Silurian", *Glamorgan Gazette*, 16 July 1926).

A further quotation from the same newspaper (17 December 1926), and the same writer, gives some more information about Morien and an unflattering description of a Druidic gathering in 1879 :—

> "His first love was Welsh Calvinistic Methodism, which, to his honour be it said, he never wholly deserted. To the end he valiantly tried to reconcile the two theories (by equating Taliesin with Jesus Crist), but he might as well have attempted to mix oil and water . . . The full-blown Druids were wonderfully and fearfully clothed, but Mr. Owen (proprietor of the *Western Mail*) and a few others appeared in ordinary garments. The service was supposed to be held in the face of the sun, the eye of light—yn ngwyneb haul, llygad goleuni. Torrential rain, however, prevented all from seeing the sun that day. The little crowd presented a miserable and woebegone appearance, and all hurried home like half drowned rats . . ."

As a historian Morien was wholly unrealistic, and would invent an incident, such as a battle, on the flimsiest possible pretext. An example is the mythical Battle of Pontypridd, of which he gives virtually an eye-witness account :—

> "The trumpets of heroic Siluria sounded the charge, with General Idwg in the foreground of his army. The Silures in serried ranks, marching down, filled the valley from mountain to mountain. They advanced slowly, chanting a now forgotten Welsh war hymn, and, as their custom was, tapping their sounding shields with their short lances, in unison with the notes of the tune and their own strides". (*History of Pontypridd*, pp. 134-5).

Morien's reliance upon fanciful interpretations of place-names is a grave weakness, as witness his derivation of "Craig Evan Leison" from "Kyrie Eleison", but in dealing with events within living memory he is a most useful source. He died, the last of the Pontypridd Druids, on 16 December 1921.

Serpent and Rocking Stone, the Common, Pontypridd, *c.* 1900

Rocking Stone, the Common, Pontypridd, *c.* 1900

COELBREN Y BEIRDD
HERWYDD
DOSPARTH IÒLO MORGANWG

(Tynnedig o'i waith Saesneg ef dann yr enw, "History of the Bards")

"The Welsh Bards have, from time to time immemorial amongst them a remarkable method of writing, inscribing, or engraving on slender billets of wood. The following is their Alphabet, with an explanation of it; it is retained now only by the very few that remain of the genuine successors of the Antient British Bards, who have, o flate ages, existed unknown to the world, and who are able to give very respectable accounts of their Predecessors; but, being unknown, they have, consequently, never been consulted by the too many Historians of the Antient British Bards that have lately appeared, who, unavoidably, know very little of their History."

Bards' Alphabet		Modern Welsh Alphabet	
1	Λ	A, à, short	A, short, as in the English words, bad, sad, can, man, &c.
	Λ	A, â, long	A, long, and something broad, in the *Silurian* and *Venedotian* dialects, as in calm, balm, &c. English.—In the Dimetian Dialect it is very broad as in—hall, call &c.
2	↲	E, è, short	E, short, as in the English—pen, den, bed, fed, &c.
		E, ê, long	E, long, as in clean, bead, heal, &c.
3	I	I, i,	I, as *ee* in the English—Queen, seen, feel, feed,—or *i* in machine, &c.
4	◇	O, ò, short	O, short, as in God, nod, rock, sock, &c.
	◈	O, ô, long	O, long, as in bone, stone, hole, stole, abode.
	V	W, ẁ, short	OO, short, as in good, wood, stood, &c., and as *u* in bull, full, pull, &c.
	Ψ	W, ŵ, long	OO, long, as in fool, cool, moon, rood, brood.
	Y	Y, ỳ, short	Y, Greek ϒ, V, short, or French *u*; *i*, in *this* is something like it.
	⅄	Y, ŷ, long	Y, the same. As the French—mûr, &c.
	Ψ	Y, ẏ,	As U, in bud, gun, burr, sun, mud, dull, &c.
5	L	B, b,	B, common.
	ⱪ	F, f,	B, soft, the same as *v* in vain, brave, &c. No radical.
	⅄	M, mutate	M, the mutate of B.
6	W	M, radical	M, radical, varying in form from the foregoing, for etymological reasons.
7	Γ	P, p,	P, common.
8	ᚠ	Ff, f,*	PH, or F, as in—Philip, fill. The aspirate state of P.
	Ᵽ	Mh,	MH, liquid state of P. No radical.

VOWELS

LABIALS

*Tradition says that the original Alphabet consisted of only sixteen characters, which are those distinguished by the Arabic numerals.

Bards' Alphabet	Modern Welsh Alphabet	
GUTTURALS 9	C, c,	K, or C, in can, call. Never as in City, &c.
	Ch, ch,	X, χ, Greek. Guttural aspiration of C. No radical.
	Ngh, ngh,	Naso-guttural aspiration; or a kind of liquid state of C, or K. No radical.
10	G, g,	G, common, as in—God, good, &c. Never as in George.
	Ng, ng,	Liquid state of G. No radical.
11	T, t,	T, common.
DENTALS	Th, th,	TH, the aspirate state of T. No radical. Hard as in faith, &c.
	Nh, nh,	Liquid, or nasal state of T. No radical.
12	D, d,	D, common.
	Dd, dd,	Soft state of D, or as the English *th*, in father, bathe, &c.
	N, mutate	N, common; but in this form, for etymological reasons, as the liquid, or mutate of D.
13	N, radical	N, radical, common.
LINGUALS 14	Ll, aspirate	L, aspirated, as in the Spanish, or nearly so.
	L, l, liquid	L, common, liquid state. No radical.
15	Rh, rh,	R, in its usual aspirated state, as it is, perhaps in all languages when radical.
	R, r, soft	R, soft, as the last R, in rare, &c. No radical.
Sibi 16 lant	S, ss,	S, common.
ASPI-RATES	H, h,	H, common, aspiration of vowels.
	Wh *or* chw	Pronounced in the Silurian dialect, as *wh*, in the English words—what, where, why;

but in the Venedotian dialect, it is always guttural, and pronounced, as if to these English we should add the Greek χ, and pronounce χwhy χwhat χwhere, &c. There is no word in the Silurian *radically* guttural.

Yn gymmwys ar ol y Ddosparth ddiweddaf, mae yr hen Bencerdd, fal pei buassai ei enaid glew yn ymarfogi yn erbyn gwrthwynebwyr amgylchynniadol, yn cyfeirio at un o'r Cyhoeddiadau cyfnodol Seisnig, ac yn rhoddi y tynniad canlyniadol o hono; gann ei farnu (ac yn gyfiawn) fal dywediad tueddol i feithrin *ymbwyll* ym meddyliau Dysgedigion ag oeddynt wedi penderfynu, mor fyrbwyll, yn erbyn gwir hanfodoledd Coelbren y Beirdd; a hynny trwy ddiffyg iawn wy bodaeth ar y pwngc.

"We deprecate the rudeness of self conceit that can *brave* CONVICTION, as well as that determined spirit of discovery that can *surmount every* obstacle.

Crit. Review, Nov. 1804, of the Oxford Homer

William Price, M.R.C.S., L.S.A.

Born 4th March 1800.   Died 23rd January 1893
Cremated on East Caerlan, Llantrisant, 31st January 1893

By permission of Pontypridd Public Libraries

With the passing of Morien ended a movement which had its roots in the antiquarianism of the Renaissance and its full flowering in the wayward genius of Iolo Morganwg. It was the dream of men who refused to accept the recorded view of the history of their land. For them it was unthinkable that the common life of their fathers had been only a patient plodding from day to undistinguished day ; so they refashioned the past to mirror their own longings, and peopled it with giants.

The author wishes to acknowledge the valuable assistance he has received from Mr. T. J. Hopkins, B.A., of the Central Library, Cardiff, and Dr. J. H. Cule, M.A., M.D., of Camberley, Surrey.

GLAMORGAN COMMUNICATIONS:

(1) THE STORY OF THE ROADS

by

THOMAS BEVAN, M.A.

SINCE the dawn of civilisation communications have played a vital part in the development of trade and communal life. In Glamorgan today, where an expanding industrial economy is dependent upon good communications, the roads are of paramount importance. Their history, briefly related in this chapter, is the story of man's endeavour from earliest times to the present day to establish contact with his neighbour.

Archaeologists have discovered and excavated several sites of ancient settlements in Glamorgan, but most of these are either low along the sea-line or high upon the mountain ridges. The intervening country was often a mass of matted forest or deep marshy ravine where lurked fierce animals which were a positive danger to primitive man, who was virtually defenceless against their attacks. The first attempts at outside communication must have been over the channel to and from the opposite shores of the Severn Sea or creek by creek along the coast to the west and to Ireland.

High above the valleys rough tracks could be made from ridge to ridge where there were no rivers to cross, no bogs to negotiate nor forests to penetrate, and many of these ancient "ridgeways" can still be traced across the lonely uplands. As an instance, one could stand on the top of that big, round bulk of Margam Mountain and see radiating for miles in all directions a veritable "Piccadilly" of deviating routes. The discovery of ancient stones with markings, like the "Bodvoc" (*c.* 600 A.D.), along these pathways would suggest that man once travelled these high ways from settlement to settlement. An old British camp in the same vicinity known locally as the "Bwlwarcau" is probably a relic of one of their defences and from it a straight course can be followed through the Cymer-Corrwg,

146

Craig-y-Llyn, Rhigos eminences right into the heart of Breconshire. Many more such mountain trackways exist in Glamorgan, forerunners of some of the recent well-engineered heads of valley roads.

From these ridgeways, when men became better equipped to clear the forests and deal with dangerous animals, side tracks were forced down into the valleys. In most cases these routes were predetermined by old streams and ice-age glaciers, forming "hollowways" into the lower lands where the soils were easier to cultivate and the animals better domesticated to everyday use. Down these slopes the first use was made of that wheel-less vehicle, once so characteristic of Welsh upland farms, the "câr-llusg". It was dragged up and down by the same sturdy breed of mountain ponies as those which have been fetching high prices in the export market in recent years. Along these tracks, too, in early years of coal-getting in Glamorgan teams of mules trekked, bringing sacks of fuel dug out of the outcropping quarries high above the valleys.

Many legends are told of how these old routes were sometimes used by pilgrims bent upon penance as they journeyed to and from their holy shrines, and how some of them perished on their way through sheer exhaustion. They were probably buried in the stone cairns now lying about in scattered heaps alongside the old trackways. One well preserved memorial of such a traveller may be seen today in the south-eastern corner of the chancel at Llandyfodwg Church in Glynogwr. Certainly a good many of these mountain churches, whose square towers still dot the sky-line, had their origin in little hermit cells of the Celtic Church. The paths the saints trod became later the parish roads along which enterprising cattle-dealers and vociferous stall-holders trudged to establish the popular mountain fairs which to this day are held around some of these churches on the festival days of their patron saints.

So one can say that early inland communications in Glamorgan were just rough tracks following the natural contour of the country. But when the Romans came to South Wales in the first century A.D. to subdue the Silures, the most stubborn tribe they had yet encountered in their invasion of Britain, they brought with them all the skill and science of constructing straight roads regardless of undulations. Although one can still find here and there short stretches of such routes in Glamorgan, the Romans did not leave behind any Watling Street with paved surface nor Foss Way on raised causeway. Rather were their ways a series of boundary barriers linking up lines of small forts one with the other. This had always been their method of controlling a troublesome people. They would split the tribes into smaller units, a kind of ruling by fragmentation and a strategy that had paid them well in previous campaigns in Gaul and Spain. Their roads were therefore just rough tracks along which their legions would march in full battle dress to demonstrate to the unruly natives their overwhelming supremacy.

Their plan for the subjugation of Siluria was first to establish a big major camp at the head of the tidal waters of the Usk which they named *Isca Silurum*, the present day Caerleon. Then following the coast straight west and building small forts on all river crossings, they set up a large square enclosure on the left bank of the Taff which later became a chief base. Portions of these walls may still be seen in the outer defences of Cardiff Castle. An account of a special visit to Britain, now known as the *Antonine Itinerary*, refers also to a small fort further west in the Vale of Glamorgan which they called *Bomium*. Its exact position has not been ascertained, but in all probability it must have been near a crossing on the Ogmore-Ewenny estuary. It was quoted as fifteen Roman miles east of another camp *Nidum*, a site definitely located now near the mouth of the Neath river. Another outpost is mentioned as *Leucarum*, being on a crossing of the Loughor, together with several small stations as far as *Maridunum* on the tidal river of the Towy near Carmarthen. These were probably linked by some kind of coastal road, but since only a few short stretches near Pyle and some two or three milestones between Margam and Neath have any signs of being Roman, it is difficult to be certain of its track. It would be folly to regard every straight piece of roadway on the present highway as Roman but in all probability the Roman road followed roughly the same course.

Again, from *Isca* but to the north, a similar line of outposts passed by way of Abergavenny (*Gobannium*) and Pen-y-gaer to Brecon (*Cicutio*), leaving the Gloucester (*Glevum*) main Roman road near Usk (*Burrium*). This was a more mountainous track which travelled the ridges of the Black Mountains through Llandovery (*Labum*) to meet the former coast road again at Carmarthen. The whole system was completed by causeways crossing the valleys and connecting the coast with the mountain roads by subsidiary tracks.

One of these has been traced from Cardiff over the Caerphilly and Gelligaer hills, locally known as the *Sarn Fid Foel*. Another seems to have followed the Neath Valley along the Coelbren Ridgeway and is called the *Sarn Helen*, meeting the first in a very commanding camp high above Brecon marked *Y Gaer*. To this day Brecon has continued to be a road centre of considerable importance.

It is evident that during the period of Roman occupation Glamorgan was provided with well-systemised communications. The roads, however, were chiefly military highways and not intentionally built for trade, with the result that when the Romans left in the early fifth century to defend their home and empire the roads fell quickly into decay. Wherever the soldier marched for conquest the way was often lost, but where the merchant carried his commerce the track remained. It is true that a few civil settlements have been traced in Glamorgan belonging to the Roman era, as at Ely near Cardiff, and Llantwit Major in the Vale, but on the whole the roads were simply routes for carrying military supplies from camp to camp. After their departure, communications in South Wales seem to have been lost in the mists of the Dark Ages and no road developments appear to be recorded for at least six hundred years.

Waves of Picts, Irish and Saxons now mercilessly attacked the helpless Britons who repeatedly begged for the return of their old masters. River estuaries like the Severn were particularly vulnerable to their raids, but wise compromise on the part of the more civilised natives made a life of co-existence with the newcomers possible. Danish place-names such as Flat Holm, Steep Holm, Tusker, Sker and Sweynsey (Swansea) are evidence that the Norsemen eventually settled and established trading stations along the Glamorgan coast. They also made clearings in the interior, and narrow winding lanes, hap-hazardly made, connected settlement with settlement. Where the Roman called his way a "street", meaning a track scientifically laid down in layers or strata, the Saxon introduced the new name "road" signifying a journey, or ride (Old English *ridan*) on foot or horseback.

The Norman, too, when he arrived in the eleventh century needed no broad way, and as his chief means of movement was his horse he required only narrow bridle-paths for passing to and from his various manors. As these, too, were more or less self-sufficient, very little interchange took place between village and village. Indeed, even down to the eighteenth century, means of travel were not very urgent, for the domestic system assured that every township could support itself in most of the essentials of life by its own home-crafts and the produce of its neighbouring fields.

There is the evidence of travellers in Glamorgan after the Norman conquest testifying to great difficulty of movement even along the main road of the county. Giraldus Cambrensis, for instance, gives this vivid picture of a journey with Archbishop Baldwin during a preaching crusade in March 1188, led by the Bishop of Llandaff :—"We immediately pursued our journey" he says "by the little cell of Ewenith (Ewenny Priory) to the noble Cistercian monastery of Margam". From here to Neath the way was fraught with many dangers, especially across the marshes and sands of Kenfig and Margam. We "proceeded along the seashore towards the river Neath, which, on account of its quicksands, is the most dangerous and inaccessible river in South Wales. Yet, although we had Morgan of Margam as our conductor, we did not reach the river without great peril and some severe falls". He tells how one of his pack-horses floundered and sank into the sands but was at last extricated with great difficulty "and not without some damage to the baggage and books".

When John Leland made the same journey c. 1538, the highway "from Pont Remny (Cardiff) to Cremlin brooke (Swansea)" was still open and many new bridges had been built. Cardiff Bridge, over the Taff, was a sound timber construction, but by 1544 "by means of the outragiousness of the water it is fallen into greate ruin and decaye". Later, in 1578, Rice Merrick in his work *A Booke of Glamorganshires Antiquities* gives an account of the "port-way which leadeth from Cardyff to the Wester townes" and notes that "In this Soyle then stood only three market Townes, Cardyff in the east, Kynfyne in the west, & Cowbridge betweene both".

From these references one can imagine that the old Roman coast road still provided fair access to the west. From Cardiff to Margam it seems to have retained its character to some extent, for even Giraldus could say "immediately" as far as Margam Abbey, and both Leland and Merrick could testify to "fair" travel through the Vale, but further west, no doubt, conditions were almost impossible.

Matters had certainly improved by the end of the sixteenth century after the Reformation, and wherever there was a parish church the pathways of the congregations gradually widened and made good approaches for the worshippers. Even to-day as one winds one's way through the maze of minor roads in the Vale there is an obvious convergence on the parish churches. Indeed, Dr. F. J. North in his publication on Llandaff, *The Stones of Llandaff Cathedral*, points to such a concentration on the cathedral and even hints that the ancient route from west to east might possibly have crossed the Taff somewhere in that vicinity rather than over the treacherous mud-flats nearer the mouth of the river. In any case, tribute must be paid to the medieval church for its part in establishing and maintaining communications in Glamorgan at that time.

In 1555 Parliament passed an Act ordaining that each parish should be responsible for its own roads and should appoint from among its own number one to act as "Highway Surveyor" to organise the maintenance of communications in the parish. By the Statute of Labour six consecutive days had to be spent each summer on the roads by all parishioners, in scouring ditches, gutters and drains, cutting back hedges and overhanging trees, and generally keeping clear a passage for travellers and carriages from one end of their parish to the other. Defaulters were fined and their names read out in church immediately after the sermon on the very next Sunday after the operations.

In time it was realised, however, that such compulsory service placed an unfair burden on local residents who had to repair roads used by travellers from distant parts. The Justices of the Peace often showed their sympathy with the parishioners by refusing to proceed judiciously against defaulters, and the method of appointing an unpaid surveyor once a year without any special knowledge of road construction was very unsatisfactory. The central government knew that a good system of transport was an essential preliminary to any agricultural or industrial advance and now turned to the principle of private enterprise by passing a series of Acts authorising individuals to form companies with powers to raise money and charge actual users of the roads with tolls at gates erected at convenient places across the highways.

The first Act of this kind affecting Glamorgan was passed in 1764 and a later amendment apportioned the chief highways of the

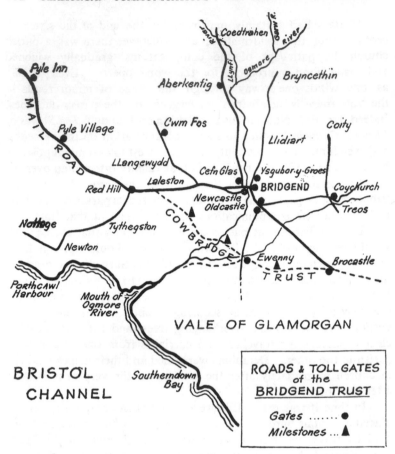

county between five "Trusts"—Cardiff, Cowbridge, Bridgend,
Neath, Swansea—with powers "to raise capital and make charges
by gates and toll-bars for the more effectively making and improving
the roads of Glamorgan".   The gentry of the county took up the
work with enthusiasm and invested capital readily.   They also
established "The Glamorganshire Agricultural Society" which held
shows and offered prizes for improvements in land cultivation and
road construction.   In its report for 1780 there is a record that
Joseph John of Llantrisant and Akijah Hugh and David Bowen of
Llangynwyd were judged to be the best highway surveyors for the
year.   Earlier, in 1775, John Popkin was awarded a silver medal

"for cleaning draining, and making profitable seven-and-half acres of black, peaty land in the parish of Bettws".[1] It is significant that these places were off the main highway and therefore a beginning of penetration into the heart of the hilly country which later saw such complete industrialisation.

Then, in 1789, "The South Wales Association for the Improvement of Roads" was formed. It is true that its chief object was "to secure an improvement of the main road from Milford to London" but it gave encouragement for general roads extension in Glamorgan. In its report, details of bridge building, road widening and surface improvements are given. A typical example is the following estimated account for repairs to Ely Bridge in the Parish of Llandaff:—

Ely Bridge, 10 feet wide.

Lengthening arch by 1 ft. 6 ins. on south side	£1	0	0
Lengthening second arch 2 ft. 6 ins. on south side	£1	6	0
Lengthening gutter and parapet wall on south side		15	0
Breaking stones and gravelling 1,940 yds. of road	£97	0	0
Lengthening arch and parapet wall on north side	£1	0	0

Much detail is available on the working of Turnpike Trusts in Glamorgan. Each of the five mentioned above was an independent unit levying its own tolls, the variations often causing annoyance to travellers passing through several trusts in the same day. Gates were put up at any point at the discretion of each trust, and chains were temporarily stretched across the roads whenever thought expedient, usually on market and fair days. The Acts, however, fixed maximum charges as follows :—6d. for every beast of draught with vehicle, 2d. without vehicle, 20d. per score for droves of oxen and 10d. per score for sheep with other minor details regarding carriages and coaches. Double tolls were demanded on Sundays. The main highway was apportioned to the five trusts as follows :—

Rumney Bridge to Bonvilston (Cardiff), Bonvilston to Laleston (Cowbridge), Brocastle (Crack Hill) through Bridgend to Aberafan (Bridgend), Aberafan to Crymlin Brook (Neath), Crymlin Brook to Loughor (Swansea).

In the course of time smaller trusts, such as Llantrisant and Merthyr, were formed to manage minor roads. Cardiff handed

1 John Garsed. *Records of the Glamorganshire Agricultural Society*, Cardiff, 1890.

over to Llantrisant, for instance, at Capel Llanilltern in the Ely Valley and to Merthyr at Tongwynlais in the Taff Valley. Cowbridge covered much of the Vale, and Bridgend looked after Mid-Glamorgan. Neath and Swansea developed the west but there were often in the Gower peninsula "long lines of barren, desolate, uninhabited tracks".

In 1844, according to the *Report of the Commissioners of Inquiry for South Wales*, Swansea was reputed to have had four gates in eleven miles of road in one section and three gates in nine miles in another. Bridgend was also a bad spot with as many as fourteen gates within a radius of six miles. Llantrisant was the worst offender where eight gates and four chains had to be negotiated every market day to get into the town. It was here that a rising of the same nature as the dreaded "Rebecca" took place in October 1843 when three of the gates were destroyed in less than a month and all the keepers brutally assaulted by unknown persons in dark masks. Such attacks were not as frequent in Glamorgan as further west, but in July 1843 outbreaks occurred near Pontarddulais in the Swansea trust when the Bolgoed Gate on the Goppa Fach road and the Rhydypandy Gate at Llangyfelach were pulled down. Three men, in this case, were arrested and after making confessions in Cardiff gaol on 1 November were transported for life.

It was inevitable that transport costs should sometimes be excessive, but it was only fair that those who used the roads most should pay for their upkeep. As most of the goods carried were bulky and the conveyances usually small, duplication of journeys through the same gates was unavoidable. This was particularly aggravating to small farmers and little tradesmen. For instance, giving evidence before the Commissioners in 1844, three farmers near Pyle protested "the quarries of limestone are to the eastward of the gate and the collieries to the westward; they pay toll taking the coal to the limestone quarries . . . then they have to pay toll again when they bring the lime down. They think it a hardship upon the farmer to pay first of all toll for bringing his coal up, and then to pay when it comes back again". Again, Thomas Richards, a vegetable vendor in Pontypridd, complained "I have a small donkey-cart. I go to Llandaff twice a week to buy roots of all descriptions and garden stuff in order to sell them again, and when I bring my donkey-cart from Newbridge (Pontypridd) to Llandaff (ten miles) I pay 3/- in gates . . . I cannot bring more than 15/- worth of goods in the cart. I cannot get out of the village without paying 1s. 6d".

Vivid descriptions of conditions of travel are also given by tourists such as the Rev. Richard Warner who made two walks through Wales at the close of the eighteenth century.

Great were the hazards of the roads in the days of the trusts, and although modern calamities may be considered much more serious and tragic, the discomforts experienced can hardly be more irritating. However, a certain amount of glamour and compensation enters the story when we think of the stage-coach rattling along with the scarlet-coated driver high in his seat in front and the burly guard with blunderbuss and horn in the rear. The clatter of the iron-hooped wheels, the galloping beat of the horses' hooves and the penetrating notes of the horn must have brought the villagers out in numbers to watch the coach "flying" past at ten miles an hour! There is much interest, too, in reading the names and perusing the time-tables which appeared in the current newspapers. For instance, the *Bristol Gazette* for 28 August 1788 announced that "The Diligence" would run every Sunday, Wednesday and Friday from the *Mackworth Arms*, Swansea, at four o'clock every morning to arrive the same evening at the New Passage, where a good boat would be ready to take passengers over the Severn, and that a coach would be waiting on the other side at eight o'clock next morning to carry them to Bristol. The fare was thirty shillings. Again, *The Cambrian*, a local newspaper, published notices on behalf of "The Duke of Wellington", "The Enterprise" and "The General Picton" which were plying between Cardiff and West Wales. Even the London *Times* in its issue of 10 September 1811 declared "Spencer's coaches are the only day-time carriages doing the run direct from London to South Wales and if the journey be taken through Ross and Hereford will only take two days".

It was in this age, too, that the "hostelry" became a characteristic institution in England and Wales. In Glamorgan the most renowned were the *Angel*[2] at Cardiff, the *Bear* at Cowbridge, the *Pyle Inn* near Bridgend and the *Mackworth Arms* at Swansea. There were others on the minor roads such as the *Cow and Snuffers* in Llandaff, the *Porto Bello* at Taffs Well and the *Duke of Bridgewater's Arms* at

2. For other references to the *Angel*, see pages 105, 107 and 160.

Glyntaff.   Some were special coaching-stables for the Royal Mail which could always be distinguished from other carriages by its chocolate and maroon colours, its doors emblazoned with the royal arms and its horses bedecked with scarlet ribbons.   It kept a rigid time-table, had precedence over all other traffic, paid no tolls at the gates, and any keeper failing to give it open road was liable to a fine of forty shillings or imprisonment.   There was a regulation uniform that had to be worn by the pikemen : corduroy breeches, white stockings, leather aprons and tall black-glazed hats.   By 1830 the London letters were arriving daily in Cardiff by three o'clock every afternoon and leaving for London every morning at ten o'clock. A London newspaper, costing 10*d*., was paying 1/- delivery and a single-sheet letter 6*d*.

Many a tale is told in plays and novels of disasters and hold-ups of the Mail, and it is recorded that on one single day six coaches were overturned on the roads of England and Wales either by accident or intent.   Floods were a great danger in South Wales and it is known that a London coach once crashed through the parapet of Rumney Bridge into the river.   A notorious spot for highwaymen was Pantylladron near Stalling Down, a very convenient getaway point where four parishes meet.   One of the best hostelry stories is that given in David Jones of Wallington's papers regarding a "runaway mail".   The coach was coming up through Ewenny on a very cold winter night when the driver and guard halted at a small inn for refreshment, leaving the coach outside on the road. During their absence the horses moved off slowly, picking up their paces on the flat, slackening speed on ascending hills and pausing a short while before each descent, apparently giving time to attach the "drag" to brake the wheels.   The ladies inside suspected nothing unusual but great was their astonishment and alarm when the horses pulled up at the *Bear*, having travelled without driver or guard the whole distance of six miles from Ewenny to Cowbridge without mishap.   In an hour's time the two men came panting after a long pursuit up and down hill.   It is said the guard died shortly afterwards from the strain of that long chase.

No doubt, the turnpike system laid down the general pattern of modern roadways but the multiplicity of trusts and the inconsistencies of variable tolls so irritated the growing commercial undertakings that a change of policy was again due. The 1843 Royal Commission recommended in its voluminous report of 6 March

1844 that all trusts should be consolidated and placed under uniform management in each county. For Glamorgan, at a meeting in the *Pyle Inn* on 12 February 1845, a new "Roads Board" was elected consisting of twelve magistrates under the chairmanship of John Dillwyn Llewelyn. All the fifty toll-gates in the county were taken over by the Board for gradual elimination. Thomas Dalton, later Clerk of the Peace for the County, became first Clerk to the new authority, a position he held for the whole thirty years until the formation of the "Glamorgan Highways Board" which took over the main control of all roads in the administrative area under the supervision of one Surveyor for the whole county. By 25 March 1876 all the turnpike gates had ceased to function and the low, squat, double-windowed toll houses were gradually pulled down or sold. At present the County Council administers road affairs under three classifications, main highways, district roads and parochial by-ways.

The discovery of the power of steam and the invention of the locomotive ushered in a revolution in transport which eclipsed the importance of roads for almost a hundred years. Canals and horse-drawn tramways struggled on for a while, but as the load became heavier and bulkier, the "Iron Horse" forced all other means of carriage almost out of existence. It was the invention of the internal combustion engine that re-instated the roadways as a chief means of transport in serious rivalry with the railways. The motor car, the public omnibus and the petrol lorry have penetrated to the remotest villages and furthermost valleys, rendering hundreds of miles of rail track useless and obsolete.

Consciously, or unconsciously, the future road planners have reverted to recommendations made at the old *Pyle Inn* on 17 June 1825 by that great road engineer, Thomas Telford, and incidentally adopted the ideas of that unpaid amateur turnpike-surveyor, John Loudon Macadam, in producing strong, smooth, solid surfaces for their modern highways. They have spanned the Loughor by a stone bridge in place of the old timber-trestled structure, have straightened the ancient "Port Way" from east to west, have engineered a wonderful crossing over the mud-flats of the River Neath at Briton Ferry, have linked the valleys by easy gradients over the hills and are now proposing to build a grand double-carriage "South Wales Motorway" from the new Severn Bridge to West Wales, skirting all the big centres of population.

FRANCIS GROSE'S TOUR IN GLAMORGAN, 1775

Edited by

T. J. HOPKINS, B.A.

INTRODUCTION

THE journal printed here forms part of a journal kept by Francis Grose when he travelled from London to Glamorgan in the summer of 1775 for the purpose of preparing and illustrating the fourth and final volume of his well known work *The Antiquities of England and Wales* (London, 1773-76). He journeyed via Oxford, Gloucester, Hereford, Chepstow and Newport, and then returned via Newport, Pontypool, Abergavenny, Raglan, Monmouth, Lydney, Gloucester and Oxford. The original manuscript is preserved at the British Museum (Additional MS. 17398).

A biographical account of Grose is given in the *Dictionary of National Biography*. The son of a prosperous jeweller who was a native of Berne in Switzerland, he was born *c.* 1731 at Greenford, Middlesex, received a classical education but did not proceed to a university. After studying art in London he began to exhibit his own drawings and later he used many of them to illustrate his own books. Quite a large proportion, however, of the engravings contained in the *Antiquities* are from drawings by other well known artists such as Paul Sandby and J. I. Richards. From 1755 to 1763 Grose was Richmond herald, but in the latter year he became adjutant and pay-master in the Hampshire militia. His connection with the militia explains the frequent references he makes in his journal to military men. From 1778 (or earlier) till his death in 1791 he was captain and adjutant in the Surrey militia.

In this edited version of the journal modern usage with regard to punctuation, capital letters and spelling, with the exception of personal and place names, has been adopted. Everything within brackets, together with the footnotes, is an editorial addition. With two exceptions (Cardiff Castle and Llandaff Cathedral) the rough plans and sketches included in the manuscript have not been reproduced.

158

THE JOURNAL

(*Monday*, 24*th July*, 1775)—Set out (from Newport) in a chaise and pair at about half after eight for Caerphilly, Pont y pridd and Cardiff which was by our landlady reckoned altogether 36 miles and we paid accordingly.   She made it out thus;   to Caerphilly 14 miles;   to Pont y pridd 10;   to Cardiff 12.   We passed Tredegar Park which is walled in, and over one or two bridges with another new building. Tredegar Church is pleasantly situated.

At about 3 miles from Newport the road to Cardiff turns off to the left, but we proceeded straight forwards, the roads becoming more narrow and stony.   After descending a hill came in sight of the demesne of Rupella (Ruperra), and in ascending another, which was very steep and dirty, we were stuck fast and obliged to get out and push on the chaise which notwithstanding every effort made by our horses and postillion would otherwise have remained *in statu quo;* here we found that one of our horses was stone blind, a discovery which considering the rough and stony roads we were to expect gave us no great satisfaction.   At 10 miles the country was extremely rich, the view being diversified with woods, cottages, cornfields, and other signs of cultivation.

We now came to the banks of the River Rumney, at present almost dry.   The river separates the counties of Glamorganshire from that of Monmouth.   We now began to have a sight of Caerphilly Castle, which at a distance looks extremely black and dismal, and was pointed out to us by our guide with the epithet of "that Black Thing yonder".

We stopped at a small ale house, or rather tavern, for what was called wine is sold there, nearly opposite to the gate of the ruins. [1] The landlord, who seems as if he was a good customer to himself, procured us the ciceroni of the Castle, which belongs to Lady Windsor and is preserved with a considerable attention.

Having made several drawings of particular bits of this ancient structure, we returned to the inn where the landlord telling us he had some fine beans and bacon ready for dinner we agreed to take a snap.   The bacon in colour emulated gold, and the beans were of most respectable antiquity.   However by the assistance of eggs, butter, and cheese, we made out a hearty meal, and washed it down with some tolerable ale.   Then calling for our bill resumed our

1   Probably the *Boar's Head*, which has had a continuous existence as a hostelry since the first half of the eighteenth century.   See page 84.

chaise for Pont y pridd. I cannot take leave of our landlord without observing that however deficient he might be in some moral duties he was not wanting in that of considering what was due to himself, for his bill amounted to full as much as we had been charged for real good dinners at Chepstow and Newport.

On the hill to the right of Caerphilly on an eminence at about 2 miles distance stands the house of Powell Esqr. called Inner Glyn (Energlyn). It is like most in this country white, and seems a large and handsome building.

From Caerphilly we turned back and got into the Cardiff road which for three or four miles was excellent but soon grew worse and worse till it became scarcely passable for a chaise, the road being narrow with frequent and sharp ascents and descents, and full of large loose stones, or ways over solid rocks cut like steps. All this was by the banks of the Taff, which notwithstanding its boasted rapidity was now sunk almost to nothing, scarcely creeping through its pebbly bed. Passed near a horse ferry worked by ropes.[2] The left hand or southernmost bank is overhung by large woody hills, not much unlike the Warsbeck in Northumberland. At about a mile from the Bridge pass some romantic rocks on the right.[3] Nothing can be more picturesque than the spot where the Bridge stands, environed on all sides by woody hills, corn fields, most luxuriant trees, and some neat cottages, and to the north most grotesque rocks.

Return by all the bad roads and some miles of the good we had passed, mostly by the banks of the Taff. At about four miles from Cardiff on the left hand side on an eminence among some trees stands Castle Goch, or the Red Castle, of which part of the keep only seems remaining. As we were pressed for time and as it did not seem very remarkable we made a slight sketch of it from the chaise but did not get out to draw it. Arrived late in the evening at the Angel at Cardiff where we met Mr. Clerk, the Registrar of Hereford who was going to Llandaff on business, where we also proposed to go in our way to Cowbridge, but were prevented. N.B. our landlord whose name was Steward had been a soldier in Sir Peter Hacket's Regiment both in Flanders and America.

(*Tuesday, 25th July*)—We walked in the morning with Mr. Clerk to see the ruins of Cardiff Castle which are very extensive and consist

2   This ferry was at Upper Boat.
3   Probably the rocks on Coedpenmaen Common.

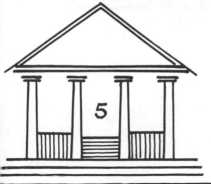

(*Above*) **Dunraven House**
S. Hooper after F. Grose, 1776

(*Left and Below*) **F. Grose's rough plan of Llandaff Cathedral**

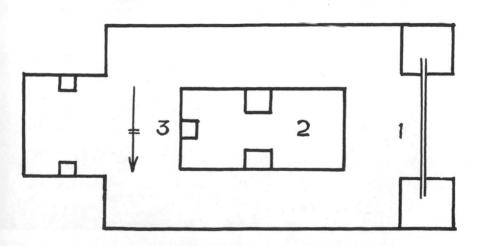

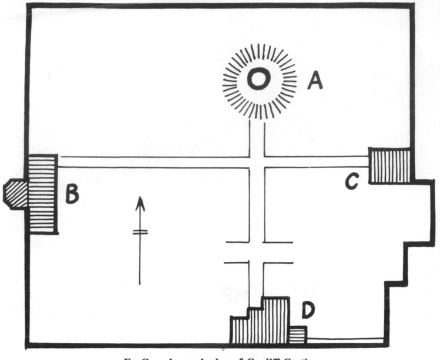

F. Grose's rough plan of Cardiff Castle

Cardiff Castle *S. Hooper after F. Grose,* 1775

of several distinct piles seemingly built at different times.   An idea may be gathered of the most remarkable of them from a crude plan taken solely by a very cursory view. [4]   The Keep A is mounted as usual on an artificial turfed mound.   This seems the most ancient part of the building.   It is called the Magazine, having been used for that purpose by the Militia.   B. The Court or habitable part of the Castle consists of a large octagonal tower very like one of those at Warwick and a long pile of building in which are many good apartments.   In one of these the tenants of Lady Windsor have an annual entertainment.   The window towards the inner part of the Castle is pointed and well finished.   This pile seems more modern than the Keep.   C. The Chapel. [5]   We did not go in, not having the keys.   D. The Tower, seemingly, is nearly co-eval with the Keep.   Here it is said that Robert, son of William the Conqueror, was confined.   A large vault at the bottom of this tower is shown as the Prison.   Adjoining to this tower is the Gate leading from the Town.   The whole area in which the buildings stood is enclosed with embattled walls.   Some other of its buildings are probably employed for domestic uses; but the shortness of our stay which was even protracted beyond our first intention did not give us time thoroughly to investigate it.

This Castle like most others has been spoiled of its squared stones for the purpose of building : many of the houses in Cardiff having been erected with the materials plundered from the Castle. The usual story of subterranean passages between this Castle and some neighbouring Religious Houses is held and affirmed by the ciceroni of the place.

Cardiff is a neat pleasant town, just now paved according to the London fashion [6]   The river Taff which runs up to the walls is now almost dry, but it is navigable to within about a mile and a half; and by the number and width of the bridges must in winter or flood time be very broad.   The tide except at Springs does not rise as far as the town.

There is a pretty market house seemingly new.   An ancient

4   A copy of the plan faces this page.

5   According to William Rees, *Cardiff : A history of the City* (Cardiff, 1962), p. 21, there was a private chapel dedicated to St. Nicholas within the castle throughout the Middle Ages.   Grose appears to be the only eighteenth century visitor to mention its existence.

6   A private Act of Parliament "*for the better paving, cleansing and lighting of the streets of Cardiff*" was obtained in 1774.

Inn called the *Red House*,[7] very like a Religious House. The Church has a very handsome tower—more I cannot say of it—not having seen it.

After dinner having laid in such things as we thought necessary for our intended stay at Dunraven we set off for that place, resolving not to stop at Cowbridge on account of the approaching races. The first part of the road from Cardiff is good, but uninteresting. Just before the five miles stone ascend a very steep hill called Rew Gochin (Rhiwau Gochion), at the top of which Sir Edward (Edmond) Thomas has a Summer House which commands an extreme extensive prospect in every direction.[8] Near it passed by a good brick house belonging to Mr. John Lewellin of Cardiff.[9]

Pass by a park on the right belonging to Mr. Wey neth (Gwinett) called Ketrell (Cottrell). Then through Boulson (Bonvilston),[10] a very remarkable village for the neatness of its cottages, the trimness of the hedges of trees, in a word for that appearance of industry, comfort and happiness which is better felt than expressed, affording a most striking contrast to a French village.

On the left pass by a handsome park, walled in with a high stone wall.[11] It belongs to Sir Thomas Aubury (Aubrey) and immediately after ascend a long and steep hill. At the ten mile stone again ascend a very long hill and over a kind of Common.[12] Cowbridge and the adjacent country appear very fine from the hill about a mile short of it. All the way from Cardiff to Cowbridge very fine. Pass through Cowbridge, which is a single street of houses, some good but the major part only thatched cottages not

---

7 The *Cardiff Arms* was built on the site of the Red House before 1800. See page 107.
8 Actually Sir Edmond Thomas, the 4th baronet, had sold the Wenvoe Estate to Peter Birt in 1774. The interesting building mentioned here is still standing, having been converted into a farm house.
9 The predecessor of the present Coedriglan mansion was only a few hundred yards to the north of the main Cardiff-Cowbridge road. A few cottages have been built on the site, and the gardens have been retained. William Thomas the diarist noted the building of the house in 1767 and described how a brick works had been set up by a well under Halvaes farm (Cardiff MS. 4.877, vol. 1, p. 124).
10 Up to a few decades ago the usual pronunciation of Bonvilston in the immediate locality of the village was "Bowlson".
11 Llantrithyd Park.
12 In the first half of the nineteenth century new stretches of road were constructed at Rhiwau Gochion (or Tumble Hill); to the north of Llantrithyd Park; and over Cowbridge Common from the present Flamingo Cafe to a point over half way down the steep hill to Cowbridge.

unlike an Irish town. Turn to the left and ascend a steep hill whence on a hill to the left are the ruins of some ancient building, seemingly a Castle.[13] Keep ascending for some time. Hitherto matters went on pretty well tho' we had stayed rather too late at Cardiff, not knowing how far Dunraven was from Cowbridge, which we had supposed only five or six miles, but at length on coming to a place where the road divided we were at fault and our postillion informed us he did not know a step of the way, never having been at Dunraven.

William who galloped before procured instructions as to our road and we again set forward, and at four miles from Cowbridge pass through an almost deserted village,[14] most of the cottages being in ruins. The roads here began to be very bad, and what was worse night approached. Luckily asking the way of two farmers who passed the chaise one of them offered his assistance to pilot us, and after leading us as we thought several miles by lanes, commons, bye-ways and through private grounds, particularly through Mr. Curr's yard,[15] at the end of a Common he declared he did not know how to proceed, the usual way being plowed up and sowed with corn. This field which was of oats we passed, and at length came to the yard gate. In ascending to the house one of the horses fell and the other had nearly tumbled over him. The boy however, recovered him, and at 10 o'clock we reached Dunraven. Had our guide left us as he once was about to do we had infallibly passed the night in the chaise. It being quite dark we could not suffer the boy to go back till the morning, and he was accordingly lodged and entertained at the house, in return for which he stole away a halter. He had in the evening soon after his arrival put all the family in motion by suffering his horses to get loose from the stable.

Dunraven is a large old house, having much the appearance of a Cell to some Convent. It consists of a number of buildings, patched on in all directions in the Gothic style. Part of it is occupied by a farmer. The remainder is kept in the hands of the proprietor Mr. Windham of Cleerwell (Clearwell), who keeps it

---

13 The "old castle" of Llanblethian, the remains of which can be seen in the Bucks' view of Llanblethian (1741). See L. J. Hopkin-James, *Old Cowbridge* (Cardiff, 1921), pp. 15-19.

14 This village cannot be any other than Llandow. It would be interesting to know what accounted for its ruined state at this period.

15 Clemenston.

for a kind of hunting seat, an old agent or steward and his wife living in it. It has a good hall and parlour, the latter commanding a view of the sea to the westward from a bow window. The house stands on an eminence, near a point of rocks called the Witches Point. The room where I slept, with the adjoining one, had it is said formerly been a Chapel; and under one of the outhouses is an arch walled up, which the agent said he heard led to a vault or burying place.

All the information I could procure respecting this House was that it formerly belonged to the family of the Butlers, who sold it to the Vaughans.[16] This family, it is said, used to set up lights to mislead sea men in order that they might be wrecked on their manor. This is, however, only asserted to make the following story tell the better, and probably has no foundation in truth.

Within sight of the house is a large rock called Swiscar (Tusker), dry only at low water, but at other times covered by the sea. To this rock two sons of Mr. Vaughan's went one day in a boat and landing did not take sufficient care to fasten the boat, which on a rising of the flood was carried away and they left to all the horrors of the fate which was inevitable, as the family had no other boat. Their distress was discovered from the house, which was filled with confusion and sorrow, insomuch that an infant which was just able to walk being left alone fell into a vessel of whey and was drowned at almost the same instant as his two brothers. This was looked upon as a judgement for the iniquitous practice above mentioned. It is said Mr. Vaughan was so struck with his misfortune that he never more could bear the house, but sold it to a Mr. Windham (Wyndham), ancestor of the present owner.

Near this house another terrible misfortune happened to a Major Windham who coming home one night heated with liquor rode his horse furiously to the very edge of the cliff not knowing where he was. The horse on the very brink of the precipice saw his danger, and stopping short threw the Major over his head who was killed on the spot, the cliff being near 100 feet high.

(*Wednesday*), 26th July—Stayed at home and finished drawing.

(*Thursday*), 27th July—Walked to the Wind Hole, and began to draw but not being well-informed as to the time of the tide came home and left the drawing unfinished.

16 Actually the Vaughans acquired it through marriage.

(*Friday*), 28*th July*—Walked to the Cave and Wind Hole accompanied by Mr. Watkins. These are two caverns worn by the sea which here beats furiously against the rocks. The Cave consists of a passage or natural piazza supported by two large pilasters or jaumbs of rock whose height is 87 feet. The opening or entrance nearly faces the east but the grandest appearance is at right angles to the rock at the second opening.

The Wind Hole is a deep cavern a little to the eastward of the Cave. It is so called because some small spiracles from it open on the top of the cliff and when the tide is up and a brisk wind blows from the south east the boys lay their hats on one of these fissures and it is blown away with great force. We visited the top to observe the phenomenon, but neither the tide being up or the proper wind blowing we with our hats covered the Hole without feeling the least effect or effort. This Cavern goes directly into the Cliff nearly at right angles for a considerable way, then turns a little to the eastward. In the whole it measures 77 yards. The inside is full of large stones which have fallen or been washed from the roof. On some of those which project over the top is that fine variety of prismatic colours like a peacock's tail such as is seen on several ores. A poor girl who had lost her way was drowned near these cliffs. She had climbed up the rocks to a considerable height.

This day Mr. Saunders of Norton[17] called on us and invited us to dine with him tomorrow and promised to accompany us to Ogmore and A Wenny (Ewenny) Castle.

(*Saturday*), 29*th July*—We set out about 9 o'clock on horseback for Norton, the road to which is both steep and stony. Mr. Saunders's horse was ready, which he mounted, and after borrowing a crupper to prevent the saddle lying on the mare's back on which I rode and which it had done quite hitherto, we again proceeded to Ogmore and from thence to A Wenny. On our way to this last place close to the road on the left hand side Mr. Saunders showed us a spring which seemed to yield as much water as that of Holywell.[18] And on the right opposite Ogmore Castle Mr. Watkins showed us several pits or shallows, being places where the earth had spontaneously sunk to a great depth. One of them, said to be unfathomable, was

17 The old house of Norton, near the mouth of the Ogmore, is now known as Norton Hall Farm. Nearby are Sutton and the renowned Sutton quarries.
18 The celebrated Schwyll well, from which a large part of the Mid-Glamorgan area now derives its water supply.

hedged in. It seemed circular and about six or seven feet diameter. It was probably like one of the Hell Kettles at Darlington.

Wenny Castle, tho' old, seems to have been a mansion erected on the site of a more ancient building of the Castle kind whose outer walls were retained and fitted to the present occasion.[19] These were square, having at the angles towers or fortified gateways venerably mantled with ivy. This mansion was very lately inhabited by an old gentleman, the last of name of Turberville, the original proprietors and founders of the Castle. A descendant of his is married to Mr. Amyand[20] who is to change his name to Turberville. Going into the house we were shown the ancient hall which though very lofty has a peculiar gloomy appearance. It was wainscotted with old oak, and had all round it racks for the lodging of arms.

From the house there was a communication with the Church by a door whose arch was circular and ornamented with the zig-zag moulding. Entering the Church was through a chancel wherein was the monument of Paganus de Turberville together with what I take to be that of his wife. The tomb is of the Altar or Table kind raised about four feet above the surface of the chancel. On it on the left side lies the mutilated figure of the Knight with the broad sword and pointed shield very much in style resembling that figure of Strongbowe shown in Tintern Abbey. On the same table, or rather making part of it, is a coffin-shaped stone round which on the margin are Saxon characters made illegible by the dirt with which they are filled, but if washed might be easily read. This church is undoubtedly very ancient, the arches being circular and the ornaments zig-zag. The inside has large massy columns. Besides this there are several very ancient tombstones. The Church is most horribly defaced by the beastly custom of making raised graves, and even the putting of headstones in the body of it. Over these it is the custom to scatter flowers and herbs, which when rotted have a very disagreeable appearance.

In discourse with Mr. Saunders I learned the following particulars: That mortuaries are not given here at funerals as in N. Wales. That burying in coffins has not always been practised here. The superstitious story of corpse candles is believed as also

19 In Grose's *Antiquities* Ewenny is correctly described as a fortified religious house.

20 Mr. Amayand (*sic*) is also mentioned in *The Antiquities* as being the owner of Ewenny. The mention is curious, for there is no reference to him in Colonel J. P. Turbervill's book *Ewenny Priory* (London, 1901).

a kind of second sight such as that of seeing the figure of a ship previous to a wreck; and the whole funeral procession as it is to be at a future burial. Also bid ales for the benefit of the new married couple who dance in the churchyard; £28 collected by a couple at Monmouth. Dined with Mr. Saunders who was a pupil to Mr. Ceasar (Caesar) Hawkins[21] and Lieut. Surgeon to the Breconshire Militia. To Ogmore three miles ; to Wenny two : total including return ten miles.

(*Sunday*), 30*th July*—Stayed at home and finished drawings.

(*Monday*), 31*st July*—Took horse at about 9 o'clock and set out with Mr. Watkins as guide to St. Donats Castle. Passed by the ridiculous house built by a carpenter called ———— Folly. A little beyond it, on Wick Green, saw the ruins of an ancient building seemingly a chapel. It is called an Armory,[22] which is all the information I could get concerning it. Passed through Wick to the Castle. The distance is called five miles, but it would be at least nearer seven. In this day's ride saw several pair of flannel sheets drying. These are chiefly used by the common people, who also frequently wear red flannel shirts. St. Donats Castle is the property of Mrs. Tyrwhitt. It is an extensive pile of buildings and has a very fine park stocked with deer and well wooded. The castle is so surrounded with trees as scarcely to admit of having a drawing of it taken except from the N.W. where I took it. West of it in the park is a small Tower seemingly coeval with the Castle, and intended for a Watch Tower or Look Out. Of this I made a drawing.[23] The Castle is surrounded by at least three concentric walls.

The Church stands near the Castle. In the churchyard are monuments of shipwrecked persons buried there. Among others that of Capt. Sackville Turner[24] of the 33rd Regiment drowned with his wife on their passage to Ireland. In searching for a place to take a view we got into the ditch, and were obliged to crawl through a trapdoor in a cross wall on all fours. This day saw a

21 A celebrated London surgeon who was knighted in 1778. See *D.N.B.*
22 The building is known as Buarth Mawr. Modern opinion is that it was a barn used in connection with the farming of the demesne lands in the neighbourhood. See Stewart Williams, *Saints and Sailing Ships* (Barry, 1962), p. 62.
23 An engraving of the drawing appears in *The Antiquities*, vol. IV.
24 Capt. Sackville Turner was of a Hertfordshire family. The tragedy occurred on the night of 5 September 1774.

wheat field near the Castle with the reapers at work. Returned to dinner, and after dinner washed and penned the outlines we had taken.

(*Tuesday*), *August 1st*—this day took a drawing of Dunraven and finished some drawings before taken. Sent a boy to Cowbridge to order a chaise for tomorrow morning.

Set out (*August 2nd*) at half after eight for Cowbridge, Mr. Watkins steward to Mr. Windham serving as our guide. We passed through the same grounds and same village by which we came and were further convinced that had we not accidentally met with our kind Welsh guide we had infallibly passed the night in the fields. Stopped and changed horses at the Bear at Cowbridge. Distance from Dunraven nine miles. In our way from Cowbridge passed through Llandaff which lies a little to the left of the great road from Cardiff—the whole difference of one mile. Llandaff itself is a miserable poor village but has two very handsome houses : one[25] belonging to that Mr. Mathews who fought with Mr. Sheridan about Miss Liely (Linley), another[26] the property of an attorney of the name of Edwards. The west end of the cathedral is in ruins and serves for the entrance into the new one which is built as it were within its walls. The old aisles are left in. There are several ancient monuments of the Bishops, and one under a window of a corps in a winding sheet, the grimmest figure I ever saw; the appearance of death brought on by a tedious sickness being admirably characterised. There are also two in white marble said to be of the Mathews family, and mentioned by Mr. Windham (Wyndham) in his Tour :[27] they are pretty well done though I cannot join with that gentleman in thinking them extraordinary either in taste or execution, or that there was the least necessity to suppose them the work of Italians. He should have remembered the rule of Horace :

Nec intersit Deus . . . etc.

25 Llandaff Court (subsequently the Bishop's Palace and now the Cathedral School). A biography of Miss Linley—*Still the lark* by Margaret Bor and Lamond Clelland—was published by the Merlin Press (London) in November 1962. It contains a portrait of Mr. Thomas Mathews.

26 Llandaff House, on the corner of what is now Fairwater Road. Thomas Edwards, who was Clerk of the Peace for Glamorgan from 1766 until his death in 1794, was greatly interested in the history of the County.

27 Henry Penruddocke Wyndham's book *A Gentleman's Tour through Monmouthshire and Wales, in the months of June and July,* 1774 was first published in 1775. It seems to have influenced Grose's choice of itinerary.

The new choir and the screen are very neat, but built according to the Grecian architecture. The Altar stands under an Ionic Grecian Temple. There are two thrones much too large for the size of the choir.[28] 1st. The Entrance. 2nd. The new choir. 3rd. A kind of temporary choir—probably used whilst the new one was building, it having two thrones and the names of the different prebends. 5th. The Altar. This church is not, like many Welsh churches, disgraced by a number of raised graves in the aisles nor are there any rotten weeds and flowers strewed over the graves. A commendable attention seems to have been had to the repairs of the ancient structure, but not guided by the least taste or propriety. The palace is entirely deserted, nothing but the outside walls and gate being remaining. The gate is surrounded by small cottages which are plastered to it. One of them is an ale house.

On the south side of the ruins is a handsome circular door case, ornamented with zig-zag work. The other arches are pointed and most of them filled up with modern and sash windows. The entrance at the west end was between two Towers. We only stopped at Llandaff to view the Cathedral, which did not take us up more than a quarter of an hour, when resuming our chaise we proceeded to Cardiff to dinner : and at the distance of a mile had a view of the ruins of the White Friars.[29] But the weather being very bad and having the appearance of continuing, we did not stop to make a drawing of it, resolving after dinner to push forward to Newport.

From Cardiff to Abergavenny

The road from Cardiff good. At three miles to the right a large tract of marsh land; to the left a view of a distant country terminated by hills. Pass a bridge on the river Rodney (Rhymney) and enter Monmouthshire. At four miles from Cardiff an extensive view all round. On the left at a considerable distance see the seat of Sir Charles Kemeys Tynte[30]—and over it the summer house of Rupella, terminated by high hills. On the right the Severn, and in front the Gloucestershire and Malvern Hills. Pass through St. Milans (St. Mellons) whose church is pleasantly situated on an eminence on the right of the road. A little farther to the left of the front, or on what a sailor would call the larboard bow, see Rupella

28 A copy of the plan inserted in the original manuscript at this point faces page 160.
29 Generally, and correctly, called Grey Friars.
30 Cefn Mably.

which from hence has the appearance of being a better house than Tredegar.[31] At about six miles from Cardiff the new and old road part, the former keeping the right and the latter turning a little to the left, but in a few yards they meet again. At about two miles from Newport pass Tredegar Park which seems finely planted with firs, a tree not often occuring in this tour. Pass a bridge, near which in the park is a tolerable water fall.

It may be necessary to observe that the roads from Cowbridge to this place—*i.e.* Newport—are what is here called "good", nay even fine, being hard and stony, having many steep hills. They are, however, at least safe. One great fault they have in common with the Irish roads, being thrown up so round that though their base occupies a considerable breadth, the road itself scarce yields room for a single carriage. In going on the side to make room one risks an overturn. In Glamorganshire they have some particular customs relative to their tillage and method of haymaking and harvest; one of which is that in haymaking they never use forks, but load, pitch and move the hay with their hands. Their rakes have a double row of teeth like a comb. In Monmouthshire forks are used. In reaping they make their sheaves placing the ears downwards. In ploughing with oxen a boy drives the oxen with a remarkable long stick, singing all the while a dismal tune.

31 The contrast between Tredegar and Ruperra is made because both mansions belonged to the Morgan family of Tredegar. In conclusion it is appropriate to mention that both Ruperra and Dunraven were demolished in 1962.

Acknowledgements are due to the British Museum for supplying microfilm of the original manuscript and to Mr. W. G. Harries, B.A., Department of Welsh, University College, Swansea, for examining the manuscript on our behalf.

THE HEALTH OF A TOWN : SWANSEA IN THE 1840's

by

TOM RIDD, M.A.

"SWANSEA," boasted *The Cambrian* in 1845, in one of its more tiresome, self-congratulatory moods, "is still in the fore front of watering places. The influx of visitors this year has exceeded our wildest expectations ; and, doubtless, it will be the same again next year". Those "jolly sons of Neptune", as the paper described all who had savoured the scenic and maritime beauty of Swansea and its immediate hinterland, "must be assured, as indeed we are, that the tide of industrialism, while rising and growing daily more irresistible, has not yet marred nor detracted from the delights which Swansea affords the visitor in search of sand, sun and sea".

For one such visitor, however, this rhapsody of praise and sanguine optimism must have appeared ludicrously inept when compared with his own impressions of the town and its environs. While others, to the evident delight of the editor of the local paper, disported themselves on the golden sands of Swansea Bay, Sir Henry Thomas de la Beche, conducting an inquiry into the state of Bristol and Swansea on behalf of the Health of Towns Commission, had been peering into fetid courts and alleyways, each with its own pool of stagnant sewage, or picking his way delicately around accumulations of ashes and household rubbish in streets, a stone's throw from the venue where *The Cambrian's* "jolly sons of Neptune" strolled and whiled away their holiday hours.

Familiarity with the euphuistical descriptions of the local topographers and guide books is scant preparation for the picture of Swansea Sir Henry was drawing. "The geological character of the Swansea district," he remarked significantly in the beginning of his report, "facilitates the formation of wells and so provides a natural water supply, but it also creates conditions which in a neglected drainage enable liquid portions of cesspools and other receptacles for refuse and filth to percolate and mingle with well waters".

171

Along with forty-nine other large towns in England and Wales, having between them a population of three million people, Swansea was now subjected to the searching, unflattering glare of a scientifically directed sanitary spotlight and as a result stood revealed in all its hideous, grisly, Victorian nastiness. The horrifying sanitary conditions adumbrated by Sir Henry T. de la Beche in his report on Swansea, and by his colleagues in theirs elsewhere, showed conclusively that in the 1840's an increasing proportion of the population of this country was living under conditions which were not only "a negation of civilised existence, but a menace to civilised society".

In view of the persistent attempts made to attract fashionable visitors to the town—attempts, incidentally, begun at the turn of the nineteenth century when the first municipally inspired efforts were made to exploit Swansea's fine natural amenities and make it a watering place equal to resorts like Tenby and Aberystwyth—the reticence of the local guide books and directories is not surprising. Much more remarkable is the silence of the local medical worthies, men like Dr. John Charles Collins, Dr. William Gutch and Dr. Thomas Williams, all of whom wrote specifically of health conditions. These writers totally ignored the bearing of sanitation on health, and nowhere in their surveys of local diseases and their treatment is there any criticism of local sanitary conditions. Dr. Thomas Williams did throw one weak punch. Writing in 1844 he remarked that the town's sewers were so badly constructed that during high tides they were flooded by the sea. Then he promptly blocked his own poor lead by saying that he considered this state of things to be a "favourable circumstance as the salt water by its antiseptic properties destroyed the malarial influence of the sewers". The plain speaking of the de la Beche report of 1845 is all the more startling by contrast.

Though there were several wretched alleys and fetid courts in Swansea, the town generally consisted of many fine, open streets ; but such was the inattention to efficient drainage and scavenging, reported Beche, that the whole town wore an air of wanton neglect. Only eight men and four carts were employed to clean some five miles of streets and these men received about half the sum which would have enabled them to perform their duties properly.

House drainage was equally primitive. The contents of privies, unconnected with the public sewers, were allowed to percolate into the adjacent soil, and as water was obtained in many parts of the borough by the sinking of shallow wells, this percolation added enormously to the other impurities in the water.

The Town Council, Beche explained, was responsible for the provision of public services related to the maintenance and improvement of public health, and had powers under a local act of parliament, the *Swansea Paving and Lighting Act*, 1804, to provide a main drainage scheme. But such had been the rapidity of the town's growth in the early nineteenth century—the population of the borough had increased from 6,099 in 1801 to 20,152 in 1841—that its administrative machinery had been outstripped and ultimately swamped by the very enormity of the town's sanitary problems. It was now blatantly obvious that the Council's parliamentary powers were not sufficiently comprehensive to be effective. Furthermore, its financial position was such that it was impossible for it to attempt any major main drainage scheme. Consequently, in many parts of the borough there were no sewers at all ; while even in those parts where they did exist they were either too small or they had been so altered as to become useless. If it was any consolation to the townspeople, even had the drains existed, reported Beche, it was extremely doubtful whether sufficient water would have been available to flush them. Beche found that this essential public service, too, had been grossly neglected. In 1845 the supply, provided by the Swansea Waterworks Company, was connected to about 470 houses out of a total of 3,369. At best, therefore, nearly 3,000 householders had to depend on polluted wells and streams, or on the services of the water-vendors who hawked it about the streets and sold it at a penny a pailful.

Of the 3,369 houses in Swansea, 1,400 were cottages with a rental of less than £5 per annum. This, Beche found, was regarded as a blessing by some members of the Town Council. Swansea, they argued, was not plagued with overcrowded tenements containing three, four, or even six different households to the manifest detriment of the health of all of them. This may have been so ; but as Sir Henry pointed out, when it is remembered that on an average there were between six and seven people to a house in the town, and that many of these houses contained only two rooms and were without proper sanitary conveniences, the presence of two or three people, let alone six or seven, was hardly less of a menace to public health than the teeming courts of Birmingham or the underground cellars of Manchester. The moral of these housing conditions, commented Beche, was unequivocally demonstrated by the mortality figures for the town : these stood alarmingly high at seventeen per 1,000.

The Royal Commission's report of 1845 provided magnificent material for public health propaganda on a national scale. Slowly at first and then more rapidly as the campaign gathered momentum, local fact-finding committees and associations were established throughout the country and they began to disseminate the facts and figures gleaned from the official government report, to organise public lectures and to compile petitions to parliament in favour of public health legislation.

In Swansea there is no evidence to suggest the existence of any such body ; but the exposure of 1845 did encourage the formation within the Town Council of a progressive party led by "Waterworks Bill", as Councillor William Henry Smith, the Manager of the Swansea Water Company, was affectionately known. It was Smith who was largely responsible for compiling the petition which led to a second inquiry into the sanitary condition of the borough of Swansea being undertaken at this time, and to the eventual adoption by the Town Council of the great *Public Health Act* of 1848.

This second inquiry, the work, on behalf of the General Board of Health, of George Thomas Clark, who was later to become the outstanding historian of Glamorgan, was made in May 1849. It is a more detailed work than that of Sir Henry de la Beche and fills out the somewhat meagre outlines of his pioneering report.

Clark, like his predecessor, saw the weaknesses of the Town Council. Its jurisdiction extended only to such parts of the borough as were within eighty yards of a public street lamp, and as large areas of the town itself were unlit, these areas were virtually outside its control. The districts which lay within the borough boundaries, but outside the actual limits of the town were still governed by their respective parish authorities, bodies which were lamentably inadequate to deal with the sanitary problems which faced them. Even within the narrow limits of its jurisdiction the Town Council, noted Clark, was hampered and crippled in its activities by the inadequacy of its rate income. This seldom exceeded £1,600 and after the discharge of interest on debts the sum remaining at its disposal was "quite insufficient to meet the wants of the town".

Quite as serious as its deficient income were its deficient powers. In the Sandfields area in the lower part of the town, a district notorious for periodic flooding, builders persisted in laying the floors of houses too low. In one street, Zion Place, the houses were even built over a partially culverted drain which was more than half full of stagnant sewage. The Council, reported Clark contemptuously, could do no more than warn the offenders; but in the absence of vigorous powers of compulsion such warnings not unnaturally went completely unheeded.

The town alone, Clark found, was lit by gas lighting supplied by another independent concern, the Swansea Gas Company. Yet, even here, in some seven or eight miles of streets, there were only 183 lamps. The continuing inadequacy of the town's main drainage was even more graphically revealed by Clark. After forty years work only 3,180 yards out of a total of 15,000 yards of highway had been sewered and very few of the houses adjoining were connected with them. Of the six principal sewers in the town, five of them drained into that portion of the River Tawe opposite the town that was scheduled for conversion into the North Dock.

The general primitiveness of the town's main drainage was surpassed only by that of the borough's populous suburban districts. Though built on high sloping ground which offered favourable facilities for drainage, these districts were "not drained at all, except by nature". The brooks and streams which traversed these localities were used extensively as public sewers, as also were the streets themselves. In Morriston, the sewage was left to find its own way along the open gutters, which in many places were clogged with it. At Landore, within an area of half a square mile, upwards of 200 houses were without lavatories. The few places which had them were shops and public houses.

The favourable impression of the water supply given by de la Beche in 1845 was not maintained under the spotlight of George Clark's more thorough-going investigation. By 1849 the Swansea Water Company supplied 924 houses and its mains covered "about three fifths of the whole town". The pressure, however, was very uneven and the supply consequently intermittent. In High Street and its adjoining courts Clark found the supply very feeble or even altogether wanting, and this, people stated, was the case for about five hours daily. In these areas the towns people had still to rely upon polluted wells and streams or on the services of the water-vendors.

A tour of the town and its outlying districts undertaken by the indefatigable George Clark as part of his comprehensive local survey, gave him a clear picture of the practical effect of these conditions and explained why it was that the mortality rate in Swansea was twenty-three per 1,000 as compared with fifteen per 1,000 in rural Gower. The worst parts of the borough were those inhabited by the poorer classes and, in particular, that known as Little Ireland, as the Greenhill district was called. This area presented a desolate scene of badly-paved, ill-formed streets and dilapidated, over-crowded houses which were totally unprovided with sanitary conveniences. Dyfatty Street, for example, had not been re-surfaced for close on six years and consequently in wintertime it could be crossed only with considerable difficulty, "the dirt being knee deep". Sixty-four of the one hundred and seventeen houses in Back Street and thirteen of the forty-three in Mariner Street were without privies. Moreover, even where these indispensible conveniences existed their condition defied description. Morris Lane, "the dirtiest alley in the town", had only ten houses but not one of them had a lavatory or a drain of any description. All refuse and household waste was thrown into the lane and there it remained, a menace to public health and an affront to decent, civilised living.

Similar sights and smells presented themselves to Clark in his perambulations in the suburbs of the borough. In Morriston, the streets and roadways were ill-made and neglected. The houses were built too close against the hillsides and were therefore very damp. Without drainage and water, this district suffered severely from fever epidemics. A fertile source of disease was the weir on the river immediately below the village. This received "nearly all the animal and vegetable filth of the neighbourhood as well as the foul waters of the collieries ; yet as the supply of water for drinking purposes in Morriston is insufficient and at a distance, the bulk of the population drink their tea brewed with this filthy water".

As Inspector Clark toured the town and drank deeply of its grisly sights and smells, another, and as it happened, not infrequent visitor had made his appearance in "salubrious Swansea" to add his persuasive force to the general movement in favour of sanitary reform—if any additional force had been needed.

In the closing weeks of 1847 the national press had reported the steady, inexorable advance of cholera across Eastern Europe. In September, 1848, the scourge appeared in Sunderland but then with the onset of the colder weather, subsided and died away. The visitation had been slight and confined mainly to the North and Scotland. With the arrival of warmer weather in the spring of 1849, however, cholera re-appeared. This time it struck like a tempest "lashing at every nook and cranny on these islands".

Cholera—the very name spread panic! Its symptoms were frightful, its suddenness appalling. Attacked by violent pains, vomiting and diarrhoea, the victim rapidly sank into a state of collapse : his breath came short, his body turned cold, his pulse rate fell away, his skin grew shrunken and blue. Some attacks lasted several days, while others, which struck terror, killed the sufferers within two hours.

By mid-June, 1849, this frightful visitor had appeared in Merthyr, Cardiff, Aberavon and Neath. The precise date of its appearance in Swansea is not known. In the first week of July *The Cambrian* was most sanguine and claimed that "Swansea was never more free from sickness than at present". Yet the possibility of a change in the forecast had not escaped notice. The police were already engaged in extensive, preparative ablutionary activities in the poorer parts of the town, and Visiting Sanitary Committees were appointed to inspect selected districts in the borough and its heavily populated industrial suburbs.

Despite the light-hearted, superficial tone of the local press which blithely continued to report the arrival of fashionable summer visitors, the epidemic mounted in severity. By the autumn it was virulent. The Mayor, Alderman Michael John Michael, approved the Vicar of Swansea's plan to hold services "to supplicate Almighty God to remove the prevailing epidemic", and designated the 10 October as a Day of Humiliation when all shops, offices, businesses and works were to be closed. "As Churchmen and Dissenters attended their respective places of worship", reported *The Cambrian*, "a Sabbath-like stillness prevailed throughout the town".

While their fellow townsmen trusted in prayer as the desired and solely feasible panacea, Dr. George Gwyn Bird and the Reverend

Charles Kavanagh, the Roman Catholic priest in the Greenhill area, placed their trust in more practical and materially successful exertions to combat the onslaught of this unwelcome and feared Asiatic visitor. Between them, in their respective capacities, these two men devised innumerable measures to mitigate the severity of the epidemic and in so doing earned the respect and heartfelt gratitude of the poor among whom they laboured. Many of these measures were of a direct and intimate nature. As the Reverend Kavanagh's priestly successor put it : "he washed them, combed their hair, made their beds and laid them out in their coffins". In the teeth of a fearful epidemic there could be no greater or more revealing testimony of devoted, practical Christianity. Thanks to the exertions of these two men and to a host of lesser, unknown local officials, the cholera epidemic gradually subsided. By the 15th November the situation had so much improved that a public day of thanksgiving was set aside and observed throughout the town to commemorate the cessation of the pestilence.

Authoritative opinion differs as to the number of deaths from cholera there were in Swansea in this outburst in 1849. William Henry Michael, the town's first Medical Officer of Health, put the figure at 139. His successor, Ebenezer Davies, put it as high as 241 or 7.7 per 1,000 of the population. On one point the experts were agreed. The upper part of the town was particularly badly hit by the scourge, no less than seventeen per cent of the total number of deaths were reported to have occurred in this locality, in the vicinity of several grossly overcrowded burial grounds.

The cessation of this epidemic may have served as a salutary reminder to the General Board of Health of the desirability of bringing Swansea within the scope of the Public Health Act of 1848. Certainly, in June 1850 the Board reached its decision and vested responsibility for the execution of the Act in Swansea in the Town Council, acting as the Swansea Local Board of Health.

The evidence amassed by the two official, local inquiries of the 1840's and from the subsequent fight against epidemic cholera, proved a most commendable and healthy shock for the somewhat somnambulent local authority. With a start almost, it awoke to the enormity of the tasks confronting it. Essential public services such as water, main drainage, street repairs, housing, parks and cemeteries, and scavenging were so deplorably embryonic as to be almost non-existent. Administratively and financially, the Local Board of Health manfully shouldered the heavy burden of its many responsibilities and as its "crash-programme" of sanitary reform got under way in the 1850's great progress was made in checking and then eliminating some of the worst horrors that had sprawled across the face of Victorian England. That there remained chinks in Swansea's sanitary armour in the next two decades was only to be expected and was conclusively demonstrated in 1865 at the cost of seventeen lives.

In the stifling, near tropical heat of the morning of the 9th September 1865, the sailing ship *Hecla*, bound from Cuba to Swansea with a cargo of copper ore, tied up alongside the Cobra Wharf in the North Dock, Swansea, and gangs of dockers began to discharge her cargo. As they did so they little realised that their charge was about to figure as the central character in a drama unparalleled in English public health history.

On the ship's homeward voyage three seamen had died—no one suspected why until a fourth man died in a dingy lodging-house in port. Then some of the more garrulous members of the *Hecla's* crew, emboldened by the inebriating effects of their beer, let it slip that their shipmates had died of yellow fever. Near panic ensued. This was a ravage without precedent for the disease-hardened local health authority or, for that matter, any other local authority in the British Isles.

Admittedly, the unusually hot weather, almost tropical in intensity, created favourable conditions for the outbreak ; but no one could predict that in any given year the summer months would not produce the same conditions, nor could anyone predict that if yellow fever did recur it would be as confined as it was in Swansea in the autumn of 1865. Anyhow, the weaknesses in the national sanitary defences which this unique epidemic revealed, together with those revealed by a fresh, savage attack of cholera which followed in its wake, attracted parliamentary attention and legislation of the highest practical importance followed. The chief measure was the great Sanitary Act of 1866 which introduced, through its provisions, a new era in the history of public health in England and Wales. Perhaps it would not be impertinent to suggest that Swansea's totally unwelcome and unwanted guests of the mid-sixties played no small part in the inception of this new sanitary era.

SOUTH WALES COMMERCIAL MOTORS :
A PIONEER GLAMORGAN BUS COMPANY

by

STEWART WILLIAMS

THE motor bus is a product of the twentieth century; its history
spans our own lifetime. Although often taken for granted its
economic and sociological effects have been profound, and most of
us, whether or not we realise it, have been influenced by its growth
and development.

Buses were not unknown in Glamorgan before World War I,
but they were considered something of a novelty, and few people
realised their potentialities. In the post-war period, however,
especially during the ten years from 1920 to 1930, the bus came into
its own and established itself as a serious and highly competitive
rival to the railway. It was a period which offered great
opportunities. The economic climate was favourable; post war
restlessness demanded a new mobility. Bus companies, in common
with most businesses, were seriously hit by the depression which
clouded the late 1920's, but by this time, buses had become, for
business and pleasure, an accepted part of everyday life.

If the decade under review gave full scope to the enterprising,
it also encouraged the sharp operator, for the licensing system of the
day, vested in local authorities, was often applied willy-nilly and was
downright corrupt on occasions. Small regard was paid to time-
tables and fare-scales. Competition was fierce and relentless.
Politics often influenced decisions. In many instances people,
totally lacking in experience, mortgaged their homes in order to
join in what became a "miniature gold rush". The system clearly
was inefficient and in the public interest the Road Traffic Act was
passed in 1930. This took the power to licence services and the
responsibility for the road worthiness of vehicles out of the hands of
local authorities and into Governmental control through the
Ministry of Transport, who divided the country into a number of
traffic areas and appointed Traffic Commissioners to administer

them. It also provided a simple and effective system to replace the clumsy procedure whereby the licensing of drivers and conductors was a matter for the individual councils through whose area a service ran. As a result of this legislation, order was restored out of what had threatened to become chaos.

This briefly outlines the colourful background against which a pioneer Glamorgan bus enterprise was born. The Company was named South Wales Commercial Motors, and its first regular service, between Cardiff and Penarth, was introduced on Good Friday 1920. It was an hourly service, operated with two vehicles, and the inaugural journey departed from the *Terminus Hotel*, St. Mary Street, Cardiff, at 10.00 a.m. From this modest beginning grew a thriving business which in 1929 was merged with the passenger road services of the Great Western Railway to form Western Welsh Omnibus Company Ltd., now the largest operators of stage carriage services in South Wales.

The story of South Wales Commercial Motors is also the story of Mr. Albert Gray, its joint managing director, for it was largely due to his vision that the Company was formed in 1919. He saw a great future for commercial motor vehicles and resolved to set up a business selling and repairing them. At the time he was employed by Messrs William Hancock and Co. Ltd., the Cardiff brewers, as their transport manager and engineer, and it was his chairman, the late Colonel Joseph Gaskell, who arranged the finance. To a conservative mind at that time it must have seemed a dubious proposition.

But let us take a closer look at the Company. Its offices, garage and workshops were housed in the present Hancock's buildings in Penarth Road, Cardiff, and its staff—fitters, coach-builders, drivers and conductors—were as new to the bus business as was their chief. This was in many ways an advantage for it gave the staff a zest which enabled them to overcome some outsize operational and mechanical difficulties.

The experimental flavour of the enterprise is perhaps best captured by the red and white painted saloon vehicles which, with their solid tyres, oil lamps, slat seats and formidable steps to negotiate, jogged their passengers at a steady 12 m.p.h. over the three and a half mile route between Cardiff and Penarth for a return fare of 1/6d., reduced to 1/2d. as business picked up. These early buses were home-made—a couple of second-hand coach bodies were purchased and altered to suit the R.C. Commer ex-Army chassis. Breakdowns were common and it was customary for a driver to start out with a kit of tools, oil can and a tin of grease to lubricate the sprockets and chains.

Judged by present day standards the operational shortcomings appear considerable, but if recognised they were disregarded by the public who gave the new Company encouraging support—so much so that Mr. Gray was soon able to think in terms of fleet and route expansion. The frequency of the Cardiff-Penarth service was increased from hourly to half hourly before 2.00 p.m. after which a 20 minute service was operated; an hourly service was introduced from Cardiff (*Tresillian Hotel*, Penarth Road—which, incidentally, was "blitzed" during World War II) to Barry Island via Cogan and Dinas Powis—1/6d. return (later withdrawn); and, most far reaching of all, a service was established over the main road between Cardiff (Westgate Street) and Bridgend—3/- return.

This brought the bus to the country-dwellers' doorstep, as Ashton's, the Cardiff fishmongers, were quick to appreciate. Advertising in the Company's first timetable they declared "For your health's sake have a fish meal at least once a day. Living in the country this was not always possible. These Motor Buses will now bring it to you".

Private hire was commenced in 1921 and to meet the anticipated demand from outing organisers, several charabancs, described as "comfortable and easy riding", despite their solid tyres, were brought into service. These were often used on stage carriage services, giving conductors of the day a problem in the collection of their fares as they edged along the footboard from one compartment to another while the vehicle was in motion.

Looking around for fresh fields to conquer, Mr. Gray soon realised the possibilities of Bridgend as a bus centre, situated as it is at the foot of the Llynfi, Ogmore and Garw Valleys, and within easy reach of the popular coastal resorts of Porthcawl, Ogmore-by-Sea and Southerndown. By 1921 he had opened an office at the *Wyndham Hotel*, Bridgend, and obtained a garage in Brackla Street which was sufficiently large to accommodate ten buses. From this Mid-Glamorgan hub, services radiated to Porthcawl, Ogmore Vale,

Maesteg and Pontypridd. A further extension from Porthcawl to Port Talbot was introduced in 1922.

The conveyance of parcels on the buses was a profitable sideline, and by 1922 agencies, where parcels could be collected or delivered, had been established in every town and village served by the Company. Parcels could also be handed to conductors on the buses. "Large and bulky packages will only be carried subject to there being room on the bus, and for which an extra charge will be made" stated the regulations. This was a necessary safeguard in view of the many and varied articles brought for transit.

At first, a weight limit of 56 lbs. was imposed and parcels weighing between 28-56 lbs. cost the consigner 2/6d. The cheapest rate was 6d. for small parcels of 1-6 lbs. weight. In 1923 the charges were twice lowered, special rates applied for distances of between one to twenty miles, and the weight limit was increased to 112 lbs. Later the rates were further reduced, vans were purchased and an "express parcel delivery service" augmented the parcel service provided by the buses.

It was at Bridgend that history was made in 1923. In this year, the original bus station, a wooden structure with corrugated iron roof, situated between Wyndham Street and Market Street approximately opposite the present bus station, was opened. It was the first bus station in Wales. With the expansion of the business, new office premises on the corner of Market Street and Dunraven Place had been obtained in the previous year.

By the summer of 1923 services had been extended from Bridgend to Ogmore-by-Sea and Southerndown (three departures daily with an additional journey on Saturdays, although the seasonal potential was recognised by the time-table footnote which stated "On Fine Days Extra Buses Run Frequently"); the Garw Valley had been opened up with a service from Bridgend via Aberkenfig and Llangeinor to Blaengarw—ten departures daily, three on Sundays; a link was forged between Maesteg and Caerau; and for the first time the Company ventured into Monmouthshire with a new service from Newport (Rodney Road) to Chepstow via Caerwent. In actual fact few journeys worked through to Chepstow. Most terminated at Caerwent.

Pride in their job was always noticeable among the staff, particularly during the early years. It was a common thing for men to give up part of their leisure time to polish radiators and lamps, clean the paint work and generally tinker with their vehicles. In those early days duty scheduling was a comparatively simple matter so that buses were frequently manned by the same crews. As a result they came to regard their vehicles with something amounting to affection. This helped to create a "family spirit" and was encouraged by the management. Indeed, there can be no doubt that S.W.C.M. was in every respect a happy organisation.

As already stated, Mr. Albert Gray was a visionary. He was also a man with an inventive turn of mind. In 1924, after introducing the idea to the local travelling public, he successfully patented in Canada and the United States of America an invention for "Improvements in hoods for single deck omnibuses and other road vehicles". In effect this was the forerunner of the present day sliding roof, a standard feature on luxury coaches. In his petition Mr. Gray stated "This invention provides a roof with an entirely open space when desired and thereby permits of a plentiful supply of fresh air for the passengers". The Commer vehicle (bus number 36) with the roll-top canvas roof was a nine-days' wonder. It was the first public service vehicle in the country to have an open top. But owing to the vagaries of the weather the idea failed to gain favour with the travelling public of those days, and the design was eventually dropped—only to be taken up, most successfully, in modified form years later.

The pattern of services remained more or less the same during the mid-twenties. Fresh ground was broken in Bridgend with new services to Kenfig Hill and Sarn, but the Porthcawl-Port Talbot service was withdrawn. At the Monmouthshire end of the Company's area strenuous efforts were made to consolidate services between Newport and Chepstow, and a new route via Magor and Portskewett was introduced.

Even allowing for the comparative prosperity enjoyed during these early years, the fares charged were excessive. This was due to the high cost of operation. The petrol consumption of the Commers was a particularly costly item in the balance sheet. However, the switch-over from solid to pneumatic tyres and the introduction of more modern vehicles—Leyland "Lion" and Lancia saloons—helped to bring operating costs down, and the

This solid tyred, chain-driven Commer saloon was used on the first regular 'bus service operated by South Wales Commercial Motors between Cardiff and Penarth. It was introduced on Good Friday, 1920

Bridgend 'Bus Station, 1923

This Commer saloon with the roll-top canvas roof was the first public service vehicle in the country to have an open top

Mr. Albert Gray, joint managing director of South Wales Commercial Motors and inventor of the open-top roof

A 'bus body in course of construction at the Penarth Road, Cardiff, workshops of South Wales Commercial Motors

---

Photographed at Sycamore Cross, near Cardiff, two contrasting types of saloon vehicle operated by South Wales Commercial Motors. *Left :* a 1925 SG11 Leyland 36-seater. *Right :* a 1926 Commer 3P 28-seater

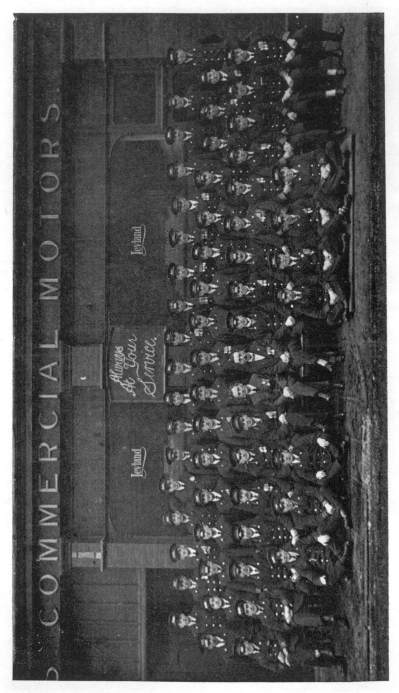

The combined Cardiff and Bridgend staff of South Wales Commercial Motors photographed outside the head office in Penarth Road, Cardiff

management prudently reduced some fares and offered cheap day return fares on selected routes.

It was due to an individual by the name of Klewer Williams, who lived at Caerleon, that the Company operated an extended tour of Britain in 1926—the first from this part of the country. Luxury holiday tours of fourteen days duration are now commonplace, but in 1926 they were largely a dream. The itinerary of the tour, which embraced some of the most beautiful scenery in Britain, was planned by Mr. Williams. When it was completed to his satisfaction he approached S.W.C.M. to supply a bus, together with a driver, for fourteen days. The vehicle, a 3P Commer 28-seater saloon, had its seats removed to make room for dining chairs and a table, which were screwed to the floor of the bus. In this way it was possible for the party—they numbered eight—to have a private meal anywhere at anytime. During the two weeks they were on the road the party covered 1,200 miles—a considerable feat bearing in mind the 20 m.p.h. speed limit obtaining at the time.

Since its formation in 1920 the Company had faced in most areas continual and sometimes unscrupulous opposition from other operators. One-man businesses and taxis "muscled-in" at every turn, undercutting fares and poaching passengers with the result that a business as dispersed as S.W.C.M. had to be efficiently managed if it was to survive. But persistence and a genuine desire to provide a good public service finally resulted in the consolidation of a network of services which made the Company outstanding among its contemporaries.

When negotiations commenced in 1928 for the purchase of the Company by the National Electric Construction group, thirteen services were listed in the timetable. These included a through service which linked Penarth—Cardiff—Bridgend—Porthcawl (hourly—4/- return); a service from Penarth to Ogmore-by-Sea via Cardiff, Cowbridge, Llantwit Major and Southerndown (hourly—4/- return); Cardiff—Barry Island via Sycamore Cross, where an immediate connection was made with the Bridgend—Barry Island service (a highly remunerative link-up); and a service from Beddau to Barry Island via Pendoylan (four journeys daily—2/6d. return). Elsewhere the services were much as before. A combination of adverse trading factors—low receipts and high operating costs— killed the Company's hopes of establishing services in Monmouthshire, and the Newport—Chepstow services were reluctantly withdrawn.

From the amalgamation of S.W.C.M. with the road passenger services operated by the Great Western Railway emerged in 1929 the Western Welsh Omnibus Co., Ltd. On this sure foundation, and with Mr. Gray as its first general manager, the new Company prospered and grew, absorbing other firms and widening its horizons until services covered six counties in the Principality. Mr. Gray continued to manage the new Company's affairs until his retirement in 1938. By a happy coincidence his son, Mr. Ivor L. Gray, is the present general manager of Western Welsh, while another son, Mr. Leslie A. Gray, assistant chief engineer, has worked continuously from the formation of the Company until the present time. The family can, in fact, claim an unbroken link with the bus industry in South Wales, dating from that historic Good Friday in 1920.

INDEX

Aaron, Christian martyr, 122.
Abercynon, 22, 23.
Aberdare, iron industry at, 21, 22, 25; Canal, 22; Roman marching camp at, 72.
Aberdare Valley, coal industry in, 23.
Aberdulais, ironworks at, 20; Mill, 46, 48, 51, 52.
Abergavenny (Gobannium), Roman fort, 148.
Abernant ironworks, 20, 22.
Aberthaw, cement industry at, 26; Cowbridge, Llantrisant railway, 116.
Aberyscir (Cicutio), Roman auxiliary fort, 70, 72, 148.
Act for the better Propagation and Preaching of the Gospel in Wales, 64.
Act of Union, 28.
Afagddu, 138.
Afan, lordship of, 42.
Agriculture, effect of industry on working population, 110, 113, 114, 117-8; Glamorganshire Agricultural Society, 110-1, 152; premiums to farm servants, 110-2; Bridgend Labourers' Friend Society, 112; harvest customs, gleaning, 112, haymaking, 170; driving oxen, 170; high wages in the Vale, 114-5; numbers of agricultural labourers, 117-8.
Alcock, Leslie, 37-8.
Ale biddings, 167.
Allen, S. W., Reminiscences, 104, 107.
Amayand, ——, of Ewenny, 166.
Anderson, Amelia, 96.
Anderson, J. G., "William Morgan and X-rays", 95.
Anglesey (Mona), 137, 138.
Annales de Margan, 39.
Antonine Itinerary, 70, 148.
Archaeologia Cambrensis, 1961, 40.
Archenfield, see Erging.
Ariconium, see Erging.
Ashton, T. S., 19.
Asiatic Society of Bengal, Asiatic Researches, 142.

Astley, Sir Jacob, commander in South Wales, 59.
Aubrey, family, of Llantrithyd, 54, 65; Sir John, Commissioner of Array, 60.
Aubrey, John, antiquarian, 137.
Avebury, 137, 138.
Awen, sacred symbol, 140.

Bachan, Irish scholar, 125.
Bacon, Anthony, 21.
Baglan Bay, 46, 48.
Baldwin, Archbishop, 150.
Bale, John, Bishop of Ossory, 137.
Barker, Thomas, artist, 46.
Barry, population, 113; railway links, 86, 116; St. Barrwg, 126.
Barry Railway, 86.
Bassett, family, of Beaupre, 54; Sir Richard, appointed Governor Cardiff Castle, 58, 60; leader of demonstration, 61; mentioned, 65.
Baxter, Thomas, artist, 46, 52.
Beaufort, Duke of, Progress through Wales, 47.
Beaumont, Henry, attack on castle of, 38.
Beaupre, Bassett family of, 54.
Bede, Ecclesiastical history of the English people, 124.
Bedford, Jasper, Duke of Bedford, 31.
Bedford, John, 20.
Beneventum, 128.
Bessemer, Henry, 24.
Bettws, 153.
Bird, Dr. George Gwyn, and Swansea cholera outbreak, 177-8.
Birt, Peter, 162.
Bishopston, dedications, 126, 129.
Black Death, in Swansea, 28.
Blaenau Morgannwg, Roman penetration of, 72; exploitation of coalfields, 114.
Blaenavon, 109.
Blakemore, R. G., and Co., 85.
Bodvoc Stone, 146.

187

Bomium, Roman fort, 70, 148.
Bonvilston, 153.
Book of Kells, 130.
Book of Llandaff, 132.
Booker, T. W., senior, 85.
Booker, T. W., junior, 85.
Bor, Margaret, *and* Clelland, Lamond, *Still the lark*, 168.
Bourne, James, artist, 47.
Bowen, David, of Llangynwyd, 152.
"Brecon Gaer", *see* Aberyscir.
Bridgend, light industries at, 26; establishment of bus centre, 182, 183.
Bridgend Labourers' Friend Society, 112.
Bristol Gazette, 155.
British Medical Journal, 90.
Briton Ferry, dock at, 24, 44; and J. M. W. Turner, 48, 49; and Thomas Hornor, 49, 50, 51; Vernon House, 52; Church, 52; Bussy Mansel of, 58.
Brocastle, 153.
Brock, R. C., *Life and Work of Astley Cooper*, 91.
Brut y Tywysogion, 38.
Brychan, king of Brycheiniog, 125, 126, 133.
Brycheiniog, 125.
Bryn-Rhydd, 80.
Bryncoch, near Neath, ironworks at, 20.
Buck, Nathaniel, 47.
Buck, Samuel, 47.
Burdett, Sir Francis, 96.
Burial customs, 166.
Burrium, see Usk.
Bute, Marquesses of, *see* Crichton-Stuart, *family*, Marquesses of Bute.
Butler, *family*, of Dunraven, 164.

Cadoxton-juxta-Neath, 126.
Cadwgan Fawr, 79.
Cae Colman, Pentyrch, 79.
Caerau (Caerau-super-Ely), ring-work, 38; manor, 80.
"Caerau", Llantrisant, 77.
Caerleon-on-Usk (*Isca*), Second Augustan legion at, 68; siting of fortress, 70, 148; martyrs at, 122.
Caerphilly, furnace at, 20; road to Cardiff, 21, 41, 149; Castle, 40-1, 42, 159; Roman auxiliary fort at, 76; Homer and, 143; visit of Grose, 159; *Boar's Head Inn*, 159.

Caerwal, Pentyrch, 79.
Caerwent (*Venta*), 68, 75, 125.
Caeryrfa Farm, Creigiau, cromlech at, 77; tenement, 79.
Caldey, 129.
Cambrian, The, 110, 155, 171.
Camden, William, antiquary, 137.
Capel Brithdir, 134.
Capel Gwladus, 125.
Capel Llanilltern (Llanilltern), surveys, 78; Pencoed, 80; St. Elldeyrn, 133; and the Turnpike Trusts, 154.
Câr-llusg, 147.
Caratacus, 68.
Cardiff, and the iron industry, 21, 22; railways, 23, Taff Vale Railway Station, 108; coal exports, 23-4; Dowlais Works, 24; county gaol, 35, 107; Roman auxiliary fort at, 70, 74-5; before 1890, 104-8; streets, *see* Cardiff, streets; inns and hotels, *see* Cardiff, inns and hotels; Bute Estate Office, 104, 105; Western Ground Rents, Ltd., 105; Zion Calvinistic Methodist Chapel, 104; Central Library, 104; *Cardiff Records*, ed. John Hobson Matthews, 104, 107; Canton Bridge, 105; *Havannah*, industrial training ship, 104; St. John's Church, Canton, 105; statue of second Marquess of Bute, 106; first horse tram, 106; Brecon Bank, 106; High Corner House, 105, 106; Lloyds Bank, 106; Town Hall, 106; S. W. Allen, *Reminiscences*, 104, 107; Post Office, 105, 106; London and Provincial Bank, 106; Barclays Bank, 106; Market Buildings, 107; Cardiff Infirmary, 107, 108; Corporation, 107; Crockherbtown, 107-8; Spital Cottages, 107-8; leper hospital, 108; W. Rees, *Cardiff: A History of the City*, 108, 161; University College, 108; Temperance Town, 105; Penarth Road Bridge, 105; population, 113; market town, 150; bridge, 150; visit of Francis Grose, 161-2; Grey Friars, 169; bus service to Penarth, 181-2; Ashton's fishmongers, 182; Messrs. William Hancock and Co. Ltd., 181.
Cardiff, inns and hotels, *Cowbridge Arms*, 104, 107; *Cardiff Arms*, 105, 107, 162; *Angel Inn*, 105, 107, 154,